Plays by Women: Volume Nine

Purgatory in Ingolstadt, Pioneers in Ingolstadt, Avant-garde, Early Encounter and
I Wasn't Aware of the Explosive by Marieluise Fleisser; **Tokens of Affection** by
Maureen Lawrence; **Variations on a Theme by Clara Schumann** by Sheila Yeger

Volume Nine in Methuen's highly successful series of anthologies provides a stunning
selection of plays chosen by theatre director Annie Castledine. In addition to 'these fine
new translations by Tinch Minter and Elisabeth Bond-Pablé' (*Observer*) of Marieluise
Fleisser's **Purgatory in Ingolstadt** and **Pioneers in Ingolstadt** (premièred at the Gate
Theatre, London, March 1991), selected writings by Fleisser give a fascinating insight into
her life and friendship with the young Bertolt Brecht in pre-Nazi Germany. The volume
also contains Maureen Lawrence's **Tokens of Affection**, a powerful and unsettling play
set in a centre for the containment of violent and maladjusted adolescent girls and Sheila
Yeger's dream play, **Variations**, where Louise's research into nineteenth-century
composer and pianist Clara Schumann is played against the voices of other women, past
and present, real and fantastical, counterpointing her search for her own identity.

In 1991 Marieluise Fleisser's **Ingolstadt plays** won two awards: translators Tinch Minter
and Elisabeth Bond-Pablé won the first *Empty Space Award* presented by the London
Theatre Review and the Theatre Museum and joint directors Annie Castledine and
Stephen Daldry won a *Time Out* Award.

Each play has an afterword by its translator or author and the volume opens with an
introduction by the editor, Annie Castledine.

Annie Castledine was born in 1939 and brought up in Sheffield, South Yorkshire. The
major influences in her life have been her parents, who encouraged an absolute
commitment to theatre and to reading the classics before she was fifteen; Honor
Matthews, Head of Drama at Goldsmiths' College, University of London (1961) who
refined and extended her raw knowledge and enthusiasm; theatre directors Michael
Winter, Ronald Eyre and Trevor Nunn; the work of Peter Stein and Ariane Mnouchkine
and friends like Glenys Schindler, who is still introducing her to the work of women
playwrights in Europe.

in series with

Plays by Women: Volume One (ed. Micheline Wandor)
Caryl Churchill, *Vinegar Tom*; Pam Gems, *Dusa, Fish, Stas and Vi*; Louise Page, *Tissue*; Micheline Wandor adapted from Elizabeth Barrett Browning's verse novel, *Aurora Leigh*

Plays by Women: Volume Two (ed. Micheline Wandor)
Claire Luckham, *Trafford Tanzi*; Rose Leiman Goldemberg from Sylvia Plath, *Letters Home*; Maureen Duffy, *Rites*; Olwen Wymark, *Find Me*

Plays By Women: Volume Three (ed. Michelene Wandor)
Pam Gems, *Aunt Mary*; Debbie Horsfield, *Red Devils*; Sharon Pollock, *Blood Relations*; Lou Wakefield and the Women's Theatre Group, *Time Pieces*

Plays By Women: Volume Four (ed. Michelene Wandor)
Caryl Churchill, *Objections to Sex and Violence*; Grace Dayley, *Rose's Story*; Liz Lochhead, *Blood and Ice*; Alison Lyssa, *Pinball*

Plays by Women: Volume Five (ed. Mary Remnant)
Pam Gems, *Queen Christina*; Lorraine Hansberry, *A Raisin in the Sun*; Rona Munro, *Piper's Cave*; Jacqueline Rudet, *Money to Live*

Plays by Women: Volume Six (ed. Mary Remnant)
Cordelia Ditton and Maggie Ford, *About Face*; Maro Green and Caroline Griffin, *More*; Bryony Lavery, *Origins of the Species*; Deborah Levy, *Pax*; Eve Lewis, *Ficky Stingers*

Plays by Women: Volume Seven (ed. Mary Remnant)
Kay Adshead, *Thatcher's Women*; Claire Dowie, *Adult Child/Dead Child*; Lisa Evans, *Stamping, Shouting and Singing Home*; Marie Laberge, *Night*; Valerie Windsor, *Effie's Burning*

Plays by Women: Volume Eight (ed. Mary Remnant)
April de Angelis, *Ironmistress*; Mary Cooper, *Heartgame*, Janet Cresswell and Niki Johnson, *The One-Sided Wall*, Ayshe Raif, *Caving In*; Ena Lamont Stewart, *Towards Evening* and *Walkies Time*; Joan Wolton, *Motherlove*

Plays by Women: Volume Nine

Purgatory in Ingolstadt
Pioneers in Ingolstadt
plus
Avant-garde
Early Encounter
I Wasn't Aware of the Explosive
Marieluise Fleisser

Tokens of Affection
Maureen Lawrence

Variations on a Theme by Clara Schumann
Sheila Yeger

Edited and introduced by Annie Castledine

Methuen Drama

A Methuen New Theatrescript

This volume first published in Great Britain as a Methuen
paperback original in 1991 by Methuen Drama, Michelin House,
81 Fulham Road, London SW3 6RB.

Caution

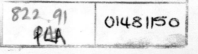

For my Mother and Father
who made me passionate about
theatre, and for my sister Sara

Annie Castledine

Contents

Introduction

'The only conundrum is that, although we are fifty-one per cent of the population, we remain so powerless.' Germaine Greer, The Late Show, BBC2, 19 October 1991

I was thinking about my introduction, and this pondering by Germaine Greer made me remember that I was so excited about editing this anthology because it gave me an opportunity to publish Maureen Lawrence's *Tokens of Affection*. I remember rushing to the telephone to tell her so: 'Now your extraordinary play can be published' I said, because for seven years we had been trying to achieve exactly that. In order to provide potential publishers with a dynamic view of it, I had even directed the play for a second time in one of my more remarkable productions at Derby Playhouse in 1989. No publisher came, in spite of the fact that '*Tokens of Affection* shows with great skill and economy, that the power we invest in caring professionals is really the power of the impotent, the enforced pragmatism of people strapped by financial constraints, and it is a power that corrupts.' *Plays and Players*, July 1990.

The play is a spectacular example of a woman playwright moulding a big idea, without fear, into an imaginative form which is sustained for over two hours. Acclaimed in national reviews, with seven bravura roles for women, it was ignored with a profound silence. Just as women's writing for the theatre is being ignored this autumn. This introduction bears witness to the fact that throughout the theatres of this whole country in October 1991 women's perspectives are not able to be seen; women's voices are not able to be heard. To be exact, a survey of the autumn season programmes of forty-eight regional repertory theatres in Britain reveals that out of 228 productions, only ten are by women.

These ten are:

1. *Augustine* by Anna Furse (commissioned by me for Derby Playhouse in 1989 but produced by Paines Plough, on tour, currently at the Bristol New Vic Studio)
2. *Our Country's Good* by Timberlake Wertenbaker at Chester Gateway Theatre
3. *My Cousin Rachel* by Daphne du Maurier at the Mercury Theatre, Colchester
4. *Merlin's Dream* by Karoline Leach at the Northcott Theatre, Exeter
5. *Worst Witch* by Jill Murphy at the Redgrave Theatre, Farnham
6. *Within the Fortress* by Gillian Richmond at the Wolsley Theatre, Richmond
7. *Buster Keaton* by Jane McCullogh at the Emlyn Williams Studio Theatre, Mold
8. *In Broad Daylight* by Lesley Bruce at the Nuffield Theatre, Southampton
9. *Mary Queen of Scots Got Her Head Chopped Off* by Liz Lochhead at the Contact Theatre, Manchester
10. *The Singing Ringing Tree* by Charlotte Keatley, also at the Contact Theatre, Manchester (woman Artistic Director, Brigid Larmour)

In London's West End, which includes the Royal Shakespeare Company in Stratford-upon-Avon, only three out of sixty-one productions are by women, with one other having a woman co-writer. The four plays are:

1. *The Mousetrap* by Agatha Christie at St Martin's Theatre
2. *Three Birds Alighting on a Field* by Timberlake Wertenbaker at the Royal Court Theatre
3. *The Blue Angel* by Pam Gems at the Royal Shakespeare Company's The Other Place
4. *Miss Chester* co-written by Florence Marryat and Sir Charles L Young at the Players Theatre

Only thirteen productions out of 289 is alarming and cannot be representative. Why, for instance, isn't Sheila Yeger's poetic and innovatory play about Clara Schumann, *Variations*, on that list? It is because, apart from Max Stafford-Clark, Artistic Director of the Royal Court Theatre, London, and fringe theatre in Newcastle and London, no Artistic Director is taking responsibility for promoting productions of plays by women. As Sheila Yeger says, women playwrights are 'forced to exist on the fringes of polite society, a beggar forever at the gate, battering, unheard, at doors which hardly ever open. Although, as a woman, I am the same sex as more than half the population, my voice is constantly treated as though it were that of an awkward and unacceptable minority, my opinions, viewpoint, emotions, considered to be of less significance and interest than those of my male counterparts.'

Brecht, when handed Marieluise Fleisser's first play, *Purgatory in Ingolstadt*, at least realised, opportunistically, that a great scandal could be created, and then went on to encourage the writing of *Pioneers in Ingolstadt*. However, it wasn't until 1960 that Fleisser, free of Brecht's influence at last, revised both the *Ingolstadt* plays, so that they received great acclaim as part of the German classical repertoire. Her voice had never been heard in this country, although Brecht's is everywhere.

Whilst at Derby Playhouse, I commissioned translations of both plays from Tinch Minter and Elizabeth Bond-Pablé. At the same time, Stephen Daldry, Artistic Director of the Gate Theatre, was reading American translations of the plays in the Royal National Theatre script archive. We were both passionate in our belief that these plays should be seen in this country and when we joined forces to produce them at the Gate Theatre in March 1991, nothing could stop Fleisser's voice being heard at last. But this 'major theatrical event' (*Time Out* Award, 1991) and 'major theatrical reclamation' was completely unsubsidised. It is surely an expression of all I have been saying in this introduction that the company had to work for three months of this year, from January to March, without pay of any kind, in order that the Fleisser plays could be seen.

The four plays in this volume, like the playwrights in volumes one to eight, prove that women can write, that they can tackle classical themes and create plays which transcend time and place and be acknowledged Great. Yet this exceptional work is marginalised or neglected altogether. Women playwrights are not given enough practice through production and have to snatch experience where they can. Unpaid performers, few resources, short rehearsal periods may result in poor showings, critical disfavour and no second chance. If women playwrights are seen, as Claire Luckham has put it, as 'rather strange ladies who are kindly allowed to speak', it is because their work is not the first choice of those in power in our theatre. Until it is, volumes like this, ignominiously called *Plays by Women*, will form the most important life-line to women's writing in the theatre.

Annie Castledine, October 1991

Purgatory in Ingolstadt

Marieluise Fleisser

translated by Elisabeth Bond-Pablé and Tinch Minter

Characters

Berotter
Olga
Clementine } *Berotter's children*
Christian
Roelle
Roelle's Mother
Protasius, *an individual*
Gervasius, *his hanger-on*
Peps
Hermine Seitz
Crusius
First Altar Server, Second Altar Server
First Schoolboy, Second Schoolboy, Third Schoolboy
Schoolboys, Schoolgirls, Crowd

Purgatory in Ingolstadt received its British première at the Gate Theatre, London on 1 March 1990, with the following cast:

Clementine	Sandy McDade
Olga	Teresa McElroy
Christian	Russell Porter
Berotter	Godfrey Jackman
Roelle	Christopher Campbell
Peps	Ignatius Anthony
Hermine Seitz	Zara Turner
Protasius	Simon Tyrrell
First Server	Mark Lewis Jones
Second Server	Robert Bowman
Mother	Beatrice Comins
Gervasius	James Dreyfus
Crusius	Thomas Craig
First Schoolboy	Will Barton

other parts played by members of the company

Directed by Annie Castledine, Stephen Daldry
Designed by Ian MacNeil
Music by Stephen Warbeck
Lighting Designed by Ace McCarron

Scene One

Living room at the Berotters'. **Berotter, Olga, Clementine,** *who is offstage at first.*

Clementine Now where's the key to the laundry-chest? Nothing's ever in its right place here.

Berotter Cat got your tongue?

Clementine Just when I've got to change the beds.

Berotter So Hermine Seitz is expected to sleep in a bed that hasn't been changed?

Olga On the tallboy.

Berotter Have you had the nerve to take something out on your own say so? How many times must I tell you that's not allowed here.

Olga Clementine never lets me have anything.

Clementine (*coming in*) You've got to yell first. Your slip's looking at me again, Olga. Look at the way you go around.

Olga You never ever let me have anything.

Clementine Whatever will Hermine think?

Olga If you ask me, she needn't come.

Berotter Frau Seitz is lying in hospital. Where else can she put her?

Olga You don't know Hermine.

Berotter She was your friend at the convent.

Clementine And she always ate your gruel that you loathed.

Olga Mama wouldn't have wanted her in the house.

Clementine She's talking about Mama!

Berotter I wouldn't do such a thing to Frau Seitz.

Olga You like seeing her.

Berotter I shan't argue with you. Too smart for your father, aren't you? She knows Latin – trying to impress me.

Clementine She didn't shed a single tear at the interment.

Berotter Got to have her say.

Clementine And she didn't go to church today.

Berotter You didn't go to church? You set me a fine example, don't you? And she's the older one.

Olga In church the evil fiend lurks around the confessional.

Clementine That's your bad conscience.

Berotter One can't be sure whether to send you there. I want no more of your mortifications. You make a point of overdoing it.

Clementine Without you what would we do?

Olga You say that every day, the lot of you.

Berotter I want to know what you come home from school for. Never goes near the kitchen.

Olga And you don't ever take me out for a drink.

Berotter You've got nothing to say.

Olga I got that from you, then. You didn't let me grow up like a human being.

Berotter I had no favourites among my children.

Olga My face didn't suit you, a child notices these things. You were always telling me I held my head askew.

Berotter It wasn't your mother who made you brazen.

Christian (*coming in*) Watcha!

Berotter People don't throw their satchels in the corner like that. Pick it up and put it down again properly.

Christian We don't use slates any more.

Berotter Less of your lip.

Clementine He's got that from Olga.

Christian Roelle's really getting my goat.

Olga Something up with Roelle?

Christian Something went on between you and Roelle?

Olga Oh, ages ago.

Christian If you ask me, you can make up stories about all the girls. I know my Olga.

Olga He's smelly. He doesn't dare go near water.

Christian He says he's got you over a barrel.

Olga Not that again.

Christian He says he's got something on you and if he wants he could turn you in.

Olga Young people always believe they can pressurise you.

Christian He'll be coming here, when he's got a moment.

Olga Big talk.

Clementine Olga held me up. Your collar's not ready yet.

Christian Convent-cow!

Clementine That's how it always is. He doesn't have a go at his Olga.

Christian Your Roelle's going round announcing that Hermine Seitz lost her slip in the middle of Artillery Square.

Clementine My Roelle wouldn't do that.

Berotter You shouldn't be so hard on young Roelle, Olga. You walked past as if he was a puff of air. Even though he said hello.

Olga He's got a neck like a worm.

Clementine But he wears those high collars.

Berotter And you're such a beaut.

Christian That's the fascination, the floppy way he nods his head.

Berotter He makes you pity him. His face went bright red. That's when I know for sure someone's interested in me. You've got it coming to you. You're hard.

Olga When I was a child he wanted something filthy from me.

Clementine He wanted something filthy from you, never. Olga always wants them all for herself.

Berotter Well, he is a human being. You must have learnt these fine manners at the convent. You're not usually so delicate.

Clementine Olga's too grand for us. One mustn't notice the way she goes around.

Christian You shouldn't have a go at her about Roelle. Roelle's a coward. And the others won't go round with him either. He won't smoke with us in case he's sick. He doesn't trust himself near water.

Clementine There you go taking your dear Olga's side. This once I'm talking. What happened with the dog?

Christian It wasn't her fault.

Clementine Somebody stuck pins in its eyes.

Olga Not me.

Clementine It stumbled about from one side to the other. You were watching.

Berotter How could you?

Olga They baited it in front of my window,

that's no way to behave. It made them believe they were strong.

Berotter Who baited it?

Olga Leave me alone.

Clementine May it haunt you one day.

Olga It was the little brown one with the floppy ears.

Christian (*to* **Clementine**) You're always casting aspersions. She's in a different class.

Clementine You think Olga loves you. Olga hasn't got a heart.

Christian Olga isn't like you.

Clementine Go to Olga.

Berotter Stop putting your neck askew. Have they got to row over you? Stop driving me mad with that face of yours.

Clementine You can be sure we'll go on thinking about her.

Berotter What happened about the dog? Were you watching? All down to – you?

Clementine I steer clear of Roelle.

Olga Are you going to beat me?

Berotter When did I last beat you?

Olga That was ages ago. And I know it's your redemption.

Berotter Don't punish me for my sainted Anna.

Olga Beat me and you'll be beating my mother through me.

Berotter I can't do it. Listen to me when I'm talking, flesh of my Anna. (*He throws a fit.*) Observe the way I'm lying here. This is the man who was so hard on his Anna. The children ought to know.

The children stand indecisively round their Father. They all pick him up.

Clementine I can see she's about to get away with it again.

Berotter You're no angel either.

Olga Am I right?

Berotter You're right. All of you are right. It's only me who's not right.

Christian Don't degrade yourself like this in front of your children.

Berotter You mustn't always leave your father out. I want to know why we've got nothing to say to each other.

Olga I can never just spout.

Berotter You're my good girl again. – If only Anna was here.

Clementine Do you love Olga more than me?

Berotter Time must weigh heavy on your hands, you just stand about. Now Christian's collar, when will it be mended? Has he got to ask again?

Clementine I'm good enough for that.

Berotter You should know your work.

Clementine Olga doesn't have to do a thing.

Berotter But she's feeling ill.

Clementine What kind of illness is it?

Berotter You're to be quiet.

Clementine I know very well you hate me. Everybody hates me.

Berotter Now she's having a go.

Clementine They're always trying to shut me up. Mama's looking down at me to see how you're treating her child.

Olga You believe that!

Clementine It's my Mama.

Olga I didn't want to do anything wicked. She mustn't think that about me.

Clementine You ran away from her, when she was dead.

Olga You can't let on to her, can you?

Clementine She doesn't distress herself over you. Mum sees into our hearts.

Olga I didn't want to make a corpse of it. It isn't a human being yet, that's how they explained it to me. It can't feel any pain. The catechist says they go to a different place.

Clementine You're scared.

Olga I didn't want to cheat Heaven of a soul. It hasn't got a soul. It's still too small for that.

Clementine You won't never go to Heaven. You'll be burning in hell whilst I'm lying in Abraham's bosom.

Olga You won't never want to know me then.

Clementine I won't hear when you cry. The gulf is too great.

Olga That's your child. That's pious people.

Clementine How are you yourself?

Olga Go on shoving my nose in it. That's what will never stop.

Christian Would you like to be somebody else, Olga?

Olga That wouldn't do for me, either. I'm not to know what's what.

Clementine Roelle's come into the house. Roelle's on the stairs.

Berotter Stop jumping around in front of me. He hasn't come on your account.

Clementine (*to* **Olga**) And you want to take this one from me too?

Olga Have I said I want him?

Roelle (*coming in*) Hello everyone.

Christian Teacher's pet, in person. Just turn round again.

Berotter Christian, you know well enough. Let him get inside first. Look after our eldest a little, young man. She's so temperamental. That must come from being anaemic. She was feeling ill today.

Roelle Of course. I'm only too happy to oblige.

Clementine What a handsome man to find here so early in the morning.

Berotter Come along, Clementine. Young man, on your best behaviour. (*Going off with* **Clementine**.)

Christian Softy. He shows a different side to grown-ups.

Roelle You'll never get the knack of superior people's manners.

Christian Olga's got her maths coaching, clear off. Peps will be here any minute.

Roelle So I'll have them both at once. I say this with placid persistence.

Christian And now he's bringing your famous Seitz with him, because she's going to stay with us for a while.

Roelle I'm not moving on for her sake. I make no bones about it.

Christian You wanted something filthy from her.

Roelle Oh yes, when?

Christian Olga doesn't want you.

Roelle She should tell me that herself. Out of my way. (*Pushing him away.*)

Christian Chicken!

Roelle Here's my autograph for you. (*He hits* **Christian**. *To* **Olga**.) My father sells snuff. That's what sort my father is.

Olga I never said that.

Roelle In front of the protestant church. You said, I'm smelly.

Olga I was a child then.

Roelle It's an overseas business.

Christian He can't add two and two together. He's putting on his feeble phiz for us.

Roelle It isn't smelly at ours. I want you to say that to me.

Olga You'll wait a long time.

Christian Let me try out my French hold, come at it. Unbutton your collar so it doesn't get in the way.

Roelle Fräulein, let me give you an overall view of the situation. In me you see no dog with its tail between its legs. You see no creature ridden with fear. But what do I perceive when I turn towards you? To my mind's eye you stand like a little heap of misery.

Olga. You've got something unpleasant in your eyes.

Roelle I'm not going red in the face in front of someone like you. You're a right beauty, good to know that. One should go and broadcast it all over the shop right now.

Olga Think you can harm me?

Roelle Well, I got it from Frau Schnepf.

Olga *tries not to show she's startled.*

It isn't bad for me. It's only bad for you.

Olga I don't know the woman. I've never been in the house.

Roelle You were seen.

Olga I don't understand that.

Roelle You probably had the idea Frau Schnepf would keep her lips sealed for your sake. – The woman has no need to be afraid.

Olga I haven't a clue what you're on about.

Roelle The woman doesn't do it any more, she told my mother. It's illegal. – The woman's had it up to here. And then she blurted out who wanted it. Women's talk. Didn't hold a thing back – you really should be more choosy with your people.

Olga You – monster.

Roelle What are we going to do now, us two? Doesn't a little dicky-bird tell you? Over here. One more little step.

Olga *goes as if senseless.*

Recite your lines.

Olga You have an overseas business that isn't smelly.

Christian Olga, how can you put up with this?

Roelle Your sister doesn't want you.

Olga Christian, can't you be tactful?

Christian My compliments – to the bulging neck. (*Going off.*)

Roelle Here I stand smiling, all meekness, my lips cracked. You'll have a bad time over me, I've worn my knees out begging for this. There's not a move you can make now.

Olga You've got these high collars. I will look at you again.

Roelle That's good. I'm deeply indebted to you. Maybe you're suffering remorse? Had second thoughts? Someone – you could say she's my heart-throb – told me I smell, maybe it was you. I'm not talking about my emotion. You went swimming and the others went with you. I watched you from afar, me, a lad who smells. But Horn was after you and he said, that one's got a pair of legs. That evening, you didn't put your stockings back on, Horn is no older than me, either. But I stood by the wall, as if my skin wasn't the same as the others.

Olga You had bad thoughts.

Roelle I'd taken a box of matches with me and waited for you to go past. I was holding it in my hand, my neck was throbbing. I thought to myself, any moment now I'll set her skirt on fire. You should have said, hey, you do look pale. What you said was, Horn, don't go around with him. And I loathed myself.

Olga I hadn't the faintest idea.

Roelle Nowadays people don't set fire to skirts. The moon goes past the window, I see your light from my room. But it doesn't matter if I smell, it wouldn't kill you, someone like you. There's always revenge. With your permission, I'll light up. It has a more calming effect on me.

Olga You know how to smoke?

Roelle Always have. (*He smokes.*)

Olga I'll go arm in arm with you in front of the whole town.

Roelle I'd rather not be seen again in this hole with one of your sort. I prefer my bad skin.

Olga What do I have to do so you – stay silent?

Roelle For once I can wield power. I suppose that sounds like double-dutch to you. I think she's going to make up to me now, 'cause I can tell the whole town just as I like. Are you reformed? You're the same. You'll treat me just as before.

Olga What do you know about me?

Roelle As your catechist I ask you, is this child of your less-than-immaculate conception an object of love or of hatred to you?

Olga It's nothing but my adversary.

Roelle As your catechist I ask you, do you deny that you wanted to eliminate it?

Olga If only my mother had done that to me!

Roelle She so to speak comes along and knocks it dead with some implement.

Olga You're always so certain you're right. What'll become of the child, you don't say. And what will become of me.

Roelle You and that perfect Peps of yours should have given some thought to that before.

Olga Thought, huh? They're all tormenting me. If you want to be free – if freedom comes in a beautiful shape and washes over you –

Roelle (*coming up to her*) You mean – like this?

She shudders.

Olga He comes here and wants to share a sin with me.

Roelle I want to say, bend the knee, and she will bend her knees and will be as a handmaid in my sight.

Olga What are you doing with a shiny face so near mine?

Roelle The neck and the arms are mine. That's something for me to hold on to.

Olga Your voice is cracking.

Roelle I'll let you notice it. I don't care.

Olga I don't want to. You make people really ill.

Roelle I'll do it. I won't do it. I'll do it.

Olga Go away!

Roelle Not going! We're bound for hell whatever.

Olga You! Feel for yourself what kind of head you've got on.

Roelle I can't hear a thing. That isn't you.

Olga You'll blush with shame tomorrow.

Roelle To me you're like the serpent.

Olga (*getting the upper hand*) Sir, you're too cross for me.

Roelle The message has reached me, what you've got to say to me. When I'm with other people, it'd make a sick dog laugh.

Olga Wash your temples in cold water and collect your senses.

Roelle Not a drop.

Olga Can you stand?

Roelle You've always got to insult me. You don't do anything else.

Olga I should have hit myself across the mouth.

Roelle If you still have something to say, do it at once, otherwise I'm gone.

Olga Oh yes, I'll even genuflect nicely to you. I'll send Peps round to you, just like that.

Roelle Go and ask if he'll marry you then.

Olga I have already asked him.

Roelle He's worse than I am. I'm warning you.

Olga He can't do as he likes, either. He's told me I'm to be his sweet reason!

Roelle It's easy for him to tell you that. He says his rosary, now he's going about with Hermine Seitz. Let Seitz give you all the lowdown. You two are so close, aren't you? (*Going.*)

Olga I knew it.

Scene Two

Later that day, **Olga**, **Peps** *and* **Hermine** *with* **Roelle** *still offstage, talking.*

Roelle I don't want to. I won't be forced.

Peps You've got to.

Dragging **Roelle** *on by force.* **Hermine** *following. To* **Olga**.

Has he asked you to forgive him?

Roelle I can't do it. It always comes out different with me.

Olga Now what is it?

Peps Olga, you don't know a thing.

Hermine He's the one who had to go to confession, but then they didn't cope with him in the confessional.

Roelle To me that's no shame.

Hermine But it is.

Roelle I'll simply go to another priest.

Hermine You'll have to confess as well that the first one denied you absolution.

Roelle I'll never confess ever again.

Peps What'll you do then when you have to go up to the altar-rail with the rest of the class?

Roelle That's my business.

Peps Well, you've got a point there.

Hermine If a man stops going to confession, he's sure to go to hell.

Roelle I can call up total remorse.

Peps Not you. The Saints can.

Hermine I wouldn't want to know what someone like him says to his confessor if something like this happens to him.

Olga What do you want from him? Leave him alone to confess what he likes.

Peps Olga, you don't know a thing. He filled the whole confessional with you. He named you by name and really dragged you through it.

Roelle That's a lie.

Peps I was standing nearby and pricked up my ears, sonny boy. I heard every word.

Hermine That's only to be expected.

Roelle You're not allowed to disclose anything under the seal of confession.

Peps I haven't taken Holy Orders.

Hermine He's not bound to secrecy.

Roelle You were eavesdropping.

Peps Do you know what you've done? You've ruined her reputation to the priest who sees her twice a week at school.

Roelle I had to come out with it. I was under duress.

Olga If only you'd left my name out.

Peps He doesn't need any names.

Roelle Next time I'll leave it out.

Hermine You're not going to confession again, surely?

Peps He'll learn, one of these days.

Hermine He can't even do a proper genuflection.

Roelle You're the Olympic champ, I suppose.

Hermine Boys never know how they're to be about the sacraments.

Roelle I went in with the best of intentions.

Hermine Did you suffer bodily torments?

Roelle No.

Hermine Well, I don't call that real remorse then.

Roelle Bodily torment is more in girls' line.

Hermine Did you hold your prayer-book right up to your mouth?

Roelle No.

Hermine There are rules, one has to obey. I'm strict about that.

Peps Hermine, being pious!

Olga She roams about with Peps long after the Sexton's gone home.

Hermine Where is it written down that I must avoid him, like dangerous company or evil situations?

Olga Nothing to do with me.

Peps Give us some peace, you've always been my sweet reason.

Olga 'Cause you've become a totally different person.

Hermine Suppose he's lost interest. He's had another one for some time.

Olga Then I'll announce the engagement in Saturday's paper. Just so you know.

Peps How big a dowry do you think Hermine will get?

Olga I must stand my ground. I must wait till my true love recognises me.

Hermine He'd be really saddled with you.

Peps With her you'd have to be first down every morning and turning the coffee-grinder with hushed eyes.

Olga Mummy, you told me so.

Hermine This is where your sweet reason gets you.

Peps This once it hasn't turned out the way she envisaged.

Hermine She thought, if she dug her heels in she'd get her way.

Roelle One doesn't treat Olga like that. Olga was like a child.

Olga Roelle's the only one.

Roelle (*to* **Hermine**) It's all your evil doing.

Hermine (*next to* **Peps**) Have you had enough of ogling the chemical attraction between us two?

Roelle For me Olga's face is like St John's, the favourite disciple.

Hermine I'll take your crummy halo away. What was it with the dog?

Roelle Well, what do you know? It's no easy matter to put something into a dog's eyes. I thought when it screamed, that's like my own poor soul. Olga understood me.

Hermine He's admitted it. You are my witnesses.

Roelle You bitch.

Hermine I'll split on him to the teacher, so he'll be slung out. These are the bad elements that must be rooted out of the school.

Roelle That's not down to you.

Hermine I'm going to split on him this very day – right now. (*Going off.* **Roelle** *goes after her.*)

Peps (*fixing* **Olga** *with his eyes*) Is it gone?

Olga No.

Peps Why not? I gave you the address of a Frau Schnepf.

Olga She's stopped doing it.

Peps You're lying, you didn't even go there.

Olga Cross my heart – I did go. She refused to do it.

Peps Then you must have gone about it very stupidly.

Olga She says she's done time for it. They keep tabs on her. She says we don't have the kind of cash she'd do it for.

Peps Then you'll have to find someone else. I can't let you have the child.

Olga I'm scared.

Peps You've got to do away with it. Nothing unusual about that. Happens all the time. A child's no use to me.

Olga You don't like me any more.

Peps Do something about it, or you'll really get to know me.

Scene Three

An avenue. **Protasius**, **Olga**.

Protasius How extraordinary, that of all people you should be walking in this unfrequented avenue.

Olga Look, you're chasing me.

Protasius The only mistake is that you're unforeseeably alone. I was convinced you'd have some characteristic companion in tow. Tut tut, tut tut, Fräulein Olga.

Olga If you don't stop pestering me, I'll scream.

Protasius Anxiety is a drive and this drive is expressed compulsively in certain human beings. I say so myself. If I were you I wouldn't want to be completely alone with a journeyman in this unfrequented avenue. With me it's rather different. You know, I'm not a man of blood.

Olga Friday is our day for beggars.

Protasius Thank you so much. I'm familiar with such cruelty. But I am not the impecunious beggar you take me for. My Doctor Hähnle, who's a figure of importance, sends me. Handle me with kid gloves.

Olga You're molesting me.

Protasius He does cling to you, Roelle, 'cause I know. You've got the biggest influence on him.

Olga If it's Roelle you want, you'll have to go to Roelle. Why come trailing after me?

Protasius I'm driven only by necessity. Fräulein Olga, let me in all patience familiarise you with the facts. That is to say, his mother, this hard-hearted woman, she won't let me near the chappie any more. And yet he gave me his solemn word.

Olga What's that to do with me?

Protasius You're my possible roundabout route to the wanted man.

Olga I don't understand you.

Protasius Roundabout route or escape route. 'Cause my Doctor Hähnle has from time immemorial sent me on the arduous errands and my Doctor is by no means a patient man. You see, I would have given you all the details nice and slowly.

Olga Why are you tracking Roelle down?

Protasius 'Cause he no longer comes by himself, I have to fetch the chappie. 'Cause it isn't done of his own free will, when he keeps on being pumped and afterwards his whole psyche is recorded.

Olga I wouldn't let a doctor peer about inside me.

Protasius But it's considered effective for the long-term healing process.

Olga Is something wrong with Roelle?

Protasius What have I been saying all this time? There is a well-founded supposition, and if this proves to be the case, then the chappie is frequently not right in the head.

Olga But he knows nothing about it.

Protasius He mustn't get excited my Doctor Hähnle says. But I say, I regard this as a common principle in the life of a human being.

Olga Then why don't you leave him in peace?

Protasius 'Cause we're left hanging. He leaves science hanging.

Olga Roelle's got his head screwed on. He's his own man that way.

Protasius It's also on account of current supervision. I say, the chappie shouldn't be allowed on the streets with this tendency of his. One cannot know how it may develop. The chappie could be a danger. But if you listen to his mother, this has always been the darkest secret.

Olga Roelle will have good reasons for not going there.

Protasius He lacks the wider view. 'Cause as things stand, when something happens to the chappie, and we can carry out our observations on him, then he'll be categorised. It's only these very rare human beings that one can categorise, says my doctor. If he stays away out of sheer bloodymindedness, where am I going to get a comparable stand-in?

Olga What can someone like him possibly offer you?

Protasius I really have to marvel at you. Your self-worship prevents you from seeing what's in front of your nose. The chappie is a dismal heathen and he dabbles in magic.

Olga Don't you start being abusive. I'm going.

Protasius You mustn't do this to us. We've only scratched this chappie's surface, that's no position for our sort to be in. We're making a study on him.

Olga But Roelle's not like a human being.

Protasius Well, I'll say this, there's no great difference between him and us.

Olga But it's better if you know it.

Protasius However, if the need had arisen, and the doctor had desperately needed someone for his observations, I'd have understudied him, I say. But that wouldn't suit my retiring personality so well.

Olga What have I got to do with it?

Protasius Tell him in no uncertain terms that he's to come and that he's doing it for the sake of science.

Olga It'll turn his head.

Protasius Oh, that's all to the good.

Olga I don't even know what sort of person you are and where he'll land up.

Protasius I am inseparably linked to my doctor. I am his procurer and his spy. Don't have a low opinion of me on that account. I procure human beings for him, and he makes his immortal discoveries on them. Without me, I say, he'd be sunk.

Olga I can see you're exploiting the chappie.

Protasius We exploit him and we stick a pin through him, but we guarantee him a kind of immortality.

Olga You're slowly making me uneasy.

Protasius From this uneasiness comes our precision.

Olga I won't carry your message, that's flat. He should be completely free.

Protasius The chappie is no longer free.

Scene Four

Side alley at a fair. Behind a gypsy's caravan.
Roelle, Two Altar Servers.

First Server
In Ingolstadt it's a fact
They've got a horse-drawn tram
And one nag cannot draw
The other one is lame
The driver's hunchbacked
The wheels are all askew
And every five minutes

The coach swings out of true.

Roelle Can't you give us a bit of peace from your idiotic bawling?

First Server Take a look at him, we aren't to move a muscle.

Second Server Watch it, or we'll dump you in it, when you make your appearance as a saint before the multitude.

First Server Didn't oughta have said that. Now he's putting on a martyred look.

Roelle You must admit, I've got to get myself in readiness. I must give ear to the voice within and get deeply submerged into myself.

First Server You get there, and after you tell me. Then I'll tiptoe off to join the heavenly choir, once I've got this off my back.

Second Server Stop puffing yourself up. You can't get along without us whipping up an audience for you. Not a single sod would hear you without us.

Roelle Then it shall not come to pass. For I know neither the day nor the hour when the spirit moves me.

Second Server Stay here. No one's sneaking away. You can do it, see.

First Server We know what you're up to. Your face has turned green.

Second Server Nothing for it, matey. If you claim you're a colour-fast saint, you gotta prove it, see.

Roelle Angels come unto me.

First Server And they shall bear thee in their hands that thou hurt not thy foot against a stone.

Second Server If you keep such company, then you're going to introduce them to us poor shits.

Roelle But it doesn't always work. I never

know in advance when it'll happen. The angels are present or the angels are absent. I can't fetch them out of the blue. The angels must move me by surprise.

Second Server Put your back into it, see. We've gone round spreading the word now and the people are keen to see real angels for once.

Roelle Angels can't be seen. Angels can only be heard.

First Server You'll have to settle that with the people, then. We're not letting you go, got that.

Roelle My children, you're blind and you're deaf.

Second Server We don't understand you, we know that all right.

First Server Well, how can we understand him, when we're not disciples of his. And we'll see to it we're not.

Second Server Wouldn't do us no good. His way, you'd be tied to your bed with the crucifix, so your sins come easier to your mind.

First Server And we're not playing, got that. We've had a bellyful of all this piety. We're bored with handling this stuff.

Second Server How long did you have to pray spread-eagled? Was your Mum standing behind you in a state of bliss?

Roelle You'd be sacrilegious, even if you handled consecrated objects hundreds of times.

First Server Look how I knock back the communion wine. (*Mimes drinking.*) 'Cause a server knows full well what tastes good.

Roelle Why have you got it in for me?

Second Server Perhaps we don't like you.

First Server This is the one in whom I am well pleased, or maybe not.

Second Server You can do it, see.

First Server You having second thoughts about exhibiting your sanctity before this sacrilegious crew.

Second Server Let's play Roelle till then.

First Server You're on.

Second Server I'm also known as Roelle. The Great Panjandrum from cloud cuckoo land. I'll lead the way.

First Server Give us permission?

Roelle I'm miles above all this.

First Server 'Cause if you didn't permit it, we'd piss on your permission after.

Second Server I am Saint Roelle, I'll lead the way. Lo! I come from the thrones and prinicipalities and call without cease or let –

Roelle Wrong.

Second Server Like this then. – Clear the path 'cause I'm coming now. You dirty dust-eaters down there show me your tonsures.

First Server
Aniseedroelle's full of pride
His shoes are wood like ours not hide.

Second Server You can slide down my unique posterior, you idolators. I say this with a heretical gesture of my hand.

First Server Hear him talk, the crazy coot?

Roelle You need your spine crushing.

Second Server My dear fellow, the Police have forbidden it.

Roelle At him. Beat him up. You'll get something after.

First Server (*beating up the second one*) One for you, one for Roelle and one for Roelle again.

Second Server That's not fair. I'm not having the ones for Roelle.

First Server What are you playing Roelle for then?

Second Server My tummy hurty me, my backbone hurty me, my words don't flow any more like a blocked gargoyle. I'm unjustly maltreated and misunderstood.

First Server Hey! Must you spit from your foetid mouth into my face when you talk?

Second Server What do I do?

First Server I'll spit back then.

Roelle He'll have to put up with it.

Second Server I'm not staying nailed up with you two any more. I'm off to the prairies.

Roelle We'll let him drop dead. Then we'll bury him.

Second Server I'm not letting you bury me.

Roelle You've got to, you've got to.

Second Server Being in command's easy. (*Over* **Roelle***'s head.*) We'll bury *him*. We'll just bury him, the real Roelle.

Roelle I'm not playing any more.

First Server No, we need him this evening.

Second Server You'll be lucky.

First Server I'm allowed to do something and you're not. 'Cause I'm the one who has to carry the Holy Book across during the Epistle, moi!

Second Server Dominus Bread-is-bum.

First Server Without us what would they do? You're the only useless lump. You're just so saintly, or want to be.

Roelle I only say, you'll see.

Second Server Let's stop talking, Kare, now he's getting down to thinking. We can't keep up with this.

First Server We're missing something up top for this, see.

Roelle I don't understand that. You've got the eyes of human beings, but you're like ravening beasts.

Second Server Maybe 'cause you're forcing it on us.

Roelle I'll figure it out for you once more.

Second Server Kare, we're about to be transfigured. Let's give our spirits into his hands, our superior spirits, then we can just renounce them. 'Cause he's pontificating at us.

Roelle Have you ever heard of the active power of love?

Second Server I don't go to picture palaces. My father takes my serving money away.

Roelle It changes you. You're not knowable any more.

Second Server Yeah?

Roelle Saul becomes Paul.

Second Server It's not easy to see in you. If anything you're becoming worse.

Roelle What you think yesterday's Roelle would have done?

First Server He would have taken to his heels and hollered from round the corner, they're too insignificant for me.

Roelle And today's Roelle?

First Server What does he get up to, then?

Roelle He positions himself so he fixes his eyes on you from top to toe and says – he says: You are the poor in spirit.

Second Server Here we go again. 'Cause you're proud got that and we are too insignificant for you.

Olga (*coming round the caravan*) I've been running all round the fair.

First Server Now I nearly whistled.

Second Server
On the first floor there's a lighty
P'rhaps she'll come down in her nighty.

Olga Roelle, come on, let's go behind the caravan, they're pointing at me.

Second Server And what if we come with you behind the caravan?

Roelle No one's laying a finger on you.

First Server This one's a shrinking violet.

Second Server This one's got to be kick started, then she'll be a good goer.

Roelle Hide, I can see the halo behind her face.

Olga Mine?

Roelle You can die of it. The heavenly light.

Second Server You can't pontificate at us, you eccentric devil, you.

First Server He's got religious mania.

Second Server You can't pass her off as an angel to us. She's known all over the town.

Roelle She wants something from me. Just be reasonable. Leave us alone for once.

First Server She wants something from him. And what do the poor servers get?

Second Server Hey, Kare, let's leave them to spoon, 'cause it's nothing to us.

First Server Let's drag our boots away.

Second Server But we're not going far. You're still under our observation, understand? You know what's in store for you.

Roelle Nothing to me.

Second Server
Go quick
The priest's sick
The sexton's donging
The billy-goat's bonging
Baa.

The **Servers** *go off.*

Roelle They know not what they do.

Olga I've come.

Roelle (*stroking* **Olga***'s forehead and face*) You must do my bidding. You must be sensitive to the least of my emotions.

Olga I immediately thought there'd be some catch.

Roelle Do you want to become saintly?

Olga Me!

Roelle Do what I tell you.

Olga But I don't want to.

Roelle You're not keeping up with me, I saw that already.

Olga That's how it is with most people, they don't want to be sensitive to each other.

Roelle That's why we got together.

Olga (*looking at him*) But you're not to make anything of it.

Roelle With your perpetual observation I'll soon get put off.

Olga I'm surely allowed to look out of my eyes.

Roelle But you are putting me off.

Olga I'm looking at the crooked curve of your face.

Roelle A person can't choose his face.

Olga 'Cause I say, you're not right.

Roelle Why am I not right, then?

Olga That's how it is with physiognomy.

'Cause the instincts paint themselves there, even if they're concealed. So I say, something is missing in you.

Roelle I never realised that.

Olga Why don't you stir your stumps? You're like an animal, that acts dead.

Roelle I always get so ham-fisted in front of piercing eyes.

Olga You've got to stir your stumps so what one doesn't yet know one can see in your movements.

Roelle If I'm stared at like that, I can't even gather a single original thought.

Olga I don't know then why I've sat myself down with you. And I want to find something out.

Roelle Who or what am I to you?

Olga That should be all the same to you.

Roelle But it isn't all the same to me.

Olga You were right about Peps. He doesn't like me any more. He's getting so mean.

Roelle He's not worth crying over.

Olga I don't know anyone. I can't see a way out.

Roelle I won't do a thing to you. For me you'll always be Olga.

Olga But I'm having a child.

Roelle That's how it is then.

Olga My tummy's getting big.

Roelle You mustn't have it aborted. The child's already alive, even if it doesn't know anything.

Olga Thou shalt not kill.

Roelle It went through my head. The child was conceived by love. Maybe, it'll become a beautiful child.

Olga Sure.

Roelle It should be allowed to live, even if it isn't beautiful.

Olga But what am I to do?

Roelle You won't let yourself be helped. Even if you don't want to face the fact – I am the important man in your life. Do what I tell you. Go to the country before anyone notices. Give birth to the child where you're totally unknown.

Olga It has to be paid for.

Roelle I give you my word I'll find a sum.

Olga You.

Roelle A beautiful child, I'd like to have.

Olga You haven't got to have it.

Roelle But I want to have it.

Olga (*bitterly*) And me with it.

Roelle It's not to become like its father.

Olga You're barging in on something –

Roelle It'll make us human beings, while it's becoming a human being.

Olga One mustn't lean on people. It leads nowhere. (*Running off.*)

Roelle But it can't be like this.

Mother (*coming in with a billy-can*) Now I've got you, you bloody-minded brat, you. Going to do what I want now?

Roelle You can't run after me with your stupid soup. You don't know what it'll lead to. I'm giving you fair warning.

Mother Now, this is to be eaten. Do I have to give you a sermon every Thursday on not leaving your sago soup. Sit in front of it for an hour, just as you like. I'm not leaving till you do.

Roelle Mum, I've the best will in the world. But it rather offends my sensitivity.

Mother And there's that good egg in it.

Roelle I can't eat out of such a receptacle. I'm an enigmatic man in that. And anyway that's an invalid's food receptacle.

Mother Have I got to spoon it into you?

Roelle What a one you are to me today.

Mother Aren't you ashamed in front of your mother? You wait, I'll lock you up in the back cellar and let you scream.

Roelle That's just classic you. Look, Mum, see how I'm forcing myself. But this is a real pigsty, it's completely cold.

Mother I poured it in for you just as you left it. Eat up.

Roelle Let me go. The soup makes me retch.

Mother Down to the last drop. That's to be eaten clean. I'm not letting you get away with it.

Roelle How can I put on the beef like this?

Mother Have I got to count? (*She feeds him spoonful by spoonful.*) Now, this one's for Saint Joseph, this one's for your little sister who's dead and gone, just take a nice little grip on yourself. This one's for your guardian angel, you never know when you'll need him. This one's for all the poor souls in purgatory.

Roelle Man needn't eat.

Mother You'll not fill out else. The flesh'll fall off you.

Roelle Perhaps that's just what I want.

Mother You're dicing with your own health. I'd be frightened.

Roelle It is to be frightening.

Mother They should never have been allowed to drive you out of the school. You take it too strongly to heart.

Roelle I do what I have to.

Mother He got that from his father, Jesus, Jesus! I'm only an ordinary woman.

Roelle The teachers cooked it up that I'm good for nothing.

Mother As if others don't get up to mischief while they're young. One grows out of it.

Roelle Only me they pick on. The others get away with it, I don't know why.

Mother It's unjust, my son.

Roelle They said, I'm the walking plague.

Mother Don't take it so much to heart.

Roelle And I'm not the walking plague. That will be revealed.

Mother We aren't the lowest of the low.

Roelle And it's not come out yet. They'll be astounded.

Mother There are other schools in another town. I'll have to afford it somehow. I'll send you to an institute.

Roelle I won't go to an institute.

Mother But you can't do your leaving exams here. You need your leaving exams.

Roelle I want to stay here. And Olga isn't away any more either.

Mother You'll drive yourself quite crazy over that person. Want to lock yourself out of life?

Roelle Doesn't go so smoothly for me. Mine are the thorns, I know that.

Mother Suffer the pricks. Go right ahead.

Roelle You can't follow me, woman. As I tell you, I've been called.

Mother My son, just don't overreach yourself.

Roelle And they'll see one day. And I can pull myself out of my slough by my own hair.

Mother Miracles don't exist. It all goes step by step.

Roelle They know not who I am. Perhaps I've made up my mind to become saintly.

Mother Saintly with a mouth like yours.

Roelle And it works. You must hold on tight to the idea and you'll do it. And you must do something for it. Others could do it, so I can too.

Mother Just you dare!

Roelle You've always got to take a grip on yourself when things become difficult. Stop eating for example.

Mother Stop eating, stop eating! Till we can see through you? Till every illness attacks you. Till you go crackers, my son? Then who'd look after you?

Roelle You've got to eat so little that the supernatural apparitions come to you in broad daylight.

Mother I don't call that healthy. I call that dangerous.

Roelle And it works. I've proved that it works. It carries you beyond the boundaries.

Mother Aren't you frightened of the risk you're running?

Roelle It is to be frightening. That's why I stopped.

Mother You see.

Roelle But now I've taken it up again. I still wasn't enough then. I wasn't saintly somehow.

Mother It's addled his brains. Jesus, Jesus!

Roelle You can't prohibit me, woman.

Mother My son, I don't wish you to be saintly.

Gervasius (*turning up from behind the caravan*)

We've nabbed him this time. He's only a mother's boy, after all.

Roelle There's nothing for you here.

Gervasius You should know, I'm everywhere.

Roelle You're short-sighted, you didn't see it that well.

Gervasius I saw it well enough.

Roelle If anything happened here, it happened under the seal of secrecy.

Gervasius Get along. The whole time I was standing at the back and it regaled my spirits. This one's for Saint Joseph, just take a nice little grip on yourself.

Roelle Look, I really don't like to say what you are.

Gervasius What am I then?

Roelle You're a soul being led astray.

Gervasius I was giving it my consideration, shall I step forward and compromise this lad for all time? In the beginning I grieved for you. But then I went for compromising the lad.

Roelle That shows your dirty character.

Gervasius So I can now spread it about amongst the classier lads in the playground. I've an inkling, classier lads show no pity to someone who's a mother's boy. One more spoonful. This one's for your guardian angel, you never know when you'll need him.

Roelle Go to your grubby playground, then. Everybody knows who you fancy there. I for one can notify the Police about your practices, then they'll be onto you.

Gervasius You'll have to supply the evidence first. (*Going off.*)

Roelle He's slunk off like a skunk.

Mother Jesus, it made my flesh creep.

Roelle Now you see, how one's compromised by you?

Mother Just tell me how this came into your head. There I was standing like eternal misery, full of remorse and grief.

Roelle Going to run after me with the soup again?

Mother I'm going to pack it up right now. But I think it's the seven gifts of the Holy Ghost. (*Going off.*)

Roelle Now to prepare myself through the dignified preparation. I always get stuck.

Clementine (*coming round the caravan*) I would have said something to Frau Roelle, but she was in such a state. She didn't even notice me.

Roelle That's my mother all over, who she sees and who she doesn't see.

Clementine Not with me. Not long ago she said, Clementine, if there's ever anything between you and my son, I've got nothing against it with you, because you're such an industrious girl and that's as good as capital. And it's true. The whole house hangs on me.

Roelle In fact I give a lot for my mum, her judgement. 'Cause I always say, just going through life makes one wise.

Clementine She's been in the thick of it and that's what I want as well. How did Olga's hair-ribbon get here?

Roelle The wind must have carried it here.

Clementine The wind didn't carry it here. It's her wide one and still looks brand new. You're beyond me, Herr Roelle. You're chasing her. The way one kids oneself about a person.

Roelle I haven't been chasing her, she came wholly of her own accord. And she went wholly of her own accord.

Clementine I'm just saying, Olga's a right beauty. And whoever wants something from her has my pity. In profile she resembles a man.

Roelle You've got her number there.

Clementine You've known me since I was a child. As a man you won't be distant.

Roelle I'd never liken you unto your sister.

Clementine Somehow I've got to get away from home. That's no surroundings for me.

Roelle I'm not the lowest of the low. I can stand up to a woman.

Clementine You know who you'll be better off with. With Olga it would be a catastrophe.

Roelle Just let me get today behind me.

Clementine You won't regret it.

The two **Altar Servers** *come on.*

First Server Time. The people are waiting for your appearance.

Roelle Out of the question.

Second Server Certain individuals are in the mind to describe it as a swindle. But then I gave them some potent food for thought.

First Server Hermine Seitz rouses the rabble most.

Clementine Now what's he got himself into?

Roelle That'd be telling.

Second Server He didn't fill the other one in either.

First Server He's just trying to say, 'cause you're the second one today.

Second Server That face she pulled she should get stuck with.

Clementine *goes.* **Roelle** *tries to get away.*

Stop him getting away. Roelle's shrinking from company.

Roelle This'll be nice. I'm about to be raped.

First Server You've got to go out front, now.

Second Server You're the alpha and omega of it all.

Roelle I'm not prepared.

Second Server You can work at it on the way.

First Server Your followers want to receive you, so do your enemies.

Second Server There is only the path set with snares.

First Server You can't run away. Your Olga's standing outside craning her neck.

Second Server Your teachers are standing out there. Your school mates are standing out there.

Roelle Two more reasons not to do it.

First Server And they all wanted to have been there when you were spouting.

Roelle Has the circle been drawn in chalk?

First Server It went clean out of our heads.

Roelle The circle must be drawn in chalk beforehand, 'cause I've got to step into it.

Second Server Everything will be drawn once you step into it.

Roelle Bound to work, then? Do the populace know they're not to address me?

Second Server Move.

Roelle A hand can be raised like this. And a hand can be raised like that.

First Server Are you going to appear like that? Tatty bye.

Roelle This is for me a peculiar posture.

Some **Schoolboys** *pass by.*

First Boy We came from the wrong side.

Second Boy Right through here. You can get through here.

Third Boy Half the school's supposed to be there.

The three go off, some **Girls** *pass by.*

First Girl There's one who believes it.

Second Girl It's not like with other people. I've heard they don't live long.

Third Girl Come off it, I see him every day passing the corn exchange.

Second Girl The organs, the internal ones, can't cope with it any more.

Third Girl But there's nothing odd-looking about him.

The **Girls** *go off. A* **Schoolboy** *comes around the caravan.*

Boy They won't wait any longer. When is this rare Saviour appearing?

Second Server We've got to lead him three times round the place, so he collects himself.

First Server The holy figure is three.

The **Schoolboy** *goes off.* **Protasius** *and* **Gervasius** *pass by.*

Gervasius I've been dying to say something.

Protasius Say it then.

Gervasius I've heard something. But how did I hear it? Under the seal of secrecy.

Protasius Then that's that.

Gervasius But I'm absolutely dying to say it.

Protasius Under the seal of secrecy?

Gervasius Yes.

Protasius Under no circumstances are you to disclose it, or it'll strike.

Gervasius Who'll strike?

Protasius Lightning.

Gervasius If I'd known that I wouldn't have got involved.

Protasius What's it called then, what Roelle's up to today?

Gervasius Don't get me started on Roelle or I become toxic. That pathetic person with his spiritualism.

Protasius What's that? Quick, say it again.

Gervasius Spi-rit-tu-al-ism.

Protasius Aha!

Gervasius But not the sort to make your hair curl. He latches onto every crazy idea.

Protasius Six months ago someone demonstrated it in the Schäffbräuhaus, to bring some lustre to the platform once in a while. I assume, he nicked it from him. Something to do with spirits. Manifestations, understand.

Gervasius Then it's above me.

Protasius They look out of the medium, out of the neck they look, and tell you what you don't know yourself. You simply have to believe it then, or the spirits wring your neck.

Gervasius And that's what Roelle's aping?

Protasius Four strong men could hardly hold down the one in the Schäffbräu. These spirits have a terrible power.

Gervasius And that's what Roelle's aping?

Protasius Through this you can become famous. Only need to interest a University man and he'll make you interesting.

Gervasius You're pulling my leg.

Protasius And you're jealous of the chappie, I can tell.

Gervasius The lad'll be arrested. I'm going to arrest him now.

Protasius I doubt if that's permitted.

Gervasius Haven't you ever read in the paper: the culprit, showing signs of mental derangement, was arrested?

Protasius Have you got a stamped photograph?

Gervasius I've never needed one so far.

Protasius Well, if you've got no stamped photograph, of course you can't arrest a person.

Gervasius Who says so, then?

Protasius You must be able to produce it every time you assume an official function, otherwise the Police'll be onto you.

Gervasius That's something extraordinary about your education.

Protasius And then you need handcuffs that snap shut by themselves, 'cause he won't come along of his own accord.

Gervasius Look, that's how it goes, I'd have arrested him now.

Both go off. Disturbance and voices.

Voice Where is this promised angel of ours? Bring on the angel at long last.

Voice We want to see this so-called angel.

Voices Bring on the angel. Bring on the angel.

Second Server They're simmering. Get going. Throw yourself right in.

Roelle I can't do it. I can't do it.

Second Server You must.

First Server I'll die laughing. This'll be a glorious fiasco.

The servers pull the resisting **Roelle** *behind the caravan onto the platform.*

Second Server (*out of sight*) Ladies and Gentleman, in these faithless times an ordinary Ingolstädter has managed to make intimate contact with incarnate angels. Without more ado, I now present to you the man who is visited by his angel just like that. With no entry fee and only to shake the doubters, only to smash the unfaithful, my man here is going to show you this characteristic heavenly being. I ask for your undivided attention. I ask therefore that you don't frighten him for me by shouting out, it could entail for him a fatal fall. Touching an angel puts your life in danger.

Voice He's already sweating.

Voices Shush.

Second Server Silence at the back. Absolute silence, otherwise the man can't hypnotise. It's difficult.

Voice Bit of silence when he's hypnotising.

Second Server I can see already and you must see it as well, the man's getting bigger. Take note of his ecstasy, 'cause this instant the angel appears. His neck gets longer, the man is literally being pulled apart, he stretches out toward what's approaching and he draws it this way –

Voice But we can't see a thing.

Voice Quiet, it's a sacred pledge.

Voice But it's all just hot air.

Voice Nothing but hands and feet.

Voice But he's standing there like a dud.

Voice He's useless. What a nerve to summon us here. What for?

Voice It's just a mean vileness.

Voices Cheat. Imposter. Police.

Voice What he's doing, this one's an out and out sacrilege.

Voice He's possessed. The devil operates through him.

Voice Such a one must be struck down.

Voice Stone him.

Voice Just watch me shy one.

Stones are thrown, stones also roll out under the caravan.

Voice I hit him. He's falling.

Voice He is dead.

Voice All just hocus-pocus.

Some **Schoolboys** *run past.* **Olga** *tries to drag* **Roelle** *away.*

Scene Five

Terrace between roofs at **Berotter***'s. Wine is being drunk.* **Roelle***, his head bandaged, with blood seeping through.* **Olga**, **Clementine**, **Christian**, **Peps**, **Hermine**.

Peps Perhaps he's learnt his lesson the hard way now.

Hermine Not a bit of it. He's becoming even worse.

Roelle It's different with me, see. I tower over the masses.

Peps Then don't come crawling to me when you're on your last legs.

Roelle It's become evident, I have my followers.

Peps More enemies than followers.

Roelle And that's nothing yet. Someone's known to me who goes as white as a sheet if I'm only in his vicinity and cast him one of my slow tiger gazes.

Christian I'd like to be introduced to him.

Roelle Every day I'm prepared for him to throw himself at my feet.

Christian Ha – !

Roelle You can go up to him and ask. Crusius.

Christian Never.

Roelle What have you got eyes in your head for?

Christian But Crusius says different.

Roelle Crusius fell on his knees in front of me and begged my forgiveness, 'cause he'd not seen my real worth.

Christian That can't be true.

Roelle He said – Roelle, Lord, have mercy he said. You weren't even there at the time.

Christian Then why haven't you got your tome back, that he took from your desk as bold as brass?

Roelle It hadn't dawned on him by then who he was dealing with.

Olga That Roelle knows better, no doubt. You weren't there.

Christian *sits down further away*.

Hermine Eccentric.

Peps Well anyway it's such a beautiful night – I'm going to get a skinful. Cheers!

Clementine Christian's got to distance himself.

Christian I don't like sitting next to you.

Clementine I'm poisonous you see.

Roelle Olga understood me. I stood there whilst they smashed a hole in my head.

Clementine That had to happen, did it?

Roelle He who can comprehend, let him comprehend it.

Olga That's just envy with Clementine.

Clementine He didn't do it for you. It was all his own importance.

Roelle Angels come unto me. But they only come through meditation. They don't go to the market-place.

Olga They just don't know that.

Hermine We don't believe in that.

Olga You are the hardened sinners. You'll see what becomes of you one of these days.

Hermine Oh yes, and what will become of us?

Peps We are of those who aren't subject to fear.

Olga And I believe in angels.

Peps You've opened a can of worms there, Roelle.

Olga And I don't bend my little finger without it being observed by Heaven.

Peps That's what you want, right?

Clementine And I'm allowed to wash the dishes all alone.

Hermine At Mass we didn't see you.

Olga I don't exhibit myself in public places.

Clementine Won't Roelle soon weary of Olga regurgitating everything he says?

Olga My Roelle's unshakeable.

Clementine Don't keep saying your Roelle.

Olga I know what I know.

Hermine Eccentric.

Clementine I won't disclose the things your Roelle divulged about you. He doesn't say them to your face.

Roelle She's trying to ruin my reputation.

Clementine Even though he won't admit it later.

Roelle When have I been critical? That's what I want to know now.

Clementine When he peers at me so closely, I can't get anything out.

Roelle You'd better think before you speak.

Olga Scandal-monger.

Clementine Who's your favoured one now, that's what I've got to know.

Olga Clementine, you're not the sort to run after someone who doesn't notice you.

Clementine I know 'cause my hands are rough, 'cause I have them constantly in cold water. I'd like to see Olga at it.

Christian He made you into a real beaut.

Clementine I don't want to go on. Olga non-stop. Mama, when she was still alive, always favoured you as well.

Christian Just be quiet in front of strangers.

Hermine I'm not the sort to spread anything about.

Clementine They're all trying to persecute me, Christian, Olga and the others. Now I'm going to have my say. Grammar school and all that wasn't on offer for me.

Peps Here she goes again.

Clementine You want to pass as a gentleman. I took out the special china with the gold rim, but you haven't noticed. I know Olga. What a real man wants is a waist. Roelle's got no taste. I've got my whole trousseau together.

Christian Push yourself off. Clear off.

Clementine I just want to cry. You can't stop me. I'm crying already.

Olga Come along, Clementine. We'll wash your face. They needn't see you like this.

Clementine It's all the same to me now.

I'm my own person. I keep myself to myself.

Olga You're coming with me.

Clementine I'm not even allowed to cry.

Going off with **Olga**.

Peps Did someone stab your bulging neck with a fork?

Roelle With her sort it could already be treachery. She takes one step and she is living in evil.

Peps Who doesn't do that?

Olga *and* **Clementine** *come back*.

Olga They know Roelle's with us. As we put on the light in the living room, they called us names from down in the street.

Christian That's beastly.

Roelle They are my antagonists.

Clementine I'm not going out of the front door again today. They'll be smashing our windows before long.

Peps They'll take themselves off soon.

Olga So they know not what they do?

Hermine You've got your Roelle to thank for this.

Roelle Nothing will happen to you.

Clementine Don't stand there as if this was your home. It would be better if one like you went away now.

Roelle I can't be chased out like a dog. I stood there whilst they smashed a hole in my head.

Peps And shoved Olga's name onto everybody's tongue.

Clementine Who made you do it?

Roelle I stood there whilst they smashed a hole in my head.

Hermine Let's put three fingers into it.

Peps He's got a wound, that's his line.

Roelle How do you know which of my delicate and sensitive members is involved.

Peps All that's of no interest to us. That's to say we don't need someone like you.

Roelle This'll be nice. I'm being passed over in silence.

Olga Oh, I've had it up to here. I can't have any more to do with him now.

Peps So the penny's dropping at last.

Roelle It's an injustice the way she keeps on staring past me at some distant point. I'm feeling sick.

Peps Haven't you got the message? We don't want any sick people here.

Clementine But he's going green all over.

Christian If something's wrong with you, go home.

Roelle On my own I won't get there. I'm giddy.

Hermine But you'd be happy now if someone held your head from behind.

Roelle I can't hold out much longer.

Olga Lie down, if you're going to be sick.

Clementine Put him out. Put him out of my sight.

Olga Not me.

Hermine We don't fancy picking him up.

Peps He's lost some blood. Might have been too much.

Clementine Sit up, you! You should sit up proper.

Roelle I didn't come here so you could have feelings for me.

Clementine I can't stomach him any longer!

Roelle I have my sorrows, therefore I must always fend for myself. See, amongst other things I'm hydrophobic, I can't go into water. I have to hold my hands in front of me, when it climbs up my body.

Olga I find that utterly repellent.

Hermine I'll burst my guts laughing.

Roelle If she won't look at me, I simply won't let her go to the country.

Peps You haven't even got the money.

Roelle (*showing money*) Who wills, who wants?

Peps You've stolen it out of your mum's till.

Roelle It isn't stolen. It's just from my home.

Peps That's what they call continuous stealing.

Olga And you come to me and let me accept money that's stolen?

Christian He didn't give a hint of it.

Olga I'll take it straight over to your mother.

Roelle Then I'll say it was you what took it out of the till. My mother would believe that at once from me.

Olga I'm breaking off relations with you, your company is unsuitable for me. (*Going.*)

Roelle That's one of those rules of good conduct. I know that.

Olga Do you know who you're talking to? (*Standing still.*)

Roelle I'll simply come for you again. You're no different from me.

Olga I'm much better.

Roelle How did you behave then when you were standing in front of me in case I had a fit.

Olga 'Cause I collect such human beings.

Roelle If it was up to you I could have just snuffed it.

Olga To me you're not a human being. You haven't the nerves for it.

Roelle I was the one who brought nerves into it and I can get over them.

Olga Oh yes? So there's nothing wrong with you?

Protasius *and* **Gervasius** *come in.*

Protasius This is becoming another orgy of eating and drinking.

Peps Who let you in?

Protasius I'm supposed to act as a kind of removals man for the invalid.

Gervasius I'm the other one. I help with the carriage.

Roelle I'm not going to be carried off.

Protasius You're not as secluded here as you think.

Gervasius We can get to you with ease.

Roelle No one here is unwell.

Protasius It invigorates me inordinately that the matter is resolved.

Gervasius How is it you're bleeding from the head?

Roelle I'm not the one whom you seek.

Protasius You're a damned provocation.

Roelle I discharged myself. You'll just have to leave me be.

Protasius You won't give us the slip. We'll come on wings. We'll come with fins. Tut tut. Not by using force.

Gervasius Let live the insects, even if they prick you.

Protasius They don't want a corpse in the gutter.

Roelle I'm not going to be abducted. I'm not going with you. I'm not falling into your trap.

Protasius You must do so voluntarily.

Roelle I'll never go along with you again.

Protasius We know too much. Have I ever told you, brother, how to regulate the sex of your offspring?

Gervasius I don't want children, and you're not my brother. You're only my tormentor.

Protasius You need one. If you don't want to know about it, I'll tell this gentleman who isn't so crude to me for I hear he's about to get married.

Peps It would interest me.

Protasius I'll stick to the intimate points: if you can't keep off your old woman it'll be a girl. That is to say, you call on her too often. It will be a boy only after lengthy abstinence. Through abstinence you regulate the sex.

Peps Who found that out?

Protasius It is an observation of a thinking man and his personal experience. I'm only passing it on.

Peps I'm convinced. Let's drink to that. Cheers.

Protasius I would designate voluntary conversions as a sign of spiritual versatility. Without spiritual versatility, I say, a man is altogether lost. Take me for example, where would I be if I weren't so spiritually versatile? For reasons of nutrition I'd soon become transparent. But that's not the case.

Roelle Now he's buttering you up. And that's the first step.

Protasius Have I ever told you, brother, that I'm nursing the intention of buying myself a hat on instalments? 'Cause my clients keep looking so pensively at my head and that's my Achilles heel.

Gervasius I hope you'll finally do it.

Protasius So far I can put cash down for the brim. Next time it'll go towards the crown. In general I say, such broad brims aren't necessary for me, I'm more concerned about the fabric. Come along, brother.

Gervasius I'm not your brother. I've had enough. The town has nothing more to offer me. I've done most of it.

Protasius You've stuck it a long time for that.

Gervasius You can't get inside my brains, you old snoop.

Protasius It's your own fault. You're wishy-washy. You bore me. You're getting on. You've run out of ideas. No one gives a toss about you.

Gervasius You sucked me dry like vampires. Then you dumped me.

Protasius You're like some dirt on the path. You're no longer discernible. You're too ordinary.

Gervasius You nourished yourselves on me. And then threw me away.

Protasius We've got you by the marrow. You've collapsed into a completely ordinary creep.

Gervasius You've removed all my stimuli. I feel drained.

Protasius It's only what you help yourself to that counts. But you don't help yourself to anything any more.

Gervasius I still help myself to lads.

Protasius They don't need your left-overs. You're done for done for done for. Hang yourself, that'd be best. Come along semi-corpse.

Gervasius I'm not your corpse either.

Protasius *and* **Gervasius** *go off.*

Peps There's something ghoulish about those men.

Hermine I can't really see properly any more. Perhaps the men weren't even here.

Roelle One mustn't get mixed up with them, I know that. It's better to steer clear of them.

Clementine Is someone timid more to your taste?

Roelle I don't go in for general questions.

Clementine Do you know how one converts a person, if he really has got an Achilles heel?

Roelle Time and again I've resolved to do that. How could this be effective on anyone else when it isn't on me? After all, I am the person concerned.

Clementine But if we two really stick together?

Roelle If you're in it somewhere and I say, you've been in it for ever, then you can only wish to get out, but you can't imagine how it'd be in another spiritual place –

Clementine Why have you suddenly broken off?

Roelle It can't be come by from outside. The right kind of help must be within you already. And it is not within me for that. It's said, also, to be a punishment visited on our generation.

Clementine One must learn to await it. It develops slowly.

Roelle Just take a look at confession. You always confess the same things. I haven't believed for a long time in working my passage up there. Perhaps it would be even better if you did something really bad. Stealing for example. And really felt good, 'cause you'd been stealing, and 'cause you'd done someone a bad turn. And didn't have the slightest fear about it.

Clementine Have you really been stealing?

Roelle But when I sink myself in meditation, in who one is in reality then I'd like to walk out on such a dreadful life right now. I want to retract it.

Clementine You can't do that, retract anything. When you've done something, then it's with you forever, and I say, it goes on looking at you.

Roelle That's the greatest injustice.

Peps I'm coming to you with my rumbling tummy.

Hermine Then it'll be as if he's transfigured again.

Clementine Now let's get down to drinking.

Hermine We've simply got to pour it down our throats.

Roelle Are you always so hot, as well?

Clementine That comes from the American heatwave.

Hermine A human being has five toes and one head. A human being has five toes and one head.

Clementine But a human being has ten toes.

Hermine A human being has ten toes and one head.

Olga Clementine, you slow down now.

Christian I'm not playing any more, when Hermine behaves like this.

Hermine But still I'm not a crocodile, but still I'm not a crocodile.

Peps And it's all getting greyer and greyer.

Roelle I'm going to take Clementine to somewhere dark.

Clementine Would you let a daughter of yours go to grammar school?

Roelle I'm not having this litany. None of you here is sacred.

Clementine We've no need of Olga. By starlight.

Roelle How is it with your so-called chastity then? You can tell me.

Clementine One doesn't talk about it.

Roelle One gets on with it. She'll be just the same as Olga.

Clementine You'll have to wait for it.

Roelle They lead you along so far, then they claim their chastity.

Clementine Christian, he's pinching me.

Christian Beg her pardon.

Roelle It's no more than she deserves. I've got this pronounced preconception. I know your every desire all right.

Clementine Now he's going to slander me.

Roelle Don't make yourself so distant. We all know.

Clementine Then why have you trailed after me and why were you so sulky with Olga? You led me to the belief it was your love.

Roelle It's not my fault you're so stupid.

Clementine Did he always have the other one in mind whilst he was making up to me? He'd better expect something now. He thought it didn't matter with me. You don't know me. I'll think up something for you.

Christian We'll make a horrifying example of him. I've wanted to for ages.

Clementine We'll dunk him in cold water.

Roelle You can't do that to me.

Peps And enmity shall be established between thee and the water.

Hermine Now we've got something. Now we can get at him.

Clementine Someone must lay hands on him. (*Going off.*)

Christian He knows full well he can't escape us. We've got him cornered.

Roelle I don't want it, I don't want it.

Christian You stupid carcass!

Clementine Here I am with my tub. Off with his shoes.

Peps She's not going to let him take the shine off her glory.

Clementine Now the other one.

Hermine Why not even more?

They start undressing him.

Roelle I'll never talk to you again.

Christian That won't kill anyone.

Roelle I'll never say anything against Olga. I've already retracted some of it.

Hermine That's neither here nor there.

Roelle I've got my guardian angel with me. Lest I dash my foot against a stone.

Olga You think Olga will help. Olga won't help.

Roelle I'll seek sanctuary with you.

Olga Grab him.

Roelle What kind of world am I in?

Olga In your own, where your neighbour is allowed nothing but to bite the dust.

Roelle I want to confess. I want to confess something, something important.

Christian What?

Roelle I'm a bad man.

Clementine We know that.

Roelle You're all bad.

Hermine We know that as well.

Christian It won't be the death of you. My man, it's water.

Roelle Stop! I'll do it myself.

Clementine (*pushing him under*) Now, you sit there.

Roelle Olga should look away.

Peps She's still got something over him.

General sobering up. They give his clothes back.
Clementine *drags the tub away.*

Clementine's degraded herself the most.

Clementine It's all Olga's fault.

Christian We've made such fools of ourselves 'cause of you.

Olga We no longer wish to detain you in our surroundings. You'll be happy to leave.

Roelle I was naked and you clothed me not. You poured scorn over me and now it's staring back at you.

Olga Ah, every day we sink further into a world of vileness, even as we have sunk into this flesh in which we dwell.

Berotter (*coming in*) Are you leaving already, Herr Roelle?

Roelle I did have a pullover.

Berotter Now he wants to go as well. Look at me, children, is something wrong with my suit? I've come back from the Ludwig. They cold-shouldered me there in an odd way and one after the other got up and asked for their bills. Nothing's happened, has it?

Olga Father, I've got to tell you something. I'm having a child.

Berotter God. (*Collapses.*)

Peps That's distressing with a daughter.

Hermine Someone help me to hold him.

Clementine We'll go in now without Olga.

Olga Now he's throwing his fit again.

Peps I understand the man doesn't get his way nowadays.

Olga There's no need to come after me. I'm going down to the – (*Going off.*)

Scene Six

Danube water-meadow. **Protasius, Gervasius**.

Protasius Olga Berotter threw herself into the water to raise her reputation. But Roelle in an inexplicable impulse pulled her out.

Gervasius That's a good one.

Protasius The chappie actually managed it. He got her clean out of the water and himself too.

Gervasius I wouldn't have wanted to follow his lead. That's not my line. Gives me the creeps.

Protasius I was standing on the bank. I actually helped to pull the last bit. In this I was human.

Gervasius Makes my guts churn just to hear it.

Protasius Afterwards she let fly at us.

Gervasius That's gratitude.

Protasius She wanted to drown herself, to get out of it all, but Roelle wouldn't have it. She's got it in for him.

Gervasius No sense of reality. How easily something could have happened to the likes of you and me.

Protasius We're just not allowed to do good. It always goes wrong on me.

Gervasius It isn't for us.

Protasius We're not cut out for it.

Gervasius It automatically goes wrong.

Protasius A slight slip and so easily avoided.

Gervasius Our sort can surely make up for it.

Protasius That's why I've placed my column in the newspaper. I'm becoming literary now.

Gervasius They'll really need you there then.

Protasius Don't say that. I've got a domed forehead and that's a sure sign.

Gervasius They'll soon send you packing.

Protasius Up with the lark, I go to the office for local affairs. There sits a certain man, who never knows in advance where to get hold of news for his columns. I hazarded a guess, the man would demonstrate his gratitude to me, but he goes on writing incessantly. Finally he does look up the once, so I can make him lick his lips. I say, you're not informed about the nocturnal incident in the Danube, but your humble servant was there. And here is the written account of it, signed a life-saver. That's yours truly, I say, with another person.

Gervasius Was he grateful?

Protasius Naturally. But first and foremost it must yield a profit.

Gervasius Did you name names?

Protasius That's just the beauty of newspapers, that one can indicate the person in question and the person in question can do nothing about it. The paper's out already.

Gervasius That'll be sufficiently unpalatable for the Berotters.

Protasius I'd say so too when one reads about oneself. I'll ingratiate myself with the man for local affairs and play the part of informer there too.

Gervasius But never the part of life-saver again.

Protasius I must protect myself on account of my info. In general I make no grand gestures. With me it all comes more from within.

Protasius and **Gervasius** *go off.* **Crusius**, **First Schoolboy** and **Roelle** *come in from the other side.*

Crusius You're forgetting, you're a pariah to your former school-mates.

Roelle I give you money. Every time I meet you.

Crusius Just don't say you're trying to buy me.

Roelle I don't want to presume on you. But you must do something for me.

Crusius I already condescend by taking it.

Roelle But I've got to steal it from my Mum's till. That's a problem for me.

Crusius You force it on people.

Roelle I thought it would help, see.

First Boy We don't like you, see. You're not like the rest.

Roelle How am I supposed to be?

First Boy What sort of phyz has dribbled down this one's forehead? Just the way he carries his noteworthy fins simply nauseates me. In this respect a man is not decorative to himself.

Roelle I don't know the first thing about that. I don't know how I carry them. I would change, believe me. But I don't notice it.

Crusius Makes no difference. The leopard doesn't change his spots.

Roelle I don't like being a pariah. I'll do anything that'd make you take me back again.

Crusius Absolutely anything.

Roelle *nods.*

First Boy But it won't happen that quickly.

Roelle But you will take me back one day?

Crusius I'm already doing what I can.

First Boy We're not exactly eager. We say, you aren't a man.

Roelle I am the father.

Crusius I've already told them that. But they're not very taken with it.

Roelle What do you object to about it? That can happen to anyone.

First Boy A lady's man he's become. That's already something to show off about.

Roelle She eats out of my hand.

First Boy You must give us a performance of that.

Roelle Shall I exhibit the girl to you, where you can give it to her? It's a trifling matter to me. I'll give her a wink.

Crusius I've got nothing against the Berotter girl come to that. But what sort of creature are you?

Roelle 'Cause you never ever believe me.

Crusius Would you, in my presence, gob in front of her, if you could redeem yourself by it?

Roelle Will you sit at my table and break bread?

Crusius You will be like one of us.

Roelle I must redeem myself. There's no other way.

Crusius You're just the one I take you for.

Roelle You won't ask for better.

First Boy Is it possible. So the Berotter girl submits to whatever you do?

Roelle She knows why.

First Boy She's always acted so reasonable. Now she's having a child by someone like you.

Roelle That's it. I am the father.

First Boy You'll be in hot water if you're having me on.

Roelle I don't tell lies.

Crusius You know I think he'll burst into tears.

Roelle I disgust myself. You drag a person down.

Crusius Have you still got some on you? Hand it over. Every time we meet I get my money. (*He takes it.*)

Roelle I think you compromise yourself by taking it.

Crusius And don't go around claiming later on I exploit you.

In the distance **Olga** *being hounded. She has been roaming about outside for a few days. Whistles, shouts:* Stop her! *Some* **Schoolboys** *run onto the stage.*

Boys The grammar school boys have caught her.

Crusius You hear? Now it's come to it. You don't even need to fetch her here now.

First Boy Come with me by my lovely side. Now prove yourself the man you're always saying you are.

More **Schoolboys** *run in.*

Boys Now she'll be cast out. We'll corner her.

Other **Schoolboys** *herd* **Olga** *onto the stage, then encircle her. When* **Olga** *wants to force her way out, they force her back.*

First Boy No way through here, Virginity.

Second Boy Now you can have a proper look at her.

Third Boy Have you got dry after the Danube?

First Boy A Pepsi pricked Olga Berotter.

Olga Get back one of you. I've got to get out.

Third Boy Want to go to your dear Papa, that you ran away from, so the whole town'll know?

First Boy Emil, from the Turkish delight shop'll marry anything, so you won't have to search in the paper for long.

Olga You've got to let me get out. I don't hate you.

Third Boy Who do you, then?

Second Boy Seems to me she hasn't got it in for us. That's her big heart.

Olga You'd better go home.

Third Boy That's good coming from you.

Olga How are you treating me?

First Boy This one's Roelle's one.

Second Boy Nothing turns her stomach.

First Boy She'll be cast out like himself. They'll just have to see what they mean to each other.

Second Boy Perhaps she doesn't like him that much.

Third Boy She let herself be pricked, or didn't she?

First Boy From now on you'll always be

alone. None of your girl-friends will go near you.

Third Boy If anyone does they'll have something to be afraid of.

Second Boy And it'll always stick to you.

First Boy Don't let yourself be seen round here much longer.

Olga You've no right to do that.

First Boy We're giving ourselves the right, see.

Crusius Someone's got to gob in front of you. Now we'll get the couple face to face.

He hauls **Roelle** *in front of* **Olga**.

Olga Now, what's he been hatching?

Crusius Look up at your heart's delight, if that doesn't turn her stomach.

Olga You've dragged me down to your level.

Roelle Drag me up, then.

Olga Stop clawing at me down there.

Roelle Yours are the only feet where I lay myself down. I want to stay lying here. You don't need to kneel down, either. You're exempt from everything.

Olga I don't belong to him. He won't let me go. You can see that yourselves. Put him away. I don't want him.

First Boy I'm gradually having my doubts.

Roelle I'm not the father. That is the truth.

Crusius You've taken us for a ride. Just you wait.

Third Boy He's told so many fibs to all and sundry the beams are buckling.

Roelle I'll never claim that again.

Crusius What we've put you through so far was only a feeble prologue.

Olga The sole reason he dragged me out of the water was 'cause I still hadn't suffered enough for him, and now he's like this. He wouldn't let me out of my affliction. It was all thought out to the last detail. If you'd left me floating the water would be running between my teeth by now. I knew why I was going in. It would all be over and you too.

First Boy This one isn't his one. So she's none of our business.

Second Boy She can have a brat from any comer, that's nothing to us. But don't have anything to do with that one. Otherwise you'll cop it too.

Crusius He's led us all by the nose. The others must hear the news right now. Let's go.

Third Boy (*on his way off between* **Olga** *and* **Roelle**) What we've put you through so far was only a feeble preparation, you'll soon feel the difference. A hint of what in general terms might happen to the youth.

The **Schoolboys** *and* **Crusius** *go off*.

Olga It came to pass and, without doubt, I have seen him amongst his own.

Roelle Don't go away, I'll scream.

Olga Scream then.

Roelle I'm going to hold on tight. Look – I've got a knife. (*Giving it to her.*) Plunge it in, until my eyeballs roll up for the last time.

Olga Destruction.

Roelle Redemption.

Olga (*wavers, but then throws the knife away*) On a mountain of disgust we have hoisted these two faces and they must stare at each other throughout eternity.

Roelle Can you not give me some relief just once?

Olga Take your evil desires away, they've sunk their fangs into my face.

Roelle Kneel down!

Olga No.

Roelle Watch it, I'll have you by the gullet. Now you'll scream for me.

Olga. No.

Roelle A bit of appreciation, just once, do it. A handsome, lovely Roelle, repeat that. Nod your head at least. Not even nodding, she's doing nothing. Roelle, what do you want?

Olga As I see it the only excuse for you is that I am on the same level in purgatory.

Roelle Sit down here.

Olga Go home.

Roelle Once I stopped giving you the glad eye, you came running after me. I just want to see for myself the outcome of that.

Olga Have you spat the lot out of your gaping maw now?

Roelle I am not the man who sings hosannas to draw pure breath by your side. I'll renounce your feelings for me. (*He gets the knife back.*) Whatever I do for you, I'm still a lump of filth to you. But I'm going to get you, I'll get you. For whomsoever the hands of the priest are hairy, must take the sacrament with closed eyes. Now I'm going to come over you in an evil shape. For all I care, you can notice the angels don't like me any more, the angels haven't appeared to me for a long time now. Now someone quite different comes. You'll notice in a minute who is living inside me. I am the devil. (*Turning the knife on her.*)

Olga Beast! (*Hitting him.*)

Mother (*coming in, she shouts out*) I'd like to see her do anything to you when I'm here in person. My son has his mind on such higher things, you notice it, 'cause really he can't lift a finger in profanity. Position yourself at a different distance from him. You offend my eye. There she stands, loftily, letting the sun shine on her without a breath of apology.

Roelle Mum, can't you see you're interfering?

Mother You've pushed things so far my son doesn't know what he's up to any longer. But I saw it coming, I had an inkling, me, his mother.

Roelle Don't you get on my nerves as well. You lay it on so thick.

Mother In my mortal fear I ran up and down more streets than there are, and then where do I find him, in what hands?

Roelle It wasn't for your eyes. This was between us.

Mother I know your between us, all right. And I don't like it, your between us. And I'm going to put paid to it.

Roelle Mum, go home right now.

Mother Not without you, my son.

Roelle How did I deserve you?

Mother Look at him, how completely scared he is and how pale.

Roelle That's a big help, when you make your cow-eyes and put me up on a pedestal.

Mother You're speaking to your mother, my son. Be glad you've still got me.

Roelle I've been punished enough.

Mother You're the seductress. No one but you dragged him into it all.

Olga No one's ripped his head off.

Mother Then who are the ones who are mistreating my son? You're going to the school with me this minute, you're going to name yourself and every one of the others.

Olga If you want to know the names, apply to your son.

Roelle You won't wheedle any names out of me.

Mother Jesus, boy, have you ever had anything from them but bruises? Well I'll go running to the teachers, and I'll simply say, it was Böttcher and it was Wimmer, then they'll jump to their own defence and it'll come out then. I'll see to it. They'll have to reckon with me. I'll demand a stiff punishment.

Crusius (*coming in*) Not one of us is a squealer. We're bound to stick together.

Mother You're one of them too. What have you done to my boy?

Roelle Not him. This one is not one of them. 'Cause it's only Crusius and honestly he wasn't even there.

Mother You're lying. What's he after with you?

Crusius I was going across. That way you see the most. I thought I recognised the Fräulein from afar.

Mother That's something I'll have explained to me one day in heaven, what she's got that's so special.

Crusius Excuse me, but aren't you the Fräulein, who fixed me with her eye during the Mothering Sunday service?

Olga Don't give me that pathetic line.

Roelle You can see for yourself, he hardly even knows her.

Mother Boy-glutton! – Why don't you hang onto her skirts and all?

Crusius Be so good as to excuse me, one confuses someone once in a while.

Mother That was no confusion. She keeps her menfolk warm one on top of another.

Olga I won't have such things said about me.

Crusius I'm terribly embarrassed about the Fräulein. I put her under a false suspicion.

Roelle Now then you'd better make yourself scarce by a short cut.

Crusius I'm certainly staying, now. My dear Fräulein, don't do this to me, let your gaze glide over me. You might miss out on something.

Olga That's enough of that.

Crusius There are some Fräuleins who always think straightaway you're after something from them. What am I likely to do to you on a bright-dull day? What can I be after?

Roelle She's mine, in case you don't know.

Olga And you're not like Roelle.

Crusius I'm not like the one behind you. I'm of a different kidney.

Mother He only has to come along and she flings herself at him.

Crusius How are things with us, then?

Olga I'm looking out for one, to emigrate to America with.

Crusius Yes, I don't think I've understood that. – You – America's a long way.

Olga I just want to go to America 'cause no one knows me there.

Mother If she belonged to me.

Roelle *tries to remonstrate.*

Crusius If you're going to dig your trotters in, you won't get very far with me. I can tell you now, to my mind a female should have spiritual strength.

Roelle If she goes with this egotistical person, he'll really drag her down.

Crusius On that account we won't shed a life-sized tear straight away. America's not on. Anyway, you didn't really mean it.

Roelle I'd like to know how you detected that.

Crusius I detected it. Why are you looking so half-witted? Lost for words?

Olga I belong at home.

Crusius Well, that was a revelation. Why are you still standing there?

Olga I'm on my way.

Mother I won't put in a single good word with your revered Papa, so he lets you in again.

Olga I can do that myself. I can take his beating. (*Going off.*)

Crusius She won that round.

Roelle Likes me, likes me. And I've got to hear that she's my friend again, that's what ears are for.

Crusius Shut up, it could never have got anywhere with the Latin swot.

Mother I'm pleased, 'cause she's just made such a grand exit and doesn't know what's waiting for her at home.

Crusius She knows all too well.

Mother She might just arrive as they search the house.

Crusius What for?

Mother Feel free to broadcast it. I've long had my suspicions about that person. I always say, you can get in at the back, you only need to climb over the roof terrace.

Roelle At our house?

Mother But this time she stepped right in it. It's only ever notes. This time I've written down the numbers, and given them to the Police in advance, and I've reported

her into the bargain. And now something's gone from the till again.

Roelle Mum, it was me every time taking your money.

Crusius That'll be put about.

Mother Lordy, that mustn't be true. Well, my boy, whatever were you thinking of?

Roelle 'Cause they keep hounding me and 'cause I have to give to them.

Mother I must go straight back and tell them, I only mislaid the money and meanwhile it's turned up. I'll have to climb down on that. Now.

Roelle Waste of time if Crusius circulates it.

Mother As if I care.

Roelle He's got the money 'cause he took it out of my pocket.

Crusius The money was given.

Roelle The money was taken. There were people around.

Crusius We don't want thieving fingers like yours amongst us.

Roelle What about the book you swiped out of my desk? I'll split about that too.

Crusius You didn't have to put up with it. And anyway it was an experiment. (*Going off.*)

Mother Jesus, boy, listen to me –

Roelle That's the punishment. She's gone. She won't ever want to see me again. You've all taken her away from me, you too.

Mother Let her be gone.

Roelle I don't like you any more. It's over between us. To me you've died.

Mother You're sinning, my son.

Roelle To me you're dead, let go of me.

You're dead, you're not to hold onto me. You're heavy, let go of me.

Mother He's possessed by a devil, that's what it is.

Roelle Yes, make the sign of the cross over me three times and spray me all over with holy water from the graveyard. The devil's everywhere. Keep away, why don't you keep away? I can't cope, I didn't know that, let go of me.

Mother I don't recognise you any more.

Roelle When I die I'll go to hell, I'll be damned, I'll be with the devils and all the people in perdition. And that never ends, never ever. There is no greater cruelty.

Mother Jesus, Jesus!

Roelle Pigswill-face, always bursting into tears, 'cause a square table makes him cross, evil table, everything's evil, you should have thought of that.

Mother Be gone, unclean spirit, be gone into a swine, be gone into your swine.

Roelle With all your prayers you haven't ripped it out. I don't give two hoots about your prayers, you never stop praying. You can't help me any more.

Mother A priest. He's got to be redeemed. (*Going off.*)

Roelle I'm in a state of mortal sin. I've got to confess, I've learned that. But I don't know anything, I've forgotten how it's done.

Taking out a piece of paper.

I, a miserable sinner, confess to the Almighty God and to you priests in God's stead, that since my last confession many months ago I have committed the following sins: against the fourth commandment, how many times? Against the sixth commandment, how many times? I must be in awe. Against the seventh

commandment, how many times? Against the eighth commandment, how many times? This is my note for myself, I might eat it right now. Against the seven deadly sins – I ask for an edifying penance and for the priest's absolution. I'll try that.

He swallows the piece of paper.

The End.

Purgatory in Ingolstadt

Written in 1924 when she was a student, Marieluise Fleisser's first play stems directly from her own experiences. Born in Ingolstadt in 1901, she alone of four sisters went to grammar school – a convent at Regensburg. 'The convent was a barracks or a prison to me. There was no escape into the outside world, there were only escape routes into one's head.'

The Washing of Feet, the play's first title, highlights its Christian context without focussing on the introspection or emotional and moral suffocation of a small, walled town. Changing her title to *Purgatory in Ingolstadt* for its first performance, Fleisser made the connection with her home town public and permanent. The play brought her another connection which also resounded for the rest of her life; she met the up-and-coming Bert Brecht who engineered the first production – a single performance on 25 April 1926 in Berlin by the Junge Bühne.

The critics agreed hers was a shining new talent. 'It is totally without predecessors. A visionary eye looks straight through the real world.' *Purgatory*, the most personal of her plays, fuses her own age – the Weimar Republic – with the past, from mediaeval mystery plays to Catholicism and with her own childish fears. These twin themes are expressed through a highly original and idiosyncratic style – both elements which would remain crucial to her throughout her life. In 1972 she wrote to her publisher: 'I have nothing against corrections to my orthography. However I must insist that my sentence structures which give my language its liveliness and character and which have always been peculiar to my work must not be changed into normal literary German, and thereby mutilated and sterilised.'

The play is about pack-law and non-conformity. Her generation whose childhood was perverted by the First World War was disillusioned with their fathers' ideals. But their education took no account of radical social changes. She saw her own six years in the convent as a ludicrous refusal to prepare young people for the real world ahead. Her characters are products of the environment Fleisser grew up in, Germany after the First World War, when young people were crying out for their own heroes, for new standards which a shell-shocked society could rely on. Both Roelle and Olga are misfits in a narrowly conformist age. Roelle attempts to redeem himself through becoming 'saintly' – with hindsight we can view him as the leader her contemporaries craved. All that draws them together is that both are misfits which allows them only a perverted kind of relationship. This further challenge to the pack determines their continued exclusion. Being so disturbed, Olga and Roelle can never fulfil each other. So they visit on each other what has been visited on them, a vicious circle with all the permanence and remorselessness depicted by Dante. Fleisser makes the individuals who form the group quite as important. Their manic need for a redeemer distorts their critical judgement and opens the door to a false redeemer. It is not just purgatory for the central couple but for the whole community.

Until Fleisser was unearthed by Fassbinder in the last sixties *Purgatory* sank without trace, just as she had sunk into her 'dead' but vindictive home town. She started reworking the play in December 1970. Three years later she died. Now that her plays are back in the repertory of the German speaking countries there are roughly four times more performances of *Purgatory* than of *Pioneers*.

Pioneers in Ingolstadt

A Comedy in 14 Scenes
(1968 Version)

Marieluise Fleisser

translated by Elisabeth Bond-Pablé and Tinch Minter

Characters

Alma
Berta
Fabian, *17-years-old*
Zeck, *27-years-old*
Bibrich, *a young joiner*
Unertl, *Fabian's father, a businessman*
Korl Lettner/Münsterer/Rosskopf/Jäger/Bunny, *Pioneers*
Sergeant
Second Sergeant
Photographer
Pioneers, Girls, Citizens, Policeman

The comedy takes place in 1926.

Pioneers in Ingolstadt received its British première at the Gate Theatre, London on 22 February 1991, with the following cast:

Berta	Sandy McDade
Alma	Teresa McElroy
Münsterer	Mark Lewis Jones
Jäger	Will Barton
Rosskopf	Russell Porter
Korl	Robert Bowman
Sergeant	Christopher Campbell
Zeck	Ignatius Anthony
Fabian	Simon Tyrrell
Unertl	Godfrey Jackman
Bibrich	Thomas Craig
Policeman	Godfrey Jackman
Photographer	Godfrey Jackman

Directed by Annie Castledine, Stephen Daldry
Designed by Ian MacNeil
Musical Director Stephen Warbeck
Lighting Designer Ace McCarron

Note: Square brackets denote translator's addition to stage directions for purpose of clarification.

Scene One

Near A City Gate.

I

*The **Pioneers** march in. Music. **Berta**, **Alma**, **Citizens**.*

Berta Why aren't they singing, *Oh du schöner Westerwald* then?

Alma If you'd gone with them, then you'd know. Can't tell you a thing. How old d'you now? You've missed out on a year already.

Pioneers [drill].

Berta Alma, I ain't picking a fight. But Alma, no one can hang about with you.

Alma Yeah? So?

Berta Has your mistress given you time off, too?

Alma She can't give me time off no more. I got the sack.

Berta What'll you do then? You're in it now.

Alma Don't worry me. The Pioneers is in town.

[Sergeant] 'Tention! Eyes left!

Berta Don't want to know, Alma, what'll become of you.

Alma It won't be your look-out.

Berta Easy to get dropped in it.

Alma Still, I've not led you off the straight and narrow. You can't hold that against me.

Berta You'll be the first to do the dumping. When the rest get something on me.

Alma Never Berta. I won't never do that.

Berta Alma, we'll talk it over. Our friendship must go on.

Alma Berta, and I wouldn't never leave you! (*Giving her her hand.*)

[The] soldiers [set up a] camp kitchen.

Berta Alma, I got to ask you something. Tell me straight, how you do it.

Alma Do what?

Berta Get to know one.

Alma I get them like that.

Berta Don't want to be like you. But I do want to know a man.

Alma Well, there's always your master's son, huh?

Berta I don't know.

Alma But you must know if he wants it with you.

Berta (*shrugging her shoulders*) Well, I've got different ideas.

Alma 'S'not for you to choose.

Berta But it is for me to choose. I want to know a man.

Alma Why not say a Pioneer. It's not all that hard.

Berta I just run away if one looks at me.

Alma Well, go and have a butchers, when they're building the bridge, obbiously. It'll happen all by itself, obbiously.

Berta What bridge?

Alma The new one over the creek. Town's supplying the wood, Pioneers building it. The town's not having to pay.

Berta The devil has all the best tunes.

Both going off.

II

Zeck and **Fabian** *talk man to man. They both come in wearing the same hats,* **Fabian**'s *looks odd on him.*

Zeck At your age I done it blindfold. At your age I was a dab hand.

Fabian I'm not pulling none.

Zeck Oh, I wouldn't say that.

Fabian You see, you got to get the hang of it. Girls today are frightening.

Zeck And they put the fear of God up us.

Fabian If you want to get it, they make an ass of you.

Zeck You don't have to take it lying down.

Fabian Have to chew it over, then chew it over again.

Zeck Wrong. Why don't you pull your finger out, young man? Got no guts?

Fabian Got to give it to you straight. I can't hold out no more.

Zeck So you've got the hots.

Fabian (*bragging*) The next girl I meet, I'm grabbing.

Zeck Keep your eyes and ears open, and it'll just happen. You'll get there.

Fabian You've got to pick the right one.

Zeck That Berta's – in flower.

Fabian Got my doubts there.

Zeck It's easy enough there. You can have it away with servant girls in the house. You just snap your fingers. It's not like with a stranger. Keep in mind what you're after, young man. Only natural, in't it?

Fabian I've been hot on Berta for ages.

Zeck If that's the case, then watch your step.

Fabian But I don't want to watch my step. I'm going in right up to my neck.

Zeck That'll land you in the soup. When it's love, men keep their cool. That's the way to manage it.

Fabian But not the first time, surely.

Zeck The path of love is set with snares, where nasty man-traps lie in wait. You know, that's absolutely typical of love.

Fabian I'll never get the hang of it.

Zeck Naked self-defence. Be warned.

Fabian But that's horrible.

Zeck You or me. You'll just have to get used to it. A man doesn't lose his head over it.

Fabian You've just made it harder for me.

III

Berta and **Alma** *sitting on a park bench, singing a kitchen-girl song. They hold hands and swing their arms backwards and forwards.*

Alma Bit too quiet around here today.

Pioneers *pass by.*

Alma (*standing up*) There's the first swallow.

Berta What are you up to?

Alma It's on its way.

Berta You can't leave me.

Alma (*turning towards her*) Well, if I was you, I'd jump.

Berta (*calling after her*) Alma!

Alma Help yourself. I'm not handing you one on a plate.

Berta You're bad through and through. (*Turning and going back in the opposite direction.*)

Pioneers *pass by.* **Münsterer, Rosskopf.**

Münsterer Before we report to the bridge-head at eleven, we got to get to know one.

Rosskopf Missed our chance today.

Münsterer There's one still out and about.

Alma *saunters across his path.*

Rosskopf Fräulein, what's a pretty girl doing out so late on her lonesome?

Alma You called Paul?

Rosskopf Why, you waiting for one?

Münsterer (*pulling him away*) Well, I'm called Paul.

Alma 'Cause I've just given two the push, one of them was called Paul, too.

Münsterer You don't look like you do the choosing.

Alma You got a cheek, if you don't mind me saying so.

Münsterer Let's split. We're not gonna waste time here.

They both leave.

Alma (*calling after him*) Kiss my arse!

Jäger (*pushing his bicycle on, ostentatiously ringing the bell*) Fräulein, I'd have got over the hill without getting off. But because of my mates I took it slowly. Just so you don't think I can't ride a bike.

Alma If you hold on a bit, a pretty Fräulein's coming this way, you can give her the same line.

Jäger What for? You've let me trail after you a long way.

Alma That was somebody else.

Jäger That was you.

Alma Turn your lamp, so I can see your face.

He turns his front wheel.

S'not true. And you haven't got his voice.

Jäger The one you had a date with ain't coming.

Alma He is coming.

Jäger (*doing figure-riding on his bike in front of her*) No falling off! You got to get the knack. The bike obeys its master.

Alma (*impressed*) You know, the one I'm waiting for might have gone past already. Anyway he looked completely different. Can't hardly remember the man now.

Jäger There isn't no woman who can't be won.

Alma So they say.

Jäger Cigarette? (*Giving her a light.*) Girls have liked me now and again.

Alma Not saying I don't like you.

Jäger (*tapping his bike*) Jump on!

Alma *gets on the bike behind him, they go off with her standing.*

Sergeant *comes in and crosses the stage alone. A girl meets him, he tries to latch onto her, but she turns away.*

Sergeant The town isn't friendly. (*Going off.*)

IV

Korl *and* **Berta** *coming in.*

Berta And I was betrayed.

Korl (*pointing ahead at a bench*) This one's ours. We've waited for it.

Berta It don't belong here. Someone's moved it.

Korl Let's see if it's clean. (*Lighting up the bench with a match.*)

Berta I've got my cream dress on.

Korl I'll put my hanky on it.

Berta (*sitting down on the hanky*) Look, it's got no back, that's why it's not occupied.

Korl Well, it's not like I'm not here. What's my arm for? (*Putting his arm round her, she leans back on it.*)

Berta (*languishing*) Now I've got a back, and I don't know what it's called.

Korl Korl.

Berta (*languishing*) It's called Korl.

Korl You sat here before.

Berta Not like this.

Korl Make the next one believe that, I don't.

She is silent, he gives her a little nudge.

Don't give me that line. So, you were betrayed.

She stays silent.

Now you don't know nothing.

Berta I gotta think how to put it. I'm not talking about no man. I'm talking about a girl.

Korl (*not believing her*) What d'you say she's called?

Berta Alma! (*Blurting out.*) Because she betrayed me. First she needed me, now she won't even look at me.

Korl Tell me another. Fine by me without a shred of truth. Don't have to be true.

Berta But it is true.

Korl (*nudging her again*) Girls always think they can get something out of us.

Berta I'm not like the others.

Korl That's what you think! I'm like all the others.

Berta I don't believe that.

Korl How'm I supposed to be?

Berta Don't know.

Korl Well, can't change my ways. Any case, I won't.

Berta Mind striking a light so I can see you?

He lights up his face with a match, letting it go on burning quite a long time.

Not so's you burn your fingers.

Korl What's that to me. A Pioneer never feels pain. (*Holding his hand out to her.*) Put your hand here, there's a skin for you.

Berta (*feeling it with her hand*) Nice.

Korl You gotta name too?

Berta I was born a Berta.

Korl Berta.

Berta (*jealously*) You had one already, a Berta?

Korl (*mocking*) Straight up, no.

Berta I wouldn't like it if you had one already.

Korl Think I'd tell you. Must you always know everything about the one you're with?

Berta Stop running yourself down.

Korl I'm not really running myself down. But I'm telling you it ain't none of your business.

Berta But it is my business.

Korl (*grasping hold of her*) Say it isn't your business!

Berta You're hurting me.

Korl I know.

Berta I'm getting up.

Korl If I let you! (*Trying to touch her up.*)

Berta Don't! You don't do that!

Korl Why not? Get used to it.

Berta (*becoming frantic*) I ain't never done it! I don't go with men. If a man does that, I report him.

Korl (*letting her go*) You'll want it soon enough.

Berta (*standing up*) I'm not sitting down on this bench again.

Korl The next one then.

Berta Korl, I'm not sitting down.

Korl What makes you think I'll go with you, then?

Berta (*like a charm*) I won't listen to what he says, 'cause he doesn't mean it.

Korl I'm not having you worship me with your worship.

Berta Far from it. I'm not worshipping you. You need telling off.

Korl It works or it don't work. If a girl isn't willing I don't hang about.

He goes off, she stands there thunderstruck, then runs after him.

Berta Don't go away. I don't want to quarrel with you and I don't know how it happened.

Korl What's it now? We doing it or not doing it?

Berta (*in a corner*) I can't tell you straight away.

Korl But I can tell you straight away, you haven't got much time. Come tomorrow, we won't know each other. (*Going off.*)

Berta (*calling after him*) Korl!

Scene Two

Unertl's *household.*

A covered balcony, with washing hanging from it. **Unertl** *in a rocking chair,* **Fabian** *looking at the roofs.*

Unertl (*shouting*) Berta! Serve! – I'll scream myself hoarse. Where's that bit of skirt got to?

Fabian She took time off.

Unertl I'll give her time off. That bit of skirt gets time off on Sunday, not during the week.

Fabian She said she needed some air.

Unertl Take the washing in from the terrace and she'll get all the air she needs. Housework offers the healthiest variety. Statistics prove it.

Fabian Even she wants a chat now and again.

Unertl What good's chatting to her? All she wants in her head is what her master wants. Everything else is a luxury.

Fabian With soldiers swarming about, she can't bear staying in. She's afraid of missing out.

Unertl She'll get her a bastard soon enough.

Fabian But she's still a human being.

Unertl Trust you to stand up for her.

Fabian Berta's a decent girl. Berta doesn't sell herself cheap.

Unertl You could make an effort for her, if she's after one. She won't get on her high horse then. No one'll know.

Fabian She's got her head screwed on.

Unertl We'll put paid to that. I'm not letting her swan off leaving me high and dry. Does she expect me to go to the cellar when I want a beer. What's the creature for?

Fabian She's hard at it all day long.

Unertl She's not turning me into a lodger, for everyone to just ignore. I rule the roost in my own home. No one's shitting on me in my own four walls. My habits suit me all right.

Fabian Why don't you get married again?

Unertl I haven't taken leave of my senses yet.

Fabian You can get married for all I care. Won't land me in the poor-house.

Unertl I can, can I? Women don't do the running around. They get you by the short and curlies. Get married and your Mark's only worth fifty Pfennigs.

Fabian You'll hardly starve.

Unertl Get your fingers burnt once and you're on your guard.

Fabian I won't hear a word against Mother.

Unertl She doted on you. Not me.

Fabian There's no crime in that.

Unertl I'll marry a woman who can run the business for me, or not at all.

Fabian Must be some about.

Unertl I've got certain standards. I'm not having one who's never been away from here, I know about here. She's gotto be the sort to add to my glory. But that sort will never have me. Haven't the first idea why.

Fabian No one will have you the way you are!

Unertl I just remember my third shop assistant, the good one, who gave me the cold shoulder. Wanted to see for herself, she went abroad, she was pretty canny. She had one who wrote to her from America. America'd be too far off for me. She could have it right here. But not likely!

Fabian Did you propose to her properly? I doubt it.

Unertl Marry within the trade, I said, the two of us could make a go of it, with your experience and all that. That was a hint, wasn't it? You'd suit me well enough, I said, you and I could rub along together.

Fabian That's the first I've heard.

Unertl When you're with me, I told her, all your troubles will be over. Or just starting, she said. Straight to my face. Or just starting.

Fabian This creature had no faith in you.

Unertl The tart! – Never have one from the shop. The girls know too much about you. If it's for life no one's keen. They think you're using them.

Fabian As if things'd get worse for them than before.

Unertl She said, things suit me better as a shop assistant, because there's nothing final about it. It's not the end of it. That's how it is. I'm the end of the line. But I don't know why.

Fabian You only think of yourself.

Unertl Everyone does. Even if they don't make a song and dance about it.

Fabian Yes, but you make it obvious.

Unertl Not on your life, young lady. I'm not that smitten. If things go my way, I'll wait three years, set myself up as a wholesaler. Then I'll be forty-two, right. I'll still be a man in demand then. And I'll not have to play at being a lodger. I'll get myself a maid, she can do the running around.

Scene Three

Swimming Pool in a Men's Sports Club.

Changing rooms, duck-boards.

Zeck (*from inside a cabin*) Haven't heard enough. How far you got with your bit of fluff?

Fabian (*from inside another cabin*) Don't ask you about your bit of fluff, do I?

Zeck Too early for such cheek from you.

Fabian Stop stirring, Chief. (*Coming out.*) In any case. I'm on my way.

Zeck Better not get unstuck on the way.

Fabian Stop having a dig. Got nothing to complain about. She'll be my heart-throb. It's clicking.

Zeck (*coming out. Sceptically*) Oh yeah, where d'you get that idea, young man?

Fabian There are certain signs.

Zeck Our man about town! Tee hee!

Fabian I'm asking you to take me seriously.

Zeck Not till you come up with her very own petticoat.

Bibrich *tiptoeing across the boards gets stuck with one foot in a hole, and falls over.*

Bibrich Oh, ah! Charming!

Fabian One's had it.

Zeck And it happens to a joiner.

Fabian Don't you know every single board is lying in wait for you?

Zeck Why don't you look where you're going, you ass?

Bibrich Love listening to you. Please go on. Oh, Oh!

Fabian Lost your foot?

Bibrich Leave me alone, I don't know.

Zeck The cherubs will sing it to you.

Bibrich Not making any promises.

Zeck Don't look over there, there's a corpse.

Bibrich You are mean. Mean, aren't you?

Zeck Tough luck. For a start we know how to manage rotten boards. Don't give under us.

Bibrich The boards'll nab you soon enough.

Fabian Hope not.

Zeck If you must know, that'd make the third broken leg. This bloody board's nothing but a trap.

Bibrich The club don't give birth to no boards.

Zeck The club don't have two brass farthings.

Bibrich Not for us, it don't. Hare-brained lot. (*Limping downstage.*)

Zeck Once a month the trainer puts in his bid. The trainer don't get our boards no nearer.

Bibrich The club should pull its finger out, dammit. I'm not getting my limbs smashed.

Zeck The club has put in to the town for new boarding. Four times already. Town turns a deaf ear.

Fabian A swimmer, a dumbo.

Bibrich Can't even organise a diving gala when you got nothing to put your spectators on. No diving gala, no gate.

Zeck No gate, no dough.

Fabian Can't mint your own.

Zeck This is a citadel, mates. This used to be a defensive trench. Not built for sports and display. We took what was there.

Fabian Wouldn't be no swimmers otherwise.

Bibrich Swimmers don't count, do he? This club treats swimmers like cripples.

Zeck Only footballers pull in the cash.

Fabian Footballers don't give us a thing.

Bibrich We swimmer never get our duck-board.

Zeck Not the faintest chance.

Bibrich Gotto bite the bullet. The Danube's out of the question.

Fabian Too many whirlpools. The Danube tells lies.

Zeck The Danube fakes the figures. We just got to put up with our sluggish trench.

Bibrich The town can stuff it. We swimmer going on strike.

Zeck That ever bothered the town? They don't never miss us.

Fabian But we get out of condition.

Zeck They got things up their sleeve. They put up a notice for us: No entry. All we're left with is crumbling duckboards and nowhere to swim.

Bibrich We'll be right suckers, then.

Zeck What do we do then?

Fabian It's the end. And only because they shit on swimmers.

Bibrich Then I've gotto say, let's knock up our own board. I'm a joiner, I'll show you how.

Zeck Wood's got to be had.

Bibrich Do overtime.

Zeck You can borrow tools.

Bibrich It'll be a hard slog. But we haven't got no wood.

Zeck I know some wood, if you got guts. This wood's off limits.

Fabian (*generously*) So what!

Bibrich You gotto have guts.

Fabian No one here's a nark, it won't get out.

Zeck Along this creek, not quarter of an hour away, there's wood. Just have to pull it along.

Bibrich Pioneer's in town!

Zeck Pioneer build a bridge. Give the bridge to the town. Get the wood from the town.

Fabian The town sit on the wood.

Bibrich The town don't give the swimmer the wood.

Zeck Swimmer helps himself to the wood.

Bibrich Only justice after all.

Fabian Because he's in hot water.

Bibrich Club mustn't know.

Zeck Duck-board don't take even a small wood. Course the town can afford a small wood.

Scene Four

Beer Tent.

Citizens *and* **Pioneers. Berta, Fabian** *and* **Sergeant** *at a table. Coming in,* **Korl** *avoids saluting the* **Sergeant**, *sits at another table. But the* **Sergeant** *has noticed. Outside near the tent a circular pissoir with a sign saying 'Pissoir'.*

Sergeant That bloke acts blind in one eye but I'll turn a blind eye. I could tear strips off him.

Fabian You're not a spoil-sport.

Sergeant (*hypocritically*) Never. How d'you call this, a jar?

Fabian A jar for the military! Mother's milk.

Sergeant You standing treats all day?

Fabian Fine by me. Father pays the lot. Needn't give it a thought.

Sergeant Thinking's devil's work. I'll get my own back.

Fabian I'll keep you to it.

Sergeant Something's wrong here. Why's the dewy skinned party sitting in the wrong place? The military feels left out. She gotto sit between us.

Fabian The girl's all right where she sitting.

Sergeant Don't think so 'cause she don't open her mouth. You had a row?

Fabian We never row.

Sergeant I for one haven't got nothing against knowing the girl. She'd open her mouth then.

Fabian Perhaps she's got something against it.

Sergeant 'Fraid she's sick of you.

Fabian Of me? Pah! She eats out of my hand.

Sergeant Don't look like that to me.

Fabian You making a fool of me, Berta. Don't you want something to drink?

Berta Nothing, thanks.

Fabian Then why did you come with me Berta if you don't even look at me?

Berta I can't look your way all the time. People'd notice.

Fabian They're meant to notice.

Berta You gotto be in the mood.

Sergeant No one talks to me like that. You need winding up.

Fabian In your shoes I'd never let a man like me out of my sight!

Berta Who are you, then?

Fabian Berta, that was a snub.

Korl *whistles for her.*

What's that mean?

Berta *is about to stand up.* **Fabian** *holds her*

back. **Korl** *whistles again and signals to her to come over.*

Sergeant The cheek! From our table!

Fabian How long d'you know that one? You're not going just like that because he thinks it's gotta be.

Berta I got to. (*Breaking loose and going over to* **Korl** *on another table.*)

Sergeant But she can't do that. Get your fiancée back here at once.

Fabian She's not my fiancée.

Sergeant We look like baboons.

Fabian We can still get pissed.

They knock their beers back.

Sergeant Anyone laughs at me, don't like it.

Fabian It's not you he's laughing at.

Sergeant I know the man. He's too fast off the blocks, snatches virgins away from his superior. That's how it was in Küstrin, now he really gets up my nose. I got him in my sights.

Music: Stolz weht die flagge schwarz-weiss-rot (Proudly waves the flag that's black white and red).

Berta Hey, the ones with pips are different to you, aren't they?

Korl That's my superiors.

Berta What d'you call them when they your superiors?

Korl You call them non-commissioned officers, and you call them Sergeant. Say NCO and Sarge. Sergeant-Major and the whole caboodle right up to the General, who's an old ass, but eats you up for breakfast.

Berta Say NCO and Sarge! (*Laughing.*) But a pioneer's much more handsomer than a Sergeant.

Korl 'Cause he's younger. In the army it's a drawback. Our superior says, if he's not been a Pioneer for ten years he don't even count as a Pioneer.

Pioneer Don't even count as one.

Berta That's pretty hard.

Korl A Pioneer must be more able than his superiors, but he mustn't show it. (*Taking* **Berta** *in his arms.*)

Fabian What's your name, Sergeant?

Sergeant Willi.

Fabian I'll call you Willi. And buy you another jar.

Sergeant Mother's milk. You can tell you're one of the big-wigs.

Fabian I'm only just on the first rung, but I'm on the ladder.

Sergeant Fancy footwork!

Fabian I'm following my old man. Growing into the business. One day I'll be the boss.

Sergeant You've got a safe billet.

Fabian Girls'd throw themselves at me if they had any brains.

Sergeant Girls always throw themselves at the wrong ones.

Fabian (*drinking*) A jar like this holds a good lot.

Sergeant It'd better hold a lot. Drown all my black moods in it.

Fabian Boozing brother, you too?

Sergeant You haven't got no clue.

Fabian Boozing brother, booze! (*Fraternisation, militarily.*) Next the world!

Fabian And the last shall be the first.

Sergeant Don't look like that from where I am. 'Cause we're all arseholes, right, and we're all under someone else's backside. They give it me in the neck about the wood, right?

Fabian You say wood?

Sergeant I said wood, but really, it's half a bridge.

Fabian Not another word. Got my suspicions.

Sergeant I've always got my suspicions. Got to. Isn't so easy to do things right by me. It's my damned duty. Gotto be like a scourge, me.

Fabian Don't understand what you're on about.

Sergeant Count yourself lucky.

Fabian I got a dark suspicion, my little finger wants to tell me something.

Sergeant I'm not your little finger.

Fabian Don't be like that.

Sergeant I could explode. Standing in front of you's a man, who had half a bridge stolen from him 'cause he's in command of the construction-unit. Can't explain it better to a civvy. Standing in front of you's a broken man.

Fabian I heard a rumour about some disappearing wood and I believed it, that's how I am.

Sergeant Like the earth swallowed it, and I can tell you it was heavy.

Fabian People really are evil.

Sergeant That isn't the whole story. I got bawled out in a way you could only imagine under torture. Standing in front of you's a man who got nothing more to laugh about.

Fabian A pile of wood like that'd be guarded, surely?

Sergeant Who's to guard something like that? Can't be lugged away. Guards itself.

Fabian One man on his own can't do it.

Sergeant That was a gang more like. I must have men in my own unit that sold it on the spot.

Fabian Organised.

Sergeant Daylight robbery. I'll tear their heads off of their shoulders.

Fabian You'll tear their heads off of their shoulders.

Sergeant First I got to get 'em. And I'll get 'em. I know damn well who it is, but I can't pin it on them. I can't just come out with it, son of a bitch, you did it. I feel powerless, even if I do hide it behind bullying.

Fabian Who are you going to hang it on?

Sergeant He who looks is sure to find.

Fabian So you're not going on building, Chief?

Sergeant I always go on building, dammit!

Fabian Where d'you get the missing wood from?

Sergeant The town, who else?

Fabian Might as well whistle for it.

Sergeant They might as well whistle for it. Do they want their bloody bridge over the water or don't they want their bloody bridge?

Fabian Perhaps they don't deserve it. Perhaps someone very different deserves it.

Sergeant Come what may the town will replace it. But the town isn't happy about it. Them in town aren't friendly.

Fabian That's the way of the world.

Sergeant Costs me my promotion, this way of the world. Made me carry the can, this way of the world. In cases like this the General turns into a mad bull, the Major turns into a mad bull and the Captain turns into a raging mad bull. The lower down the more furious the rage, and the more it affects you. We're all under someone's backside.

Fabian What d'you do with it?

Sergeant I pass it on, the pressure.

Fabian I see!

Sergeant And I'll find one to carry the can, and if he isn't guilty I make him guilty.

Fabian (*holding beer out to him*) We two beauties can always get drownded.

Sergeant Don't help enough. Damage is already done. Worm's in the bud.

Fabian The tommy who's with the girl now, what's he like in private?

Sergeant I don't talk to privates.

Fabian But the girl was to your taste?

Sergeant If the girl prefers a Pioneer, I can't debase myself with her.

Fabian Has he got to stand to attention to you even in this dive? I've gotto see that.

Sergeant And you gonna see that. 'Cause he's the sort that pilfers, walks away with the swag and holds nothing sacred.

Music: Wood-cutting fellows.

Korl *leaves the tent with* **Berta**. *Again he doesn't salute. The* **Sergeant** *stands up menacingly.*

Korl (*outside*) I gotto run off some beer, girl.

Korl *disappears into the pissoir.* **Berta** *waits by the tent. The* **Sergeant** *also goes into the pissoir. He comes out right behind* **Korl**.

Sergeant Private, you there! How long

have you looked straight through your superior?

Korl Didn't see the Sarge, Sir!

Sergeant You salute me like you're a recruit, I'm not letting you get away with that, and now we gonna make up for it. I for one gonna have a salute from you that sends the sparks flying. 'Tention –

Korl *has to salute.*

To me that isn't even a feeble outline of a regulation salute. Whole procedure repeat. 'Tention – 'Tention –

Korl *has to salute.*

Won't do, my man. You've gotto throw yourself into it. Let the sparks fly. Flash out of your rotten carcass. Gotto put a match under your arse? And back! Left and left and left –

He makes **Korl** *march up and down fast, saluting each time he passes. While he's bullying* **Korl**, *a* **Man** *goes to the pissoir and watches.* **Citizens** *and* **Fabian** *stare from the tent. One sings with no apparent motive:* Die Fliegen, die Fliegen, die kann man halt nicht kriegen. *(The flies, the flies, you just can't catch them.)*

Berta I'd be ashamed. Let the poor man go, you.

Sergeant The girl won't help you. She'll see who's the loser.

Berta You're an evil man.

Sergeant Leave the girl out of it.

Korl She's my girl, Sir.

Sergeant They aren't girls for the ranks. They're girls for the NCOs, got that.

Korl I'm off duty. When I'm off duty I give a girl the eye and it just happens.

Sergeant It don't just happen. For a start off it costs more than you got. I for one think that's suspicious.

Korl Different with me. Get it for nothing.

Sergeant (*having difficulty swallowing this, he takes his revenge*) Down! Crawl!

Korl *has to lie down and crawl on his elbows.*

Citizens What's going on? Never seen the like! Bully!

Sergeant The town isn't friendly.

Alma (*sauntering in*) Why're you so tetchy, darling?

Sergeant Not always like this. But when someone nettles me I trample him down.

Alma But not before my very eyes.

Sergeant (*sensing his chance*) On your feet! Dismiss!

Korl *gets up. The* **Sergeant** *gives him a sign to dismiss.* **Korl** *sits down with* **Berta** *on an isolated bench.* **Fabian** *goes into the tent and drinks.*

Alma (*to* **Berta**) Your fancy man can thank me.

The onlookers disperse.

Alma (*to the* **Sergeant**) Well, how are tricks?

Sergeant Don't get it up as often as I did.

Alma That's what you think.

Sergeant You're looking good, Fräulein. But one just passed me by, who said I'm not worth knowing no more. Can't get along with myself.

Alma You're in mortal danger then.

Sergeant And you won't look like you do in ten years.

Alma What's that to me? 'Cause I'm having my best time right now.

Sergeant How old're you, Fräulein?

Alma Twenty.

Sergeant Still just right. Where d'you live, Fräulein?

Alma On the Lower Moat.

Sergeant Just near my place.

Alma I'm very popular with the gentlemen. Know most of them. I'm a woman of the world, don't you know.

Sergeant I'm not frightened off by nothing.

Alma But I don't fancy all comers.

Sergeant Why so hard? You can always make an exception. Anger's chewing my guts. Fräulein, put me back together again.

Alma Not 'cause of your lovely eyes, if that's what you mean. In other words, there's a kitty, darling. I'm out of work.

Sergeant A man don't like hearing that.

Alma We're only young once.

Sergeant You're a nice one, aren't you?

Alma And I give good value.

Sergeant I gotta say, that's all I need

They both go out. **Korl** *and* **Berta** *on the bench.*

Korl Don't you go falling in love with me, doll.

Berta I'm not falling in love.

Korl Lots have said that, but still fell in love with me.

Berta We're just having a joke, aren't we Korl?

Korl I'm not joking. I can't be tied down.

Berta You're silly. You're the one I want. You're the one I picked out of the whole lot.

Korl Don't you go falling in love with me, or you'll suffer.

Berta I want to suffer.

Korl You don't know me. I get nasty if a girl's nice to me. Woman get torn to shreds by me, got that. I've not got no soft centre.

Berta You just like it, that right?

Korl You could say that. I only want to know what all the others are like.

Berta But suppose I want to fall in love with you.

Korl I know that, or you're not all there. But I've told you.

Berta It does you good too having a soul mate. (*Pause.*) And what scares me most is you falling for another one.

Korl Not all that crap again. Don't like that. Stop talking, it's a waste of time. Get more comfortable. (*Fumbling about her neck.*)

Berta The stars shine down on us. They shining in your eyes too.

Korl Keep your mind on the job and stop talking.

Berta Korl, is that nice?

Korl Now I can't go on, don't feel like it no more. Can't take all this pontificating.

Berta (*covering herself*) Am I to go?

Korl Yes, go. Lost the urge.

Berta *stays.*

See, I just don't feel like it no more, the way I am.

Berta Yes, you do, but then something slipped out.

Korl Nothing slipped out.

Berta It's to do with the heart and you don't know.

Berta *goes.*

Pause.

Scene Five

Swimming Pool in a Men's Sports Club.

Zeck *doing light gymnastics. From the back, noises of an unseen swimmer.*

Bibrich (*coming on*) Who've you got in the water?

Zeck He knows nothing. Only Ratz. He's here every day.

Bibrich Can we trust him?

Zeck He's the youngest but he knows what the club can do to him. He's under our thumb.

Bibrich It's got to be OK with the wood. Police are snooping about already outside the club. They'll be down here too.

Zeck Won't be seen. It's wedged in by the wall in the shadows. The wood's lying too far in.

Bibrich Police'd have to dive in.

Zeck Our Police don't go about diving. Any case they haven't got a lead.

Policeman (*coming in*) Routine search, gentlemen. This part of the area has not been checked yet.

Zeck The Police have our best interests at heart.

Policeman The Police can make no exceptions.

Zeck (*taking him round*) Take care on the duck board. Someone's laid fresh planks. Still got to be nailed down.

Policeman (*becoming suspicious*) I see.

Zeck Our joiner's out of action.

Bibrich *suffers.*

Policeman (*bending down*) These boards are well worn. (*Writing.*)

Zeck From the brewery. Buckshee.

Policeman (*opening cabin doors*) What's behind the doors?

Zeck We don't have ladies here.

Policeman It's not ladies we're after. What escape-route does the ladder lead to?

A ladder is leaning next to the cabins.

Zeck The ladder only goes to the walls.

Policeman I'll satisfy myself what's on the walls. (*He climbs onto the rampart.*)

Zeck (*insidiously*) It's the highest point. From up there you look down.

Policeman (*looking over the area, then climbs down*) Rampart fallen down. No escape-route. (*Writing in his book.*) How deep is the water?

Zeck Four metres or so.

Policeman Informant indicates the depth of the water as four metres.

Zeck Could be more. I've not measured it to the nearest centimetre. You'd have to dive in, Constable.

Bibrich *suffers.*

Policeman (*writing*) Informant's name – what is your name?

Zeck Ludwig Zeck.

Policeman Date of birth?

Zeck 1899, twenty-two November, here.

Policeman Permanent residence?

Zeck Seven Goldsmiths Lane. The club has me on file.

Policeman (*bending over the water*) You can't see the bottom.

Bibrich You never see the bottom here. – Have you ever eaten chocolate underwater?

Policeman No. Why?

Zeck Don't taste of a thing. Like having a mouthful of shards.

Policeman Interesting. I'm not a diver. (*Taking his leave.*)

Zeck Ass!

Bibrich The Police didn't even give it a proper once over. Stroke of luck.

Zeck Wood stays with us.

Bibrich We lift it out as we need it.

Zeck It won't go rotten on us in the water, will it?

Bibrich Wood's treated.

Zeck Till the Pioneers' gone, we've gotto hide it.

Bibrich I'm totally KO'ed. I'm a wreck.

Zeck I'm toddling off too.

Scene Six

Building Site.

Night-time, just before the last post. The skeleton of a bridge being built. **Korl** *and* **Bunny** *approaching cautiously.*

Korl I can't put up with that bastard picking on me no more, and I've got to put up with him picking on me. Bunny, it's driving me mad.

Bunny I hate his guts too, 'cause he's a cyclist.

Korl (*climbing up the bridge skeleton*) If someone comes: our bird whistle. (*Climbing higher, he undoes screws.*)

Bunny You can't loosen all the bolts, you're mad, they'll notice. You'll drop yourself in it.

Korl Stop butting in, Bunny.

Bunny At the least it's sabotage. Know what you'll get?

Korl That bully's gotto know it's war between him and the men. (*He is back down again.*)

Bunny If he gives it a once over, he'll put it on you.

Korl He won't never know for sure.

Bunny *quietly whistles the bird whistle.* **Korl** *whisks round and can't see anyone.*

What're you whistling for, idiot?

Bunny Putting the wind up you. Let's go. He's got all the cards, you'll always get a bad hand. You're the poor calf, believe me, he'll play butcher.

Korl His sort always get bumped off from behind in a war. (*They slope off.*)

Scene Seven

Unertl's *household.*

Unertl, **Berta**, **Fabian**.

Unertl It does astonish me that we exist at all for you. All we're good for's paying wages. Compared to the military we're mere orphans.

Berta I do my work. Master can't complain.

Unertl You can't count. For the second time this week the Fräulein just flitted out, and the Fräulein wasn't to hand.

Berta Well, I've washed up every evening after your meal. After that I'm meant to be free, aren't I?

Unertl Your work mustn't suffer because of it. (*Picking up a plate to vex her. To* **Fabian**.) Look at this tide-mark sitting there.

Berta No tide-mark sitting there.

Unertl She's in such a rush, she doesn't bother to heat up the water.

Fabian This mark has always been there.

Berta People always harbour false suspicions.

Unertl Man reveals himself through his work. For one thing you could have taken the curtains down long ago.

Berta I did the wash a fortnight ago. Curtains too.

Unertl They must be white as a daisy, they must totally glisten. Cleanliness must jump out at you, that's what I call running a household. That's what I call battling against bugs.

Berta I can't change the sheets every day.

Unertl Don't you imagine you can diddle me. When I'm the one who's paying I expect people to do the job or I'd be stupid.

Berta You're always having a go at me, making me rush about.

Unertl In a household something always wants cleaning if you look out for it and if you really dig into it. That's a lifelong task.

Berta You get eaten away by it.

Unertl If you don't do it right, you're nothing but a slut to me, nobody'll cry over you.

Berta You ask too much.

Unertl I'm well aware you've got protection.

Berta The least you've gotto do is let me breathe.

Unertl Don't you go telling tales at the Labour Exchange! You'll only make a fool of yourself. You haven't the first idea what to say there. If you start picking holes in me, then you better look out.

Berta I can't never do nothing that makes people notice me.

Unertl There's absolutely nothing people need to notice about you.

Berta But I'm a human being too.

Unertl 'Cause the younger generation doesn't know what they've got handed on a plate and how lucky they are.

Berta I don't have to put up with anything.

Unertl Take your eyes off her for a minute and she's shot out of sight. And then she's late back.

Berta What do you mean late back?

Unertl I can demand certain behaviour when I take someone into my house. You're quite likely to bring us the pox. You're not on heat, are you?

Fabian Look, that's enough.

Unertl You keep out of this. – You've got to tell them, when they don't know what happens to a girl who's too trusting.

Berta No one's that bad. No cause for concern.

Unertl You're only seventeen. You know better.

Berta You make it all out to be bad. Master's gotta give me my cards. I can't face master no more.

Unertl Don't be insolent. She's got a tongue like a razor.

Berta Master's always finding fault with me.

Unertl Can't do you any harm.

Berta Whenever I go into the passage, master sends his son after me.

Unertl You getting anywhere with her? I see no signs.

Fabian You shouldn't talk about that in front of the girl.

Unertl We can give it to you too, you know. You don't have to go running far and wide after it.

Berta That's enough, if you don't mind.

Unertl Your soldier hasn't got sole rights. Where does he grope you, then?

Fabian You're obscene.

Unertl I never soft-soap. I always tell the truth. Up to her to knuckle under. Then the wind'll change.

Berta Doesn't the master know, how he's letting himself down?

Unertl The boot's on the other foot. I'll have you on your knees, you tart. I'll give you a hard time. You're gonna know I've got you in my power.

Berta If the master wants to force me, I won't be forced. (*Going out.*)

Unertl Showing her claws all of a sudden.

Fabian Not the way to go about it. Make a better job of it myself.

Unertl You've missed the boat there. She doesn't give a damn.

Fabian The girl's so confused, doesn't know what we have her for.

Unertl Let her go. Plenty more about.

Fabian I've gone off you.

Scene Eight

Building site of the bridge.

Morning mist. **Pioneers** *working.*

Sergeant You lame arses work your six hours day shift, 's not enough. From today, night shift, or we'll never get through. Put your backs into it, 's not just hot air, I never just spout hot air. Stop standing there like sacks. You trying to make out you're hard at it. Shift, shift, you lot put more life into it, I'll check on you lot. I've got eyes in my head, I'll find the skivers.

The noise of work gets more eager. He climbs up the bridge skeleton to his usual place, where he has the better overall view, and falls off. Gloating all round. A few scabs run over to him.

Rosskopf Now the sow's in the shit.

Bunny Bet he makes himself scarce!

Rosskopf You don't know that bully.

Bunny Back on his legs?

Korl Not half! No signs of tiredness, now we're for it. (*They work eagerly.*)

Sergeant (*his uniform torn*) Watch your step, you sod, I'll check on it. Keep at it!

The **Sergeant** *climbs up the scaffolding and searches for the cause. He comes down again with bolts in his hand.*

I take this as a personal attack. Group Five in line!

Group Five lines up, among them **Korl**, **Münsterer**, **Rosskopf**, **Bunny**.

Which of you mean bastards has done this dirty trick with the bolts? Safety catches undone, that's sabotage. Demands the severest punishment. Treacherous stab in the back! I expect the culprit to give himself up at once, who was it? We'll get to the bottom of it.

Silence.

I'm warning you. If no one gives himself up the whole group'll suffer. The bolts were shipshape yesterday. Who had time off yesterday evening? He'd better give himself up, I'll check on it.

He musters Group Five.

We got all our beauties together here. We give our beauties a once over. (*Turning round.*) No cause for shirking. Keep at it you at the back!

Going briefly to the back.

Korl Well, who was it then? No one wants to have done it? Is he afraid we'll shove the beam into his back?

Rosskopf We're in the clear. Wasn't one of us.

Münsterer See enough of the landscape by day.

Rosskopf Don't never come anywhere near the building site otherwise. We've had it up to here.

Münsterer But I can think who'd be happy to wipe him out.

Korl Thinking's a waste of time. Knowing's what matters.

Münsterer Someone plays the fool. All the rest gotta eat shit.

Korl Christ! What am I always saying?

They look each other up and down antagonistically.

Sergeant (*coming back*) I'm waiting for every son of a bitch to supply evidence where he spent his free time yesterday. Anyone who can't provide no witness to stand up for him, is in for a good time. Anyone who hasn't got no witness had better tell me at once. Our man hasn't come clean yet. But I'll make him come clean. And that goes for the whole group because it's covering up the culprit. Group Five line up for fatigue-duty. To the beam!

They take up positions one behind the other along the beam, the shortest at the back.

Beam – lift! With the beam – forward march, march. Backwards march, march. Knees bend – stretch – at the double, forward march, march! I said at the double. Section wheel. At the double on the spot.

They run on the spot.

Knees higher, higher! You lousy traitors remembered who the culprit is at last? Who's gonna come forward?

Silence.

Who's gonna give him up?

Silence.

Münsterer Lord have mercy on whoever done it.

Sergeant Group Five on night shift today. No tea-breaks. We work through without stopping. And keep at the double on the spot, quick march, march.

Scene Nine

From the ceiling a bed comes down, swaying in the air throughout, otherwise the stage remains empty. From behind the stage, spoken in uncouth soldiers' voices.

The truth, so help me God, Kreszenz Pichler
The truth, so help me God, Hansi Mittermeier
The truth, so help me God, Karoline Perger
The truth, so help me God, Luise Bachl
The truth, so help me God, Maria Motzer
The truth, so help me God, Beatrice Haberer
The truth, so help me God, Paula Vogelsang

Sergeant (*VO*) Go to Hell the lot of you!

Scene Ten

Park.

Distant parade music. **Citizens** *in their Sunday best and* **Pioneers** *meet on intertwined paths, stand together, part, then form new groups.*

I

Sergeant *seeing* **Alma** *coming towards him would dearly like to turn into a side path, but she plants herself in front of him.*

Sergeant The nicest day is spoilt for me, because all my Pioneers have alibis. They're all eels, I can't get no grip on them. Now this she-cat crosses my path.

Alma That's the con-man who paid nothing but the tip, isn't it? Not so keen to remember, eh?

Sergeant Fräulein, you must be mistaken.

Alma See someone once, and I know him again.

Sergeant Fräulein, I don't want nothing from you. You've muddled me up.

Alma Once they've done with you, they don't want to know.

Sergeant Tough. All soldiers look the same under their hats. We're like peas in a pod.

Alma Not to me. You still owe exactly what you've already paid. The gentleman told me he hadn't got the rest with him.

Sergeant You're driving too hard a bargain, Fräulein.

Alma Got it with you today?

Sergeant No. If a man won't settle, what can you do?

Alma We settled it in advance, you and me. I know my rights.

Sergeant Tough. I deny it. Nothing to do with me.

Alma I only want what we agreed.

Sergeant You got something out of it. Got nothing to complain about.

Alma To me it's the rights of a woman. I'm either worth it to you –

Sergeant Fräulein, not a chance after.

Alma You bastard.

Sergeant You must work with photos, if you're into blackmail.

Alma Yeargh!

Sergeant Get yourself a pimp, to look after you.

Alma I don't know what you mean, Mister.

Sergeant 'Course you don't know, you're still a beginner.

Alma Think you're cock of the walk round here.

Sergeant That's how it is. I got the experience.

Alma And you're older.

Sergeant Right. I'm not that raw no more.

Alma (*sneering*) Poor man! What a poor man you must be.

Sergeant Lady Muck. L M. (*Goes off.*)

Alma Earning a crust isn't no shame. (*Goes off.*)

II

Berta *and* **Münsterer**.

Berta He told me he'd wait by the bench and now he don't come.

Münsterer *stalks towards her.*

Münsterer You called Berta?

Berta There's nothing for you with me.

Münsterer Anyone can stand by the bench.

Berta But I got a date here – you haven't.

Münsterer What dickey bird told you I haven't got a date too?

Berta I was here first.

Münsterer (*towards her, she dodges him*) No need to kid ourselves. I soon get it if a bird's keen. I'm right in then.

Berta Don't you dare!

Münsterer Come here, Fräulein, I won't do nothing to you. A soldier's word of honour. Cross my heart.

Berta Suddenly you –

Münsterer Best wishes from Korl, and he can't make it today.

Berta Why don't you say that before?

Münsterer I gotto winkle it out what effect I'm having on a Fräulein with my effect. Instinct with me.

Berta It's nice when someone thinks of you like that.

Münsterer Like it better if you didn't think him so handsome. In his shoes I'd've come.

Berta No need to run him down.

Münsterer Yesterday he was with you, today he's having it away with another one. They all get their turn.

Berta Who'd you think you're talking about?

Münsterer You want to bring up his children, huh?

Berta He hasn't got no child.

Münsterer Well, he's got a missus.

Berta That's not the same Korl.

Münsterer Korl Lettner, there's only the one. He's got children scattered about in every town.

Berta I don't believe that.

Münsterer I'm not going to split on a pal to his girl.

Berta You're no pal. You just want to get one back at him.

Münsterer Think you're his only heart-throb.

Berta *stays silent.*

How'm I to know he keeps you in the dark, about his dependents. Thought he told you ages ago.

Berta He tells me everything.

Münsterer Then why's he stood you up?

Berta He's got his reason.

Münsterer Got to get used to it, you're only one of many. You've got a lot to learn, Fräulein. (*Going.*)

Berta So I'm not respected. (*Going.*)

III

Pioneer, **Alma**.

Pioneer Fräulein, can you spare time for a poor soldier?

Alma No longer available. Understand.

Pioneer Pity. We'll meet again.

Alma You don't understand me. No longer available. Things can change for me too.

Pioneer Putting a stop to it? Think it'll be a great loss. The others are just chickens. (*Going.*)

IV

Some girls watch from the distance. Two approaching.

First Girl Alma's got her nose in the air.

Second Girl You know, us girls want you to know, it's not very decent, the way you flaunt yourself.

Alma They want to watch they don't flaunt themselves. I haven't gotto flaunt myself. Got admirers, anyway.

Second Girl We'd all have admirers, if we went on like you.

First Girl Just don't imagine you've got such good looks.

Alma They're good enough for what I want, Fräulein.

Second Girl We know what's good enough for you. Call that good.

Alma So you're saints, are you?

Second Girl That's the whole point. We know how far to go.

Alma Yeah? But you was on the city wall with Pockface yesterday evening.

The **Second Girl** *is dumbfounded.*

First Girl You was on the city wall yourself then. Couldn't have seen her otherwise.

Alma (*to the* **Second Girl**) With that lad, I get further than you in half an hour, I can tell you.

Second Girl I very much doubt it.

First Girl You're a right one to talk. You took some money by the hedge.

Alma When did I take money?

First Girl Oh come on, we saw it.

Alma My friend forced it on me. The soldiers want me just like that.

First Girl No one's ever forced anything on me.

Alma Well, you aren't exactly in demand. And you're not even intelligent.

First Girl Oh come off it, I am intelligent.

Alma Besides, you're all suffering in the head.

All the Girls Tcha!

The girls retreat. **Alma** *goes off in the other direction.*

V

Berta, Korl

Berta Then I can't help you?

Korl Not when you cling to me.

Berta I don't want to be a drag.

Korl These days a girl's got to take as she finds, 'cause there isn't enough men about.

Berta There's me and there's you.

Korl You're missing the right angle. You know, surplus women, too much of a good thing.

Berta There's me and there's you and we don't need no others.

Korl You haven't got to love me like this, it drives me mad.

Berta But I can't do it different.

Korl 'Cause you're not smart.

Berta How d'you be smart?

Korl If you want something off of a man, don't let him know how far he can go with you.

Berta How'm I supposed to be?

Korl Hasn't it never got through to you, you can't just sink your claws into a person? Doesn't do you no good.

Berta But it does do me good. You don't want to give no leg-up.

Korl All day I gotta put up with being bullied. I take it out on the birds. You gotta get it.

Berta Yes, but –

Korl Just play the game.

Berta If you got things to wash, bring them. I'll get up in the night. I'll go to the wash-house.

Korl People mustn't have it all. We do it in work time.

Berta What can I do for you?

Korl Let me be a free man.

Berta You know what that leads to.

Korl Don't give a toss. Shouldn't have made yourself so easy.

Berta If a man gets a girl so she don't look at any others, then he asks her to marry him, because that's the next step – marriage.

Korl That's the way you see it. Then the trap'd snap shut.

Berta You can't be like that now.

Korl Not with me. That's no use to me.

Berta You've let me down.

Korl You gotto believe in us men. Then we'll let you down. Then you can cry, if you want, and then you still gotta believe in us even more.

Berta Until you're done for.

Korl The right ones hold on.

Berta But you must feel what you are for me.

Korl We've gotta turn you all into rags. (*Going.*)

VI

Fabian, Bibrich.

Fabian There's one who can't go home.

Bibrich What's been done to the girl? She's usually a very good girl. Bound to be going crazy. They lead her a dance. Then they dump her.

Berta You can't just sink your claws in. Doesn't do you no good.

Fabian Fräulein Berta, don't you see now, he don't give a toss for you.

Berta But it's quite the opposite. He just don't know.

Bibrich His sort don't want to know.

Fabian You're not going to stand up for him.

Berta But it's something very deep in me. And I'm not doing no harm. Somebody will need me, I know that.

Bibrich Stop fooling yourself.

Fabian There isn't no helping her.

Bibrich Let her go. That one's got all jumbled up.

They both go off, she runs away.

VII

Alma, Korl.

Alma Like the way I pulled it off?

Korl Pulled what off?

Alma Outside the beer tent. Chummy. You must know me. I tore you out of the clutches of that tin-pot Napoleon.

Korl You were the bird in flight?

Alma And what kind of bird are you?

Korl No better than you. I get by.

Alma We all ask too much.

Korl Maybe.

Alma That Napoleon got it in for you?

Korl We got it in for him. The whole squad knows we gotta put a stop to that little dictator. But – square bashing never changes.

Alma Surely you can do something.

Korl Things happen to squaddies every so often, but the right one never gets it. That'd be a turn up for the books.

Alma But no one turns up to do him in.

Korl Can't be done. System makes sure it can't be done. Always has.

Alma I suppose you know best.

Korl These buggers in uniform hide behind regulations. You can't never get at them. Only complain, that's all. Better not to. Better hold your tongue.

Alma What if you all gang up?

Korl All gang up, no chance. Can't do a thing. Gotto stomach him.

Alma To me he's the right old dictator. Plays the wolf, then don't pay a bean. He diddle me, understand?

Korl Made a mistake there. Don't never make that mistake. I never make promises. I do even less than I promise.

Alma Yes, but you say it before. That's the difference.

Korl You haven't been on the game long?

Alma And I'm stopping soon. It isn't no life for me. I'm deeply disappointed. The gentlemen only satisfy their own lust.

Korl Didn't you know that?

Alma I was working for a lady before. I'll never work for a lady again.

Korl Believe that.

Alma I made a bid for freedom, but it wasn't free there.

Korl When you got lots, you don't only get the cream. They miss out what's interesting.

Alma I'm still learning.

Korl Pleased to hear it.

Alma Trouble is, I'm not careful, that's the whole story.

Korl Don't seem so bad to me. First steps aren't always the right steps. So what.

Alma And I jumped straight in and I'll jump out again.

Korl I call that courage.

Alma I'm still not on the right tracks yet.

Korl You don't always get on the right tracks.

Alma I'll get on them, I know that. I always dreamt they'd take me along. One, two and jump! I could jump all day long. You too?

Korl Once upon a time.

Alma It all helps me on my way, that's what I believe. And I'm going to Berlin and I want a life that flings me about and grabs hold of me.

Korl If only I could come with you.

Alma Perhaps you can't see it, but I got something in me that pushes me through thick and thin. All I need now's that special something to drive me through.

Korl You'll get what you want.

Alma No problem. But he's gotta have some sort of spark. Otherwise I wouldn't come alive, would I?

Korl What about work?

Alma For me, work's something special, believe me?

Korl I can think of something nicer.

Alma Such as?

Korl I like you, girl. (*Embracing her.*)

Scene Eleven

Street near the Danube.

It's getting dark. **Rosskopf** *and* **Münsterer** *in a slightly drunk condition. They're rolling a barrel in front of them.*

Münsterer Smart soldier's rolled up in his pit safe and sound, don't know what he's doing no more.

Rosskopf But we still know.

Münsterer Almost. Pinch me and I'll sober up.

Rosskopf Don't never pinch.

Münsterer Idiot!

Rosskopf And I don't want to be safe and sound, I want my freedom.

Münsterer Isn't no freedom for us. Except with our girls and that's only half the fun.

Rosskopf Every lousy civvy has a better time than us. That's why I gonna play a trick on a civvy today.

Münsterer Yeah, you're gonna play a trick on one.

Rosskopf If I get it in the neck, why can't I give it to a civvy in the neck? Logic. (*Looking at the barrel with surprise.*) Where did this thing come from?

Münsterer You nicked it.

Rosskopf (*offended*) Re – quisitioned it.

Münsterer Helped yourself.

Rosskopf You treat me like a thief. Your Worship, you're too hard on me.

Münsterer I'm not hard on you.

Rosskopf Your Worship, don't keep rolling that way. That's the way to the barracks.

Münsterer You forgot the way to the barracks long ago.

Rosskopf I'm fed up with the barracks. I demand my per – sonal freedom.

Münsterer You demand your personal freedom.

Rosskopf I gonna have my joke, dammit, or I'll go mad. Your Worship, want to join in the joke?

Münsterer Then I'll want a good laugh.

Rosskopf You'll laugh, all right. Perhaps not at once, but later on in bed you'll laugh.

Münsterer I don't know, how'll you do it?

Rosskopf I gonna gobble up a civvy. I'm not really gonna gobble him up, my barrel's gonna gobble him up and then I'll do what I want with him.

Münsterer Oh yeah, how?

Rosskopf We grab that one behind us. I'll show you.

Münsterer No blood, Max.

Rosskopf No blood, Your Worship.

Münsterer Go right ahead then.

Fabian *approaching.*

Rosskopf Here he comes, all innocence.

Münsterer He's still wet behind the ears.

Rosskopf All the better.

They lie in wait and confront him.

What d'you think we got here?

Fabian A barrel.

Rosskopf This is no ordinary barrel. What d'you think's inside the barrel? – A naked lady.

Fabian Right up your street.

Rosskopf It's a certain Berta, if you know her.

Fabian That's just like you.

Rosskopf You don't have to believe it.

The barrel is standing on end, **Fabian** *peeps inside, at the same time they grab him by the feet and tip him head over heels into the barrel. They clap the lid on.*

You landed nice and softly on your naked lady? Are you lying on her already? Couldn't leave her alone, eh?

Fabian Open up! Open up at once!

Rosskopf No way. Now you're in it.

Fabian I'll scream. Help! Help!

Münsterer You better stop that. Only make things worse if you scream.

Rosskopf Be a good boy now, civvy.

Fabian *is stunned.*

Münsterer Whoever's already in it, has had it. Better take that on board.

Rosskopf You shut your trap, civvy. You be quiet or we make you quiet. You got a choice.

Fabian Please, let me out.

Münsterer It's only a joke, civvy.

Rosskopf Yeah, we might be dead earnest. But we're not dead earnest.

Münsterer We're only playing. You playing with us?

Rosskopf We gonna play war.

Münsterer And you gotta volunteer. In a war we always slide in as volunteers.

Rosskopf Can't do nothing about war.

Münsterer We're gonna show you who you are in a war, civvy, watch it.

They tip the barrel over and kick it.

When the war comes, then you're a louse.

Rosskopf To me you already a louse. (*Kicking the barrel to* **Münsterer**.)

Münsterer I'm a louse too, but you aren't gonna see it. (*Kicking the barrel to* **Rosskopf**.)

Rosskopf What do you do in a war? You're shit scared and that's all.

Münsterer Don't get excited. That's what we all get.

Rosskopf You frightened?

Fabian *is silent.*

No? You still not frightened?

Münsterer Just won't own up. He's fibbing.

Fabian Stop! I was in the wrong. Let me out.

Münsterer If you was in the wrong, we can't let you out.

Fabian What do you want to let me out?

Rosskopf Come again, the man's going to pay.

Münsterer But not in money. That'd be too simple.

Rosskopf Why not?

Münsterer We got other ideas. Tell us, who stole our wood, then we'll let you go.

Rosskopf Your Worship, you're a genius. Answer in there!

Fabian It wasn't me.

Münsterer It weren't us neither. They put it on us and give us a hard time.

Rosskopf Who was it then?

Fabian I don't know.

Münsterer You really don't know? Then we keep going. (*He kicks.*)

Fabian Stop it.

Münsterer You say it wasn't you. Sing, little bird, sing.

Rosskopf Let's say it didn't stick to our fingers, soddit.

Fabian I don't know, I don't know, I don't know. You mustn't do such things.

Münsterer (*genuflecting*) Forgive us, little one. For they know not what they do.

Fabian How'm I supposed to know anything, I wasn't there. Just as likely to be you.

Münsterer Back to square one.

Rosskopf You won't get it out of him. He weren't there.

Münsterer The lad's got such barefaced luck, we believe him. (*Lifting the lid.*)

Fabian Why are you doing this to me? What harm have I done you?

Rosskopf You're one of the nobs, you

won't have it hard. When you're having an easy time, we're having it hard.

Fabian Not 'cause of me though.

Rosskopf All the same. I bear grudges.

Every time **Fabian** *wants to clamber out,* **Rosskopf** *shoves him down again.*

And you're the kind that don't want to get involved. But you are involved. Hell on earth! Harried and hounded up and down wall bars and rough terrain in full equipment –

Münsterer – endless kilometers creeping through wet fields and ditches –

Rosskopf – and you don't never get involved in all this. But it's just what you need, and I'm letting it out on you now. (*Clapping the lid down again.*)

Fabian That's cowardly. You're cowards.

They kick him a longer distance.

Murderers. You're murderers. Murderers!

Rosskopf Say that, and I'll roll you to the Danube and throw you in.

Münsterer No blood, Max! You've had your fun. Let him go. (*Pulling* **Rosskopf** *away.*) It's raining. (*To* **Fabian** *in the barrel.*) You're in the dry. Count yourself lucky.

They go off. **Fabian** *opens the lid.*

Scene Twelve

Danube.

Strong wind. **Fabian** *alone on the bank. Noise of oars from a Pioneer boat. We hear the voices from the boat.*

Sergeant One two. One two. One two. Oars at rest. Let anchor down.

Jäger (*repeating*) Let anchor down.

We hear the anchor being unwound and then a scream. **Fabian** *is terrified.*

Jäger Man overboard.

The cable is unwound further and then stops.

Korl Stay sitting down! Too dangerous.

Münsterer The Sarge is hanging with one foot in a loop. Can't get free on his own.

Korl He's as good as dead.

Jäger But we've gotta do something. Gotta cut him out of the loop. Someone's gotto go down.

Korl If you got big lungs, go ahead. I haven't got big lungs.

Münsterer No one can. The cable's too tough. Current's too strong.

Korl Stay sitting down, for Christ's sake! The boat's listing so much.

Münsterer The boat's turning turtle. Cable's pulling us down.

Korl Cut the cable. Why don't you cut it? Cut the cable.

Münsterer We'll all get drownded.

The cable is cut.

Fabian The bastards are leaving him there.

Korl To the bank and out in a flash. One two. One two.

They row towards the bank. Some jump out and pull the boat to the land. All of them jump out. They are worn out.

Fabian How do people look, when they've done something like that?

Korl We haven't done nothing.

Fabian Nothing wasn't enough. You were watched.

Korl So?

Fabian Letting him drown so near the bank.

Korl You don't need distance for that.

Jäger We would've dived, but we couldn't dive. The current was too strong.

Fabian You should've done it straight away, while the cable was pulled taut.

Korl Nice and cosy in the dry, eh?

Fabian You wouldn't even have had to look for the man. The cable would have led you straight down to the man. Instead you cut the cable.

Korl We would've, we would've! Then we'd have been drownded too. The cable was already pulling us under.

Fabian Nobody will believe you, that you haven't killed the man. The corpse has a witness.

Korl There's always a court-martial. But not with civvies.

Fabian The man stepped backwards got one foot into the loop, and the cable tugged him head over heels into the Danube and he got trapped by the cable.

Korl His own fault. It was an accident. We didn't put the loop in the man's way.

Fabian You only thought of yourselves when it happened. Saving your precious skins.

Korl That isn't against regulations. Nearly went under ourselves. It would have cost more human lives. What on earth do you want? It was an accident. They'll buy that.

Münsterer That's what happened. Anything can happen. We can't choose what water's there.

Korl In a war if we have to cross a river, we don't put the water there either.

Jäger If we lost our heads at every accident we'd not never do our bloody duty.

Korl It was an accident. That's the whole truth, they'll ask questions and that's what we'll say.

Fabian You talk too much for me.

Jäger It was an accident, they'll buy that.

Korl Go and report us, if you've got the nerve. But we got it too.

Fabian But you didn't try everything.

Korl Try everything, beg your pardon, who for? We could've killed ourselves for that man. That's overdoing it.

Münsterer It's a hard life.

Jäger The man just drowned.

Korl Thanks be to the Danube.

Fabian You've got a tongue like a razor. Well, what's it to me? I'm not in the Forces.

Münsterer The man passed on.

Korl The man isn't gonna stay under.

Münsterer Wait till the water goes down.

Korl Won't leave an anchor like that behind. When the anchor's weighed, the man'll come up on his own.

Scene Thirteen

Park.

Alma, Fabian.

Alma Is it true the soldiers attacked you?

Fabian They didn't just attack me. They put my life in danger.

Alma But they're nice people. I can't believe it of them.

Fabian Once in a while it's dead earnest.

Alma But you're still alive.

Fabian D'you blame me for that?

Alma I don't want to do you down.

Fabian You're not doing me down. No one does me down. I was blind to put myself out for one who didn't want me. That's over and done with.

Alma You're better off without her.

Fabian I'm not gonna run for my life any more if I fancy a girl. I'll make it easy for myself.

Alma That's even better.

Fabian Why put yourself in the wrong, just so someone else is in the right? Why play games you don't have to. I'm worth something too. An eye for an eye.

Alma Seems common sense to me.

Fabian Course it is. We all want to lord it over others. Who'll swallow who?

Alma It's often not very nice. – Was it the first girl you put yourself out for?

Fabian Somebody's gotto be the first. – But nothing was going on. I wasn't getting through to her.

Alma Then there wasn't much to it.

Fabian And she'll live to regret it. I imagine . . .

Silence.

Alma What?

Fabian I'd get more out of you.

Alma I've always hoped for the man who'd take me as the first one. I only ever come after the others, don't know why.

Fabian Now don't act funny.

Alma Somebody's gotto to be the first.

Fabian Sure.

They go into the bushes.

Scene Fourteen

Bridge building site.

The bridge is almost finished. Pioneers are putting on the finishing touches. Spotlights.

Rosskopf The bridge'll be opened tomorrow. But we won't be here by then.

Münsterer We're always the advance squad.

Jäger The password is: Off to Küstrin.

Münsterer I'm already forgetting that we've been here. Not here any longer.

Rosskopf One town's just like the next. Sergeant's the same anywhere.

Münsterer Like having ants in your brains. Decampment's in the air.

Rosskopf By then we'll get new girls.

Jäger Something always turns up.

Münsterer But the rivers are always the same rivers. Early in the morning the air's always bleak.

Rosskopf A rank and filer's always a rank and filer, and an officer always comes up trumps, and wins the trick.

Münsterer Don't get to be gentlemen squaddies. Just sharper.

Berta (*coming on*) I've gotto speak to someone, Korl Lettner.

Rosskopf Korl, a girl wants you for something.

Korl That won't take long. Where's the Sarge?

They point into the far distance.

Cover up for me, I'm going off. (*Going over to* **Berta**.) Now you're running after me again.

Berta Yes, and it isn't easy. It's just that I can't help it.

Korl Wedding gotta be at once?

Berta What wedding? I know I'll never win that one.

Korl I know these stories. You aren't the first and you won't be the last. That game don't work with me.

Berta I don't believe that any more. – I can't let you go.

Korl Suit yourself.

Berta I'm all yours.

Korl We can do it straightaway, if you want. Ready for anything.

Berta But not here. I've got myself the night off.

Korl Pity, I'm under orders. I can only spare a minute. If the Sarge comes I've gotta be in line.

Berta I feel sick.

Korl Don't want to know about that.

Flinging himself with her into a bush. The **Pioneers** *go on working. Some time passes. They sing.*

Pioneers
What good's a beautiful girl to me,
When they go swimming in her – one, two,
three?

Rosskopf (*maliciously*) Spotlights to the left.

Berta *and* **Korl** *come out of the bushes into the light.* **Pioneers** *jeer and whistle.*

Korl Turn that light off, soddit, you idiots.

Rosskopf What you on about, we're only envious.

Münsterer What the hell for, we do it every day.

They move the light away.

Korl Don't give it another thought. These lads are off tomorrow. Get up now. Pull yourself together. Others gotto.

Berta *gets up.*

Berta Was that all?

Korl Why? Something missing?

Berta We left something out, something important. Love's what we left out.

Korl Hasn't got nothing to do with love.

Berta Then that's terrible.

Korl Berta, I gotta get back in line. You can't stay here. Better be off now.

Berta I can't. It can't be over like that. Why are the men going off tomorrow?

Korl Berta, I haven't told you this yet, we've got our marching orders. Going back to Küstrin tonight.

Berta I've got to have time.

Korl We're the advance squad. Always the first.

Berta Can't be true. Can't cope with that yet.

Korl You've gotto cut yourself off, Berta. Just cut yourself off. Others got to.

Berta But I can't live like that.

Korl You've gotto.

Bunny *does the bird whistle.* **Korl** *runs to the others and gets in line.* **Photographer** *approaches, wooden sides of his camera clapping, advertising through a loud hailer.*

Photographer Gentlemen, you're about to depart from this historic town. You have built us this sturdy bridge, leaving us with a lasting memorial of you. I suggest you'll certainly have the desire to take with you a small momento of the Pioneers' stay in Ingolstadt. The picture won't weigh you down, there's room for it in every wallet and it costs hardly anything, only three Marks per man in the group picture. You can take the picture out in every spare moment –

Münsterer You must be joking –

Photographer You can show it to your respective fiancées and your ever-loving parents.

Rosskopf Just what we'll do. Wouldn't miss a chance like that.

Photographer Right, position yourselves, gentlemen. Group yourselves as you choose, tall men at the back.

Pioneers *position themselves.*

Back row standing, middle kneeling, front lying down. That way I'll get you all in the picture, that way I'll bring out the best in each of you. Don't look at the camera. (*He clicks.*) May I ask you to state your esteemed addresses. I'll take the money right now, develop it today.

Münsterer Here's the address of the whole unit. You only need the names of those paying. Till's open for anyone wanting his group photo.

Pioneer Jäger – (*Pays.*)

Photographer Jäger – (*Writes.*)

Pioneer Pfaller – (*Pays.*)

Photographer Pfaller – (*Writes.*)

Pioneer Angerer – (*Pays.*)

Photographer Angerer – (*Writes.*)

Pioneer Gensberger – (*Pays.*)

Photographer Gensberger – (*Writes.*)

Pioneer Bachschneider – (*Pays*).

Photographer Bachschneider – (*Writes.*)

Pioneer Rosskopf – (*Pays.*)

Photographer Rosskopf – (*Writes.*)

Korl Lettner – (*Pays.*)

Photographer Lettner – (*Writes.*)

Münsterer Münsterer – (*Pays.*)

Münsterer *is the last.*

Photographer Münsterer – (*Writes.*) My thanks to you, Herr Münsterer. I've got the names, you've got the receipt for all of them. (*Giving him the receipt.*) I'm happy to take individual photos to order. Six framed photos only cost twenty Marks. NCOs downwards only pay half, and who's an NCO here?

Rosskopf Now, Lettner, you must be immortalised with your latest, the least you can do for her. Then she'll have you in black and white.

Korl Come on, Berta. (*Posing with her.*) You must send the photo to the lady.

Berta Berta Kobold, here, 17 Doll Street.

Photographer I'll take the money, right now.

Berta *is about to take out her money.*

Korl I'll pay. (*Paying.*)

Münsterer 'Tention.

The next **Sergeant** *comes on. He is just another edition of the drowned* **Sergeant**.

Report: bridge ready to hand over.

Sergeant I'll inspect. (*He inspects the bridge.*) Fall in, in marching order.

The **Pioneers** *fall in, in marching order.*

We all know we're going back to Küstrin. I expect exemplary conduct from my corps, and that no complaints reach me from the local populace. Every soldier must know he's a citizen in uniform, and is always in the public eye. Before leaving the barracks the soldier checks his uniform. His pockets are buttoned up, his shoes polished, his hat sits square with no natty creases.

It's forbidden to form groups blocking the pavements and force people into the road. Singing and flashy conduct isn't allowed. Soldiers do not smoke in the street. Drunks, mobs and brawlers are given a wide berth by soldiers. They are careful about their choice of bar, they don't lounge about in front of the entrance. Suggestive dancing doesn't suit uniform. Soldiers in uniform must not attend political meetings. These are army regulations, they must be second nature to you. There are no dispensations, no personal decisions. Every contravention will be subject to disciplinary action.

Ready to march. Left wheel, in step – march!

The **Pioneers** *march across the stage.*

We sing: Left and left and left!

The **Pioneers** *sing.*

The End.

Pioneers in Ingolstadt

The first person to read *Purgatory* was the novelist Lion Feuchtwanger who passed it on to Brecht. So impressed was Brecht that he urged her to write a second play: this was to become *Pioneers*. In 1926 a corps of Pioneers were posted to Ingolstadt. By this time Fleisser and Brecht were lovers, spending the summer at his parents' house: 'Brecht immediately wanted me to observe this sort of military invasion of a small town, and its effect on the population.' He outlined the play he wanted from her: 'It must be assembled like certain cars, which you see driving around in Paris, DIY cars from kits, which hams knock up almost by accident, but they do go, they go! It must have a father and a son, a maid-servant, a car that someone casually palms off on the son, because it no longer goes. Soldiers take the girls for walks, a Sergeant bullies them. At the end, the son blows the bridge up, because one of the Pioneers has nabbed the maid from him.' Fleisser said, 'I knew as little about cars as I did about soldiers. To me, soldiers were unknown beings, even when Brecht sent me to watch them, to listen to them, and to go out with them. I was young, I wasn't as politically aware as Brecht, I wrote a play about soldiers and girls. The text didn't satisfy me, it remained incomplete, simply because I knew too little about soldiers.'

Brecht made important changes to the play in his deliberately provocative 1929 production at the Schiffbauerdamm, Berlin. Fleisser felt so estranged that she stopped attending rehearsals, but she was not able to avoid the scandal, which reverberated well beyond Berlin and damaged her for life. The Ingolstadt connections are so specific and the inhabitants never forgave her. Her father's house was stoned and she was banned from it. The scandal also ended her relationship with Brecht and caused her to lose her sense of herself, first through a disastrous relationship with a Nationalist then in her marriage (1935) to a tobacconist and swimming hero back in the 'safety' of Ingolstadt. In fear of her life throughout the whole Nazi period – her books were burnt in 1933 – she found it virtually impossible to write. She had no copy of *Pioneers*, the whole experience had hurt so much she just wanted to forget about it.

Rainer Werner Fassbinder found a lost copy of *Pioneers* and started a pirated production in 1968. At first Fleisser was avidly against it, but once she saw Fassbinder's working methods she was so converted she began a new version, the one in translation here: 'It was only now I understood what Brecht had wanted of me in *Pioneers* and what I had left unsaid in my first attempt. I tried to present him with this later, even though he was already dead, to make the texture deeper and richer through social criticism. I had to keep the time – the play is set in 1926 and cannot be transposed to the present day. Men in the army are always men under constraint.' Franz Xaver Kroetz, who played the Sergeant in this production, wrote an open letter to a publisher with the result that Fleisser's plays – six in all – were published in 1971.

Pioneers in Ingolstadt is a play about the dead end lives of little people. Maid-servants who cannot defend themselves against exploitation meet soldiers who are themselves under pressure all day long, and can only get rid of the pressure by handing it on. Korl has features of Brecht in his early days and though his relationship with Berta is not autobiographical it has points of similarity with Fleisser's dependence on Brecht.

The English language premières of these two great plays have had to wait well over half a century. In this time Fleisser's 'sons', the next generation of playwrights who learnt from her – Fassbinder, Speer and Kroetz – have found their places in this country. Without her Fassbinder said he would not have become a writer. Her 'sons' agree that their own successes would not have come about without the re-awakening of Fleisser. They all share her non-naturalistic speech, short, highly-charged scenes and claustrophobic situations.

Fleisser wrote about a small town in Southern Germany and its inhabitants, but it is in many ways the recognisable background of any small town; in just the same way her language is not straight local dialect but stems from the psychological and emotional as well as the physical environment.

These extraordinary plays eventually found their expression in English in two out-of-the-ordinary productions and I was given extraordinary help by both Moray McGowan and Fleisser's nephew, Klaus Gültig.

Avant-garde

Marieluise Fleisser

translated by Tinch Minter

Avant-garde

It was not completely clear – was she his co-worker, friend, lover or would she become his wife? 'She'll be my wife' the controversial poet had said right at the beginning. But what did it mean coming from him, and what was it worth, the use he made of others? He helped himself to the freedom of a genius and it was the stroke of genius which bound her inescapably to him, something had sparked off. Cilly Ostermeier would have given her all for that, she took no precautions.

She too wanted to write. She was of tender years, a fresh student, who didn't know herself yet, her head filled to the brim with her desire, for the moment that was nothing but impudence. With this desire she came across him and was completely crushed. The man was a power, he crushed her at once. It would all come out, if she survived it. If not, then she wasn't worth it anyway.

Her way of life was already crushed. She bunked off the lectures and seminars, to be at hand when the poet needed her. She dealt with the nitty-gritty of his life. His time was more worthwhile, this didn't even need to be discussed.

Ostermeier didn't have an easy conscience when she thought about her people at home. These people paid. She would have liked to work towards her doctorate. 'What do you get with a doctorate?' he put to her, 'you can write as you are. A doctorate won't help that, first you've got to live. Just stay with me and you've got your direction just like that. You've got to make something out of chance.'

He was a man who was already on his way. She felt it deeply how he was above her, and when she was with him, she held onto a splinter of that ardent, that blazing life. She took her first steps. She learnt to write the way he wrote. Of course it was dangerous, the man sucked her up. She should have set herself against it, she was too young for that. She didn't put boundaries around herself yet. She was blessed by sensing more than she understood, she had an inner eye.

At this time she believed his every word. At this time all she knew was she was growing towards art by staying near him. For her it was filtered through this person. She could no longer imagine how to manage without him. It was an unconscious urge in the dark, plantlike and as vulnerable as a plant.

She went hungry for a few years as only a young person can go hungry, it affects the heart, but no one notices. Different ways are unknown. Between whiles, she worked for strangers so she could work for him for free. She couldn't bear it for long, being separated from him, she had to be with him.

The hunger, which couldn't be satisfied, made her so useful to him. Things could be piled on her, she could easily bear it, she couldn't turn back now. What more did the man want? She didn't interrupt him while his ideas were taking shape, she didn't prune his budding inspiration. This was the condition, it was no more than a beginning. In his search and growth she searched with him, was the desired fielder of his ball. He didn't work without a fielder. The balls only came back from her, she had no reason to get big-headed. It was him who did the giving. She'd better have no illusions, without him she was nothing at all.

He never noticed what was hard for a woman. He held her tightly by the reins and got used to her, just never made it legal. Bit by bit the penny dropped. She sensed the abyss that she'd been heading towards like a sleep-walker. She hadn't taken enough caution, she fondly believed. Right from the start, you must make demands, children of the world know that.

He'd already been through something of the sort once. He'd had it very hard and he had seen the outcome. He'd already let himself be tied down once. He recognised some of it and made comparisons. He had learned from his commonplace experience, which was to his advantage. It wasn't just his few years' headstart, it was the lived knowledge, it was the scars. He was no longer as compromising as he had been, meanwhile he got used to his scars, swallowed bitter pills under duress. He didn't beat his brains out over it, this wasn't the best of all worlds. Like a guard dog he defended his freedom of action, and no one got round him. One had to turn a blind eye, he couldn't help it. Don't make a fuss, just be there, when you're needed!

She was a simpleton at love. She didn't doubt that in the end she'd get what her hunches told her. It was like breathing to her, it would become right, force its way by itself. It had an underlying power. But he had seen the outcome, this time it would be different. He wouldn't fall for it a second time. He'd burnt his fingers, acted accordingly.

It was asking too much to lock him up, it crippled him. It simply wasn't on, even if he forced himself. The man turned nothing out in the cage, the man knew this, the young man had to run around. And if he needed someone, there'd be no cage, this time he'd be on his guard. And hadn't he got it all nicely arranged for himself?

Some are born to get a lot. Some are born to be masters, in the meantime that came to light. It just can't be ignored. Meanwhile it's already obvious.

The man dispensed with nothing, there was no reason to change anything. They didn't even talk about it, it hovered in secret. It was dangerous to name it, they preferred not to name it. He was such a tamer, he was everything to her. She would take care not to nail him down, if that would mean she'd lose him. Meeting with a genius was productive, it was in itself a thing of value already. Do or die! In the little town where she came from, the scandal-mongers had a dig, with all those sacrifices and efforts she'd become no better than she ought to be. She could turn a blind eye but still – it scorched.

Things came first. People didn't matter so much, people could be replaced. He said it straight to her face, he quite deliberately repulsed her. This was the frost of freedom, she must learn to freeze. People don't follow a lead. And people don't run away from a responsibility, once they're affected by it. Something was developing there that couldn't be had any other way. Something of the sort that isn't thrown away. Things being easy wasn't preferable. A swift side glance skimmed over her, surely they were of one mind?

The man fixed the space between them. It must never happen to him. It only ever happened to others through him. He learnt from people how to become their master. His words were a whip cracking, he didn't make it easy for you. He towered a head above you, belonged to a totally different space, one never knew what he'd come up with next. He really was someone to fear. He turned all his prickles outwards.

His powers of imagination were curiously irritable, without giving you any warning, he could be hurt in mid-sentence, wounded in a secret way. Then there was no stopping him, he immediately hit out and when he attacked he went for the soft spot, it went through to the bone, cut through to the marrow. She wasn't to move a muscle, like the Indian in the book. He played the fool. It only hurt her, if she didn't forget it: he had already forgotten it. In a single second he could jump from one position to its opposite, he could be generous just as unpredictably. It was uncanny with him. But it stood him in good stead, it seems he could afford it.

The man put himself first, the man could put himself first, it all sprang from this. You had to see it for yourself, his game was captivating, he had magic at his disposal. His half-smile said a lot, behind it lurked knowledge, you longed to experience it in the flesh. It drew back too easily, tempting you to follow, but it was in front again and it drove you on. But then he was just a human being, and the change was charming and the young man was charming. It made her go weak in the knees, when his sneer dissolved, he could have anything. It simply flattened her, let him do it or leave it undone. He wasn't shaved, and with him it was no shortcoming, the light came from inside. It was flames. It was past like a bird's flight, he had already shocked her with the lightning strike, what else was important? He had soared a long time ago because he had ordered himself into top speed, she was lying sunk, felled. It disturbed her, the way he demonstrated: a man must go on, a man just isn't a woman.

In art he was the man who was already on his way. His artistic means were so simple, there wasn't much he needed. But how he made something of them struck home, they hit the mark. He who had ears to hear, heard and found himself so deeply affected, he never forgot him. He had met with a man-catcher.

The talent far exceeded the character, in this he was a greedy child. However much the child burnt his fingers and had gone through something he remembered secretly, no one else could know, if the child didn't reveal anything, if the burnt child didn't give himself away. In all innocence someone might poke it, might poke the hidden wounds. Then there'd be the scenes you dreaded.

Going round with him was difficult to digest. He showed his weaknesses cynically. It didn't concern him, others had to put up with it, he saved strength like this. His shoe-size was just bigger, but he couldn't chop his feet off on that account. In mid-sentence of admitting his dirty tricks he made up for them with a stroke of genius, suddenly things were fine again. Suddenly you stopped being furious with him.

The man undermined and the man fascinated. It was amazing: anyone who had broken with him, never completely got over it. Anyone who was his friend had to remain one. Even so it was glorious with him, there was nothing remotely like it. And anyone who stuck by him, who lived through his special perception of his nature and conduct, knew why. He was compensated with something deep in the core. He obviously didn't go away totally empty-handed. Obviously what seemed to be a stone wasn't a stone. He experienced a phenomenon. He gained a feeling for greatness. You didn't get something like this for free. It had to be paid for. The law of the jungle here.

It wasn't clear for Ostermeier because she was going around like a sleep-walker. She was a young student and had to make something of herself. On his say-so she hadn't done her doctorate. She wanted to write, but first she had to live, and death was for free. She got next to nothing from home. The treadmill chafed, she experienced that for real.

Sometimes the talk was about royalties, which she would get as soon as he was over the worst. The promise shimmered in front of them, it fooled them. The man never had any cash. A few theatres staged him here and there, always sporadically and, as he maintained, wrongly. He put people's backs up, his plays were taken off. He hadn't made his mark yet. The man never cleared his debts. If he gave her any of his cash, then it was two Marks for food, it was a symbolic gesture. She even had to ask for them which she'd rather have avoided. Sodom and Gomorrah was another matter. She'd already atoned for her sins here.

'We'll stick at it till we pull through,' he promised. That was just it, they'd stick at it till they pulled through and then what? She was not even his wife by law, she was so stupid. For instance letters came from the people at home, warning letters, letters appealing to her through understandable anxiety, letters renouncing her if she didn't comply. She didn't enjoy getting such letters. She was fond of the people at home, something always remained there. Besides, no one wanted to pay any more, so she was as free as a bird.

It was her own fault, she didn't want it any other way, she certainly wasn't bourgeois. But it was hard not to be bourgeois. By this time it had become heartless. You couldn't step back from it, once you'd done it. You never knew the final facts. In the deeply personal sphere of your own existence was agonising uncertainty. It would still go too far. Anything could come of it, even death. Its nature was nothing but a danger. Such a person stakes everything. She could never explain that to her people at home.

Perhaps she was nothing but a silly young thing. Lying awake at night it hit her what a dog's life it was hoping for an imaginary future and that her run-up time didn't belong to her and would only be given once in a lifetime, and not again, and if the run-up time was wasted, her own life was wasted too, you had to limp along lamentably behind, where others of the same age were leading the way. She felt completely walled up, she was cruelly captive, she could see no way out. And when doubts came to her narrow bed, if she really was constructing a future, if in fact she wasn't demolished, as she was finally betrayed, she still tried to suppress her doubts and wanted to be brave and clenched her fists in her sleep.

Cilly Ostermeier lived up there under the roof like this for the poet, who was the coming man, as he was performed. The man used her, it was probably his due, a talented man helped himself. And if she was used, she inhaled a genius's air and had her destiny up there under the roof, and so was not lost, not yet. Every hair was counted, every tear fell into a cup. And he didn't make her pregnant, she could give thanks to him for this as well.

The city already made demands on your destiny, the essential plumb-line to the inner stability. The city was enormous, the houses next to each other too alien, the doors too unwelcoming, the streets too long, the squares too broad, you could drown in all those spaces. You were swept along by a hostile wind, face shrivelled, hands ice-cold. Perfect strangers didn't dodge in front of you before you looked hard at them, then they did so but even then only at the last second. They'd rather push you down into the gutter, block your way on purpose, simply from bad grace. They advanced like candles and didn't give way, they had rude names on their tongues to rattle the populace, unpunished because never recognised. Who knew anyone in a city like this? This was a metropolis, abyss next to abyss.

She came to the big city a total stranger, she hadn't been born there, so nobody took any notice of what she did. Then she worked for the poet, who was now being performed elsewhere. Lately her name was mentioned, she no longer remained hidden.

Not for nothing had she turned her antennae towards him. The poet promoted her work generously, got the right people interested in it, she started to be known about. He got her a contract with a leading publisher. ('These are our race-horses, we let them run.') He'd hardly made his own mark before he was drawing others with him, he was impatient, what came out of it.

She was discovered, it was almost too early, she didn't keep pace with her growth. She was well received with her first-born, here was something from within her. More had now to come out of it, he started to push her, she didn't go along with it, she became rather deranged. It had always been like this, with her it flowed sluggishly, she needed patience with herself. He didn't have patience, he hustled himself, he was so young in this.

He was always rather stuck into his discoveries, he had to get the best out of them easily and preferably at once.

He had his own idea of her, for her it was an order and she would have loved doing it, it was funny. He gave her a theme from a completely unconnected incident, she was to write a play about it. She would never have come up with it.

It was in the merchant Fugger's city,* where he was born – he went home over the summer and summoned her from the town on the Danube – she was at home there for that one summer. He fetched her from this stone's distance, she told him: 'The Pioneers from Küstrin are in our town, it's a proper mix-up, the girls are beside themselves and a bridge is being built across a creek. I first watched it all from one of the banks, then a man in a boat rowed over from the men's sports club, who let me get into his boat. We could see it all much better from there.' – 'Just your luck,' he said, 'that you look such a goody-goody.' – 'That was only Nickl, I've known him since he was a boy. But we were so near we had the spotlight right in our faces.' – 'There you are!' The idea for a play immediately hit him, he wanted it done, and she was to be the medium for it.

This was by the town moat, where the yellowing leaves were swimming, the swans floating in the evening light. On that spot he put an idea into her head and galloped her up and down the town moat, turning round again and again. Years ago he had scribbled a play right here, the footpath was fertile for him.

In the attic room, where the damp sponge hung from the window bars for the air to dry it, he read her obscene songs, that he'd written on a whim, he'd read them to his women, he sang them to them, crowing more than singing. Now and again he called for his Marie. He had a thing about the name Marie, and if she wasn't called that, he gave her that name. For he had taken a servant girl all for himself, to see to his washing and the two rooms under the roof. This way there was no disagreement with the housekeeper downstairs, who was solely for his father. She was a pretty thing of tender years, her hair almost shorn, so short, and it made her so impudent he was pleased with his personal girl. 'Mariiiie!' he bellowed with delight, he gave it a slightly common sound, he had her open the window and then close it again, chased her in and out, what was she to do all day long, she'd hardly work herself to the bone with him. He played a cod lord and master, she gave him back as good as she got with saucy answers, which enchanted him, he took it from her with delight, she'd already learnt that much from him.

He lay on his couch like an eastern potentate, his feet planted on the back wall of the wardrobe. There on the wooden back wall the artist friend painted the man life-size with his titfer, metropolitan-man, who had been symbolic to the kindred spirits of boyhood. Cilly lay down smack opposite him on the other couch, a wide gap between them with the table where he usually wrote in front of the window. In the nursery at home where she slept with her sisters the beds were just the same, she said, and there they told each other what was relevant to them about their loving god, that he was yellow, all sorts of childish ideas they had. They laughed themselves to sleep once over a nose they'd seen on a religious picture. 'Laughing like that,' her sister had said, 'is as good as two soft boiled eggs, that's what I've read, laughing makes you full.'

But here she laughed at his verses in the style of a carter, crowed out in a wild sing-song. He crowed at full pitch when his voice couldn't manage it. He was more out of his shell than usual and relaxed. 'Here in the house,' he told her, 'my mother was a rebel. She was an intruder in the family and a protestant.' How he loved his mother wasn't said.

---

* The Fuggers were the greatest German merchants during the Renaissance. The city is Augsburg.

'You must take advantage of big cities,' he then stated and at some time he threw in the idea 'trend-setter', they talked nonsense and sense. 'Who is a trend-setter?' she asked, wrapped up in a dream, and tapped the wall with a pencil; he knocked at the metropolitan-man with his foot. 'You'll be a trend-setter,' was all he said. He stood up to his full height, came over and made her happy. It was all like children playing.

Afterwards they went to a cowboy film, he was gone on cowboy films. 'In German films it's all second-rate and yet complex, these are different. Just look how this guy rides here, from what distance and in what air and how economical his movements are, making the point spot-on. Our people act too much, that's inner insecurity, there it's virtuosity.'

He lay with his neck buried in the seat-back, his legs stretched out in front of him under the empty rows, the large cinema was empty in the afternoons, his hands hanging cool, calm and collected. Afterwards he showed her his fairground, made a bee-line for his usual swing-boat, and they rocked up to the clouds in the swing, till the brake block engaged, forcing them to get out. It seemed to her she had more of him in the Fugger town than in any other town, here he was cut off from his set.

But then she had this urge to speak about the bridge when she saw the water in the town moat, and the idea for the play hit him.

'The main thing to me is, it's not to get heavy. It's got to be improvised and light. It must be like a motor in Paris that a ham cobbles together from bits and pieces he picks up here and there, and it doesn't even look like a car, but it does go, it goes.'

He got into a passion over his little butterfly, he described some of the characters to her, he already knew what they'd say. They went round in his head, it might be rubbish, he hadn't even thought them through, he just felt happy about it. In this respect he was a danger. You could fall for the radiance in his face, this radiance could deceive and had already deceived a good number. He was not without faults. She would have loved to promote his happiness.

It was a theme for a man. She didn't even have the basic know-how, she didn't have an instinct for politics. She had dreams. It was her instinct he tried to rouse. As if it could be ordered from one day to the next.

There were seeds and no ground for them. That wasn't a worry to him, he was such a tamer. With actors he had gone into his creative miracles, he took on Ostermeier exactly like that. But actors are built differently, it's their business to put on somebody else's skin.

He demanded of her what wasn't in her. She sensed something wasn't right, it must be down to her or was it not down to her? What was peculiar to her was wounded, precisely this counted nothing for him. He cut out all the atmosphere, he seemed to just hate it. She was to apply her efforts to something different, something from his own imagination and his cool intention. She was to put it into writing.

She would have loved to do it for him. She couldn't. It made her unhappy, she didn't know which way to turn. It totally confused her. She wasn't in his league. She plunged into powerlessness and woke up to powerlessness. She was no one. It wasn't to be wrenched out of her.

She escaped into anger. To be precise it was an intrusion. But the man lived by intruding. In the end she was as stubborn as a mule, the one thing you weren't allowed to be with him.

One day she would discover there were two creatures that didn't go together. It hadn't gone so far yet and she wouldn't have believed it from anyone. She would have gone for the one who predicted it. The shock was still asleep in the very depths of her, the shock wasn't yet roused. It mustn't come true, it mustn't come from within.

She didn't know she'd hit a block. There was the confounded play, wrenched up by the hair, she brought it to him with the greatest misgivings. It couldn't be more this time. He looked at her unhappily. She'd gone bananas. The insecurity had made her flip and become flippant, which didn't suit her in the least. 'Then be really impudent!' he said, it was too subdued for him. He said: 'We'll leave it be.'

All of it was right by her, as long as she knew no more about it. She didn't care about the play. She went around like one possessed. She was her own worst enemy. But what comes from within, soon comes from outside as well.

He had demanded it of her, so surely he must see she'd really done something. From his point of view it was totally different. He was as sober as a judge, didn't pass sentence beforehand. It was all just ladders for exercising on. A few rungs were there already, he saw the few possibilities at once, for him it only hinged on the director. He'd imagined there'd be more. Anyway it wasn't all that important, because it was all to him only a stepping stone, a reason for the better work, which always followed when one had been disappointed. The workplace didn't shut up shop.

Her whole life it was a horror, but she just didn't know it now. The thick edge was still to come. She was blind and she was deaf, she didn't notice a thing. She just didn't let it in. She had to protect herself from it, so much was down to her. In reality it was a crisis, there were signs of inner destruction.

She had gone hungry too often, she had been treated too badly, the woman had been given a stone for bread. She'd been taken for a ride, she had no right to the ground under her feet. Too much had been wrenching at her nerves for too long. Come to that she couldn't even put all this into words, she wasn't free to do so. She was under pressure. The destruction was still there within her.

She did know then about the children he had by his various women. She had already met Polly, who was an actress and the mother of his youngest son, and knew she had wanted a child by him and had chosen the father for the child, who was to be talented. It was far worse, she liked Polly. It was cock-eyed, because she noticed which way this led.

Cilly was now far more in the know. She had experience of a woman who was shrewd. Only Polly would pull it off, if any woman on earth pulled it off. She couldn't even envy her for that. It wasn't on, she liked her.

'I was a stormy person,' said Polly, 'before I met up with him.' This has been helpful for her. She told her things about her pregnancy, that were remarkable. Cilly gained a certain respect. She couldn't measure up to it.

Polly became a refuge. Without anything being said to her she knew a lot. 'Leave men alone,' said Polly, 'they are all rotten.' She said that to a woman. Cilly often went up to see her, she was allowed to use her bath, Polly had a bathroom.

While she was highly pregnant she kept going round to the lodgings office till she got a garret, which she turned into a flat. There was so much room, not one superfluous thing in it. The painter friend painted a larger than life metropolitan-man on the wall behind a rostrum, you could sit in front of the metropolitan-man. The atmosphere was spontaneous here in the room where scripts were learnt. To one side, stairs led up to a loft, it was even better to sit here, looking down into the ravine of streets beneath the window where lots of streets intersected. You could also rehearse the way of descending from step to step.

As a wardrobe she had a separate closet in the pitch of the roof, you walked into it and only walked into it when you needed a dress. Sometimes she chose something for Cilly and dressed her in it.

The poet lived more starkly in his garret, no one would have suspected there was a flat there, it wasn't even registered, and he got away with it for quite a while. 'The finance office has not asked me for any tax yet.' Between partitions you climbed up narrow steps like a hen ladder, there was always a fire risk. There in the pitch of the roof behind his iron bed stood whole batteries of bottles, built with their brewed contents. You were near heaven here.

The poet took his meals at Polly's, this was his new habit. This was often her only opportunity to see him. Occasionally Cilly came for meals as well. Then she observed how he trained him, his son. The little son had to bring his cap, when his father stood up to go, he had to notice. And he did notice, ran along the long passageway all eagerness, while still far away his little hand held out the cap, as if it had the utmost importance. 'That's right,' his father said curtly, bent down, took the cap from him. 'That's wrong,' he said quite as curtly and as briefly when something didn't please him. He trained him like this and set down the lines for his son, he didn't waste words on that.

What was thought natural wasn't fought against, the son was allowed to run wild here. When he saw Cilly, he immediately charged at her, ran headlong across the room where there was so much emptiness. He bored his head into her leg, tried to grab her under her skirt, she had to pluck him off by force, he clung to her like a tick, flinging and floundering about. 'Is that what a genius would do?' was all she said. His mother stood nearby and laughed, realizing he was a chip off the old block.

But then he got a poorly ear, needing ointment in it, which burnt badly but healed it. So his mother said: 'You put the ointment in.' She held her son only by his head, so he was still. Cilly put the ointment in his calmly offered ear, he couldn't get away. He pushed her away with his feet, he was held back by his head so the ointment didn't seep out again, it burnt badly, and it made him hate, squinting sideways up at Cilly, his eyes outraged and as brown as his father's. After that he didn't like her any more and bore it in mind that she had burnt him so.

Polly was a sly one. Only Polly would pull it off. Cilly couldn't even envy her over what was upsetting. That was the odd thing: no one dislodged her from her place. In principle there were places beside him for the chosen. He was a sun. He reached into all corners. And the shock stayed asleep.

The shock mustn't come true, it mustn't come from within. There was enough fuss with the others. There were signs of big difficulties. The man pulled her towards him like a magnet, the more he showed his true colours.

The man was a special kind of creature. As a final goal he set out to help people. In his manners he was a misanthropist. That wasn't swallowed from the man and anyway he hadn't the authority. He was to be new, but not too new and the kernel not too hard and the shell less rough, it had to be right. All in all he was to be just a little less objectionable. Perhaps you had to accommodate him, at best mollify him.

There had always been rows with everything he came into contact with, now they piled up. The rows were sure to pile up. The poet let the cat out of the bag, that was already clear. There were people who thought it a monster. At school they had called him cock-eyed. Only madmen go around looking out for things to object to. They deliberately fly in the face of what's always been there.

This poet wanted to take offence by force. It was his business if he got his fingers burnt. He was allegedly obsessed with one specific idea of his theatre of the future. Surely it was up to him where he stood in the here and now! He must have been a madman, he gave no credit to anything.

The poet simply took as his birthright. He showed his feelings stingily, which was a priority to him. He understated, he turned shortcomings into strengths. Why shouldn't he, when it worked, when he turned it into great art? He had his own personal creed, made to measure his special circumstances and still up-to-date thirty years later. And if it did the trick, the established theatre was blown apart. He was committed to imposing his creed, to blowing the theatre apart.

It was still castles in the air, as the child in the man went about it. He slapped a black titfer on, which helped him a bit with thinking, the titfer was handy for inspiration. Sitting cross-legged under the titfer he hovered on the head-rest of the mean couch, and day-dreamed like a boy. First he had to talk a large number into serving him. Then he would have his special present for people, that could no longer be disregarded. In his head under the titfer it was already there. You just had to look on while he tried it out on the boards and demonstrated it.

He measured everything uncompromisingly by his own yardstick. In fact, as things stood, nothing could be right. There were important theatres in this city, the poet didn't think they were important, he denied their reputation. He went to rehearsals of plays about to go on, to learn how not to do it. But then how would he himself have brought it off? It struck him when he was at odds with others. Down there in the seat, it suddenly became very clear to him, he learnt like a tailor and recce'd above.

He wasn't invited, but he was in there, because he knew the ins and outs. He was more important than those invited. While recceing he did more, moved an act on stage, put it right, if only in his head. Later on he would order them to the nearest centimetre. He compared and rejected long in advance, he had his own formula. He was a born director and this was roused now.

By taking offence he kept his own idea alive. No auditorium was safe from him in the grey morning light, no actor's dressing room in the evening. Not even the snappiest of porters, a very Cerberus could debar him. The poet went round objecting to any work but his own, influencing actors, planting discontent. He went all out for a director's contract, he landed one shortly, but it was never implemented. 'In my theatre I make the rows myself,' someone said of him. The man was pure dynamite. Whatever he touched something just went sky high. He pitched in with a new studio theatre, but only to slaughter it shortly afterwards.

He attracted attention. With nothing but flops he assumed a name like a costume. Meanwhile something got through, you sensed the up-and-coming man. His style couldn't be put into effect with the customary methods, it left gaps which he fell through. 'So,' he said simply, 'the methods must be changed.'

His *Lehrsätze* even baffled the professionals. They plunged you into despair and if you could give in, they guided you out of the despair again and what's more into a completely new theatre, which was fundamentally new, its foundations were laid. But first you had to take the suicidal step across the border, you mustn't skirt round it. The poet undermined the secure worthies, provoked the experts. And as he provoked, he was boycotted.

Those very things where the stage made its impact on the audience were no longer to exist, if it was down to him, if the theatre was no longer a drug it would become radically new.

He became the legitimate enemy. Famous theatres banned him, they no longer let him in to their rehearsals. The actors couldn't be locked up. He sauntered about with them in front of the stage door, kept up-to-date in the side streets. They went back infected. He spread insecurity with tiny targetted sentences, gave annihilating hints *sotto voce* and it all had a lasting impact. He knew they were receptive. 'Actors,' he would say, 'are apes.'

He had excited great curiosity and knew how to incite it. It was passed on from one person to another like on the black market. There were telephone conversations corrosive as caustic acid. He was in the thick of it a long time, the theatres couldn't keep him in their sights. This was a city. His mines were laid, he knew his loyal troops.

The theatres had realised they would be old hat if this upstart was right, this nosy-parker, this novice. Word went round that someone was making the secure worthies lose face, he was making them age inexorably. What was this rebel after? How big was he allowed to become? Did he have no respect for anything?

He had held an image of Napoleon, when his own future was unknown. The boy had his mask hung up and kept it quite a while when he was a man. He had slept under the mask, sown his wild oats, thought. It was a battle to him.

The corpses falling round him didn't disturb him. Some he thought funny, then he laughed like a drain, he had no heart. Perhaps corpses like this changed their opinions, realised at last there was no other way, you could not evade the new learning. Only learners weren't corpses. Those who learnt with him, could still be immature, finding themselves by groping their way, could make mistakes, that was part of the bargain. He didn't ask for any masters. And perhaps he wouldn't have tolerated masters near him.

He was the most reviled of men. The young quoted him in their dives. A following formed around him, which didn't understand him down to the last detail, they cottoned on to what charmed, shocked. He could no longer be wiped out, stories kept sprouting up about him. It was already apparent he would be the victor. His cold passion would change theatre.

He made it hard for his disciples too. They weren't allowed in on it with him. He scintillated on purpose, he praised artifice. He gave a lot in discussion, he fired on all cylinders. This wasn't to be deceptive. You didn't really get close to him. He kept a cool distance, when you were in earnest. The nearer you got the worse it was. He kept his back to himself, he wasn't burdened by people. They weren't to sit on him. Once he had them he shed them again, in one season, without mercy, indifferent. He expected to find them in their usual places, when he gave them a thought.

Ostermeier felt she'd been shed. He drained her instinct. In her feeling heart she fought her very personal battle with him. She could no longer bear the swarm of females who surrounded him, every one a paragon. His affairs were public – the way he carried on with Polly for a start! Cilly wasn't so clever. I'm going away, she dithered, you lose your self-awareness, I'm definitely going away. You must have taken leave of your senses to put up with it, I've gone already.

By now she was quite undermined. Hadn't he kept saying so, had she simply not heard right, not known in the cold light of day? Now it caught up with her: a person can't own another person. The scales fell from her eyes. Oh no, she had never had him at all.

No one believes it by themselves, until it's battered into them. What he had looked for first in her was talent. Love was just a sideline of it, but not to be sneered at. That was a laugh all right! She was as daft as a brush, it was lovely again, she was stuck in her fixation. It was high time she took some notice. He'd made eyes at her talent and that sort of thing never changed. She was never his wife. His wife must have raven hair.

What the hell could she do for him, really give him, that he didn't get just as well from others? If you're only good at writing! It wasn't distinctive enough. He was blessed in attracting the talent, that in fact was his magic. He always found people to write with. There was nothing special about that. It almost became too much for him.

It was an actress you had to be, so he could express himself directly through his woman. This was the true complement for such a man, he vitally needed this. He really knew what was useful to him, and that sustained him because then he could see himself in the flesh. She demonstrated to him what was performable and what wasn't, and for love of him she gave her all – and was able to warn him now and again, up to here and no further! He no longer fumbled about in the dark then. If you only wrote, you were soon gnawed clean, it was not classic work. He did that on his own.

She didn't get over it and she raged against herself for hours on end. She couldn't even open herself in him, something stood in her way. This was a verdict, no more no less. If it wasn't enough her being a martyr for his sake, then it was certainly too little. Anyone must realise that. For her there was still her own obstinate self, all the stronger the more it was under pressure.

She didn't realise it at all. It wasn't her fault. He would have had it different, if he'd wanted it different. She would have gone through thick and thin with him. But no, she must deliberately wring its neck. She could never have done him a greater favour. She couldn't find her way out any longer. She had made herself there a graven image, it didn't do the job.

What a bloody human being he was! He cut you right down to the quick, he didn't care. You were abandoned beside such a cold fish. So what was left of you then, nothing but a totally pitiable object? Rather a totally ordinary man, she said to herself, no connexion with a genius. You get something out of a genius if you keep at a safe distance, where the destruction doesn't burn you. You must be far away, only then do you come to satisfaction.

Pig-headedly she wanted to go home to the little town, it would protect her from him. She was after the distance, so she'd find herself. 'Do what you can't not do,' he said sarcastically. He recognised it again, he just didn't find it very smart. Not for the first time it happened to him. Obviously he had made too much of it. He didn't intend it to be over, therefore it wouldn't be over. At half past one in the afternoon, he was so amiable, he was ready to help her and carried her cases to the taxi. He could take a lot.

It wasn't over for a long time, he was still important. She had to keep going back, like a migrant bird. And perhaps that was the secret, you had to become a migrant bird beside him, so you weren't shattered on him. Only like this could it get a new lease of life.

II

If there'd been no Nickl the swimmer in the small town, it would easily have fallen upon another one. The rebuffed life had gathered itself together for so long, the louring storm had stood so blackly above her head, had threatened inexorably and had to break out, it finally had to fall upon one.

He bumped into her so naturally and let it be taken on board, then it simply fell upon Nickl from the shop, the last one to be right. For her father had said: 'Can't you see, he isn't at all right for you?' 'You can surely have a friend who is completely different for once,' she retorted. She wouldn't be prohibited, in this she was beyond belief, it did no good.

And he did swim so well. Being a long time in the water was such a novelty to her.

And it had to be the direct opposite, must not remind her of the dream. What tormented her she shoved away with her foot, and the water was good, almost too cold. It was like a good horror that heals. And the man was a good horror, he had to heal as well.

He seemed like a trainer to her, his face still so cheeky and distinctly from down below, from there, where it still doesn't speak its mind, never comes out with it, this was possibly his power. A Nickl near root level, it gave nourishment. A trainer has you under his thumb, even if it is entirely of your own free will. It is like a mute contract. You depend on the trainer, you can rely on him. She was deeply satisfied with the relationship for the time being.

Nickl taught her how to climb out of the strong Danube. The Danube is strong, the open bank not being suitable for the inexperienced woman. Going in is easy, she's taken along by the bouncy propulsion, but getting out the woman bounces back, it's a blow to the stomach. Then the current becomes a bull that takes her on its horns and tosses her against the boulders flung down higgledy-piggledy along the bank. This was why Cilly had Nickl, he took good care. He positioned himself full square against the flow, a few strokes ahead to catch her if she lost control, the dangerous whirlpools were two hundred metres downstream. No one had ever done this for her – it was pure joy. She kept this joy in mind. She had not had a surfeit of it.

The man didn't fight his corner longer than maybe one day or two, it turned away from him. Instead he had taken a wrong turning. No one could say he wasn't warned. Because an inner voice had warned, which throttled him and was like a taboo. He'd cocked a snook at the taboo, being far too inquisitive, the taboo had infiltrated as a sweet shudder, now he would even miss it. The floor was pulled away from under him, his misgivings went up in smoke. 'I'm bewitched,' he said to himself.

Never before had it happened to him like this. He tore his jacket off, completely wrapped Cilly round in it, in case she froze after her swim. His voice shook when he was rubbing her down. He was so carried away it sent sparks through her and she mused over his sudden surrender. He was beguiled by such exotica. He didn't know how to show her, above all he wanted to rip out his heart, which laughed and cried behind his grimaces. He went cuckoo and put fresh water out for it.

He became an addict of self-adornment. He came in gloves one Sunday though it wasn't winter, patent leather the colour of copper, his own chattels, he held them casually, tapping the palm of his hand with them so they couldn't be ignored. He tugged and kneaded the leather, he could manhandle them just as he would come to manhandle her. 'Put those gloves away,' she said prudishly. He put them away at this, still went round on a cloud, nothing put a stop to it. His luck was so broad, he couldn't keep his gob closed. He swayed and turned around, carrying himself like a peacock, as a dandy all he lacked was a hat.

He made up a lot about her and debunked all the others. Nobody else was right but she was right, he would have allowed her everything, provided it was not to do with money. He squandered himself on her. In what coinage would he demand it back from her?

And yet he was a horror. When he wasn't swimming, he was standing about in the shop belonging to his parents and if he didn't queer his pitch with them, in due course it would belong to him. This was his other characteristic that was inseparable from him, but it wasn't a nuisance yet. Cilly threw this characteristic to the wind, she wasn't that high and mighty. It must have given her a kick. He showed her – the convent girl who had been forever locked up – all the places she didn't know, they roamed about.

For ages she had enjoyed running round under the rain and against the wind, in the forest where it was dense, into all the waters. Suddenly there was this wood and this water, suddenly she was no longer alone. The stony desert was no longer there, and who wasn't right for whom?

As a friend he felt fine to her. As a friend you climbed over the rungs, that kept them apart. You didn't have to, if it was done willingly you didn't even notice them. You still travelled light. And it wouldn't lead any further. It was not to lead a step further.

She had not accounted for this maleness in his obstinacy. Nickl could not even imagine ever letting go of her, it only grew stronger. Above all he had a certain respect for her father's house. The next year he let it be known he meant business, he wouldn't let her have her own way any more.

Yesterday she was still ignorant, he came out with all guns ablaze. He made a clean sweep of the atmosphere, she had no time to see what was what, something must have given her a kick. She got the ring put on her finger, he didn't even ask. What maleness! She must have agreed when he went on the attack, closing her mouth with his kisses, now she was engaged. He really caught her napping. It was pure addiction. But this wasn't what she had imagined. Getting married had after-effects. It would have offended him saying no, she didn't want that. Because then she would have to leave him and she didn't want to leave him. She needed him because he was completely different. He was the best, but not for marriage.

This wouldn't get into his head. It had to really turn him upside down, he wouldn't have it any other way, he had flung open the portal. Nickl was ripe for change. That wasn't her fault either. A year before her, nothing had gone right for him. He had even got worse at swimming.

He didn't swim his ten thousand metres, the daily work-out he was used to, he didn't surpass himself any longer, he gradually became over age. Weren't the new generation to shop for their own titles. He had a dicky heart, he didn't admit it, in mid-stream he felt off-colour.

Then he leered up out of the water, as if he had to measure the duckboard, climbed out of the bottomlessness, because he hadn't intended to retire so early, came across like a freak, always only a single syllable in his gob and his head full of other things and at sea within. A person has to know when the sea has no more planks for him and when to give up, even if he regrets it. In fact he did regret, he never liked doing it.

He was known as an odd dog, his ears stuck out, he could perform with them, waggling them about. His brows met in profusion over the root of his nose, growing almost wild. His little iron head was too small for his body, his arm muscles below were powerfully packed, they shot up. In a way to make you laugh with him he was a bit grotesque, you remembered him against your will, at first glance he was impressive. His ugliness was like dotting the i's, when he was young and healthy, everything in peak condition, he made fun of it. The Grinning Sportsman was almost a brand name, for sure, he was imitated.

Right up in the Fichtel mountains and in the Bavarian Forest a con man passing himself off as him got money on tick in the swimmer's name for the journey home, as he put it, his parents would then settle it. He managed to get money like that.

Nickl would never have dreamed how popular he was in the country nor that he was lent money on that score, to be precise the sly look-alike grabbed the main chance by passing himself off as him. And he was really spoilt by the general goodwill, gulped it in as his rightful air. All this would come to an end once he left the club, once he stopped swimming for good, the angels gave him the message. The louring emptiness had to be filled. That's why he was so keen on change. Life had to change radically for him. The angels gave him the message in his sleep, when he didn't know a thing.

Everything offended him. At home he was as snug as a fledgling in the nest, no comparison with Cilly. His family swarmed around. He had started up a business when he came home as a raw soldier, because blacksmithing which he trained at for three years didn't suit him. He did it from the family's kitty. In the end it was the family who owned the business, he wasn't half surprised, that was not what he'd intended. Whatever he did was the same old story. He didn't decide anything on his own. He felt he was on kiddy's leads and intolerably reined in. They once let him run on his own, then they pulled him back in line.

For years he'd been persistently tapping his parents, pressuring them for his own business, then his inner and outer life would connect, he'd rather make a clean sweep. They were deaf to that. They needed their son for themselves. He bristled right through. He almost scaled the heights with a shop in the best area, he almost had it in the bag. Was he crazy? Who would he get the money from? How could he take this step when he wasn't a signatory? He hit his head against a brick wall. You had to run after him, so he didn't do anything stupid. His parents said no to him, so at the last minute nothing came of it.

If his admirers in the Fichtel Mountains could see their idol now! He wasn't treated as an idol. He'd screwed his expectations up far too high. The parents wouldn't hand out so much for their son, for a long time he couldn't grasp that. The best outcome would have been for him to grab hold of it by the hair. He would have taken it for granted.

They still owed him something, according to him. They'd pushed him around enough during school hours, when they still had the push. As a primary schoolkid he'd had to slave away at home, even more as an apprentice smith, for hours before, for hours after, at that time he hardly got to sleep. He could have put his foot down, he didn't put his foot down then either. They got a lot of mileage out of him, he had no free time like his mates and when he did the time was stolen. He was spurred on by the desire for the large sums of money, some of it must fall into his lap. He forgot his eyes were fixed with tiredness, the money-bag rang out to him, he ran like a bear being so obliging.

They'd made a heap for themselves in the 14–18 war. Up and down the whole street were soldiers sitting on the kerb for the beer, in the pub there wasn't a seat to be had. Nickl dodged at the double from one to another.

In the meantime the heaped up money just vanished into thin air. It went out as quickly as it came in, inflation lent a hand in this. And the lovely house on the street to the station, the beautiful garden where Nickl still saw himself digging, the father had sold dirt cheap in a panic for umpteen packets of cigarettes; Nickl later worked it out for him at this rate of exchange. The money-bag was a thing of the past, it had been exorcised for Nickl. He had to get by on less. He deadened it through sport. Even that left him in the lurch, even that let him down. There it was again, what had always been there inside, the worm. Nickl was not satisfied.

He thought he was inadequately paid. His work was worth more. He should take Cilly out, according to him. Nickl took only what was his right, as he saw it. He put his fist in the cash-till when things were tight, now and again he liked showing off.

But the cash-till didn't take kindly to it, it betrayed his fist. A sharp eye was kept on it. What did Cilly know? She thought it was drinking for custom by a grown-up man, which is what it was. But now there were two of them drinking.

'Have you taken out that note?' Mother asked angrily. 'Why shouldn't I?' he snapped back, revealing his own standpoint. Nickl had stood his ground against the people at home far too little, others got a better deal, his brothers and sisters for example. They got cash down. The parents couldn't keep fobbing him off for he would get the lot one day if he didn't queer his own pitch, perhaps they'd spin him another line. Nickl didn't hang about much longer. They firmly trusted in money. Now he grabbed them where it hurt.

They had always only burnt his wood, always only his wood, according to him, but he did battle over the wood. This was what he was good for. At four in the morning he was already up, having rolled the casks. They did it all nicely behind his back, he didn't want to call them lazy. In reality he was everyone's dogsbody. And when he set something up after the war, they didn't let him keep that either.

Up till now they'd had him cheap, he wasn't that cheap any longer, he'd rather queer his own pitch. He'd left his adolescence behind, when one could boss him about, didn't he have a right to his own woman, how much longer must he wait?

They were dab hands at turning deaf ears, it went smoothly for a long time. He was passed over in favour of his brothers and sisters, they had better gifts of the gab, he didn't fight his corner so well. It just couldn't go on for ever, he got down to it now! It just took him longer. If nothing did any good, he was sullen with them.

Then they noticed what sort of mess they had got him into. They'd had him cheap, now they were dependent on a thief. Luckily they could do themselves good. They'd rather put aside a marriage portion for him than be fleeced by him. That kept it within limits.

They even gave him a hand in getting the new shop which he had to take at a moment's notice. They'd avoided the deluge. Nickl was his own master. How did he come across? It suited his brothers and sisters nicely. Now he had queered his own pitch once and for all.

Things must happen fast to happen at all. They only happened by force, he had noticed and came to his shop by instinctive means. Perhaps one day he'd have to bear it in mind.

They had put him astride a nag fit for the knacker, all skin and bone, on that he was supposed to race. It didn't have to go on like that. 'We have given our son his share,' the mother blurted out, wanting to be clever enough for two, 'her old man should do something too', meaning by this Ostermeier's reluctant father.

Old man Ostermeier thought this back to front. All he knew was the man had to provide for her, the woman. This very evidence he himself had provided. His own father had only been allowed to knock on one of the old families, as he was a self-made man. He had never heard it any different. He wasn't lifting a finger for brash brats.

Once they were out of the red, he'd stop putting his foot down. But even then, whilst he was still alive, he'd put the dowry only into the household. It wasn't such a good match, it was a bad match, when you gave it a close look. He to be sure had got his own wife in a different way, but then he had something to offer.

He wouldn't be hunted out of his burrow. That was a bitter disappointment for Nickl, he gulped it down, the short-term goal in front of his eyes. His hair stood up on his head, he would never have admitted how it sickened him. He would never have admitted that something didn't work for him.

He flirted with patience, it was forced on him. He raged around in his narrow cage like a lion, restrained himself again. If the admirers in the Fichtel Mountains could just see their idol! How quickly can you spin a coin? This was still in front of him, he had to learn this bitter science.

The best thing about him was his legs, they were beautifully elongated and swift from swimming. Otherwise he was as black as night, his torso a bit short and thickset. His skin was mottled like fern, like the scarred underside of this discoloured plant and had that pungent smell of deeply fermenting wood, you could easily have put him in a wood till the moss grew on him, there among the mushrooms. He was curiously unclean and rampant, from head to foot made from nothing but earth, his eyeballs were blurred with a yellow cloudy film. He was heavy-handed and his hair was a cap of pitch, also his gaze was so unflinching, it could cling to you and not go away. It wasn't easy to shoo Nickl away, he was so raw and believed blindly in his fortune. He still called it Cilly.

At the beginning he palpitated together with her and she took it for his palpitation. Loving her lifted him up out of himself. He couldn't hold himself up there for long, then he fell back forcibly. This plopped him down into a puddle.

Ostermeier was a nobly formed person with large bones for a woman and with smouldering eyes, ashes on top of embers. It was nice to think she would have found someone else. In her was a harshness against herself, she was a bit mad. In the big city a man had wounded her too deeply, and she didn't speak about it, it never came out. She went with Nickl, as if she was not whole without him.

'Man is Man' she quoted someone else, who had given it to her earlier, in her voice was wrath. She was certainly headstrong, Cilly. It was a grotesque impulse, had a connection with art, which she herself didn't know. Something in her had stood too long on the summit, had then turned head over heels. She needed this soily dirt then, it was a secret from the womb of chaos. It was only wrong if the soily dirt was allowed to overrun her, she was throttled by rampancy.

What did Cilly know? She recognised the freedom in her life, it was the one of robbers and was hard for women if they had to do things as men did, that didn't turn out well for them. There was something murderous in this freedom.

She had had courage and often went hungry, those long years often hungry and courageous and now she was worn out and now she was stunned by a blow. In her fall she clutched at something to hold onto, it was Nickl of all people. He was put right in her path, there was no knowing who by. She held onto him in her distress, that was natural in the beginning. But then he held her in the fist that immobilised her wing feathers.

What did Cilly know? She recognised the freedom of her life, the artists. She had never seen a mouse-hole from inside, so she went inside one. Maybe they would meet, the dissimilar couple destined from all time. Maybe they had met in an earlier life and they had done to each other what was not right, and were together again, so they should do it better and each make amends to the other. It came out worse and so they could never get out of each other's clutches.

When she was a child he'd had to pass her every day, she had looked at him with sheer haughtiness and thought to herself, the boy looks like a nutcracker. But he saw to it that he got away, he just couldn't stand her.

Up to the last day he wasn't certain that she wouldn't tear herself away with convulsive wings. He had a dark presentiment of how near she was to it. Right by the portal she sensed the danger. Two voices were within her, they were in conflict, she was tired of the conflict.

By the time the poet made his mark in the big city she had gone. He had become the house-poet in an old theatre under a completely new man who had made his money in wood, who risked his money from the wood on him. The new man had within him a naive impetus for a new theatre, he was enthusiastic, he really wanted to get lost in art, he could still afford it. The writer had been looking for some such person for a long time. He had been looking for a man with courage and with a slender knowledge of the danger. He even brought him luck on the way.

Through the new boy in the theatre world he got a long-running success, which knocked out all the others, it could be thumbed through the calendar. Now there was proof. Those beaten in the battle stammered wanly: 'If only we'd done that!' Other cities performed him too. All doors swung open uncannily for the poet. What he said was taken as Gospel. He was almost beatified.

And after his smash-hit, it was there to read in all the papers, people were pleased for him, it made no difference for Cilly. She was kidding herself. For when his fame ran longer and longer, and when there was a gap, he raised her play from the dead, put it into the old theatre's repertory through the chief dramaturg who swore by him. His telegram startled her, it ordered her to the big city, she must get there hotfoot. After all the poet was the man who mattered, he only had to beckon. It sat her down in the train, she dropped everything and ran.

And now it would have done the play good, if it had gone on growing, if she hadn't pushed it away. But the foreign bodies don't go on growing, they don't have a real life, they only go in for being mutilated. She went off in a straining uncertainty, something was lying in wait.

III

She went a long stretch through central Germany, alone in a through-carriage. It was a bottle there she recalled after many years, that empty wine bottle, the way it rolled to and fro under the uncannily empty seats, in time with the carriage turning and tilting; it grew dark within. The bottle came from the far end like an event, bringing with it a density on the way, it was no ordinary bottle. Of course it was an ordinary bottle. It was a bottle, no more. Someone who'd been here before, had simply drained it dry putting it on the filthy floor, it rolled doggedly the whole length of the carriage, as the pounding train moved it, got caught on a metal foot, was silenced, got free again.

Cilly saw its greenness still blinking, saw it no longer, heard it again. Apart from the noise of the train this rolling was the only noise in the carriage, this rolling doggedly told her something, but she didn't understand. The bottle really was mysterious to her. So what, thought Cilly, that's only me making it up.

But what was she making up, wanting to come up from her subconscious? It unnerved her, not a soul coming in, not even the ticket collector. In other carriages people got on at woebegone stations, her carriage remained empty. And when someone came and was only one, things didn't improve. You could have been killing someone for hours in there without being disturbed.

Nickl was becoming a problem to her. She had to speak about him to the Jew there in the big city, to the wise man of her acquaintance. Through him she had got to know the poet, he was his follower or the poet was his follower, they stood as equals. He knew so much, you could talk to him, but not about the poet, he didn't want to hurt him. She had to talk to the Jew about the ring she had on her finger.

She did go to the Jew, who pointed out what she ought to want and what she did want, but what she was frightened by. She did like Nickl. She longed for an unbiased eye. The Jew accepted her with her internal striving – with what was special to her – and was never again stimulated by another with her personal vocation. He had the delivering word for it. The difference was striking. All at once she could breathe.

For the Jew, not for Nickl, she was a person. For Nickl she was a possession. He was to put her in the shop. He didn't bother about art. He didn't exactly hate it, it hadn't gone that far yet, art had never done him so much harm. When he wanted Cilly, Nickl fundamentally wanted himself. What did him good was all he wanted.

'Man is Man', was a lie, a battle-cry maybe. Cilly and the Jew were of one mind in this, but she hadn't got it in her fist. 'He won't let go of me, he won't do that, he'll get round me again.' – 'You mustn't wait till you're there', said the Jew under his breath to his pupil, she was like at school with him. 'You must let him come here, where he'll be out of his depth. You're not to go there again. You must part from him here. He'll only believe you here.'

It was a proper strategy. He was a sage, he'd learnt so much. Sages know how to cut things off. Let the prole come, that wouldn't ever have hit her, she kept the two worlds apart.

She knew now how it had grabbed her. Her heart wouldn't go along with it. Her heart wouldn't give him up. It fought its corner so blindly! But how on earth had he got in so deeply? She had given herself a tough job.

It can't be undone wearing kid gloves, if you're so tightly clung to. Only vehemently can you fight to free yourself. She flinched from it, but still had to do it. She liked the man. He wasn't to be kicked away. If it had to be done, kicking him away, you suffer quite as much as he does. The man cut her off from the only path for her, he distanced her from art. He wanted her for himself, to use her for his own lesser ends. She could never put up with it. She had to do that for art. It was crucial. She kept putting it off.

The poet asked for changes to the play, rehearsals were in progress. They kept her at it when she could only work slowly, couldn't work fast at all. This was the old affliction, the play gave her nothing. She went over and over it in her head and made nothing better of it, just different. The winter had been severe, walls of snow were built the length of the kerb right into April, everything made her cold. Uneasily she prowled the length of these walls. Whenever the snow towered up like this, something happened to her, which she could do nothing to avoid. She still didn't make the play better, just different. She simply didn't have the gift for it.

And when it was smashed and thrown out and when it didn't hang together, she had already run out of time, the day after next the curtain was to rise. The end of the text wasn't done, how could it be done in performance? She was persecuted by the impossibility, tormented. She went to pieces, just that. She couldn't write another word, not even her name. Every single word failed her. No more could be got out of her. Darkness fell all over her.

She dared the unthinkable, the evening before the dress rehearsal she stayed away from the rehearsal, where they only asked of her what she never had. The tap was overwound and turned itself, nothing came out. Stayed away from rehearsal, that person, when the end didn't hang together, she couldn't be found! This would not be forgiven her for a long time, she did know that. She couldn't help it. She was simply done in.

This was open rebellion at the worst possible moment against an almighty and against her personal master, if not her creator. She hadn't risked this for nothing, standing up for herself, but who against precisely, against her bad play which was her own fault, whilst others were slaving away at it? What precisely did she believe?

Here it wasn't like other playhouses, where they clung to the text, that had no interest here. The text was thrown upside down right from the start and then thrown around again, till you wouldn't recognise it any more. The method here was in learning, you didn't fall out of the sky, you tried things out. The well-worn path didn't count here for all its knowledge and resolution. A text was hardly ever done, that was its noblest characteristic and she should take note, a text was the raw material and the writer came last, every actor counted for more in this theatre.

And she was shown what could be done in the theatre, what sort of treatment you got for not even appearing at rehearsals and not fighting your corner. The direction scattered a riot of pepper onto the end, the covered toolshed rocked and inside the toolshed were the couple. They were after a pretext for a scandal, went all out for one. The play was too slight, if left to stand on its own feet. But it was not to be a flop, fifty thousand Marks had gone into it, and the silly goose went to pieces, there was nothing for her in the theatre, she hadn't the nerves for it, at the last moment too few ideas hit her. The theatre cursed itself. The play was still in rehearsal as the curtain rose.

Cilly was impossible, she knew that, and the play made her ill. She didn't know exactly what terrified her. One swallowed worse things from others, without turning a hair, just being neatly constructed made them safe from criticism. The play wasn't really that bad, looked at closely its predicaments weren't at all crass. But in the search for an understated style the words were not comfortably positioned, they were just a little bit beside the mark, they grated. The actors had too little to do, they longed for pepper to banish their boredom. A few visual audacities were put in. And the play didn't rise to its theme, that's what Cilly felt. But what did she know about soldiers? Why had she just been taken in by the poet?

It was all about soldiers here, when they invaded the town like wasps, it was logical to include the name of the town in the title, which fixed the authoress like a bolt from the blue. She had not written about the soldiers' virtue nor about the characteristics typifying the town, she had not considered what goes on between soldiers and girls in all towns a matter of secrecy, she had not stigmatised the female population with two servant-girls, nor servant-girls as a class. But a huge fuss was made afterwards.

Cilly learnt the rules of the game, and who had power over who – she was the loser. The play was attacked, the backers were the real target. The fight against this theatre by certain parties was already on the cards. It was too successful, this had lasted too long, the entrepreneur was Jewish, the house-poet extreme left and now came a weak spot.

There was a special poignancy about the time, which was already weighed down with it, what came afterwards. They wanted to take offence. The day before it was announced that you were to bring your front-door key, it would be needed. The press went there in the know. The scandal was organised, not spontaneous, the storm-troops were spread over the house to the greatest possible effect. The great unknown, in reality the known, gave them a taste of a witches' sabbath.

Cilly hadn't grasped it fully when she made an appearance after the performance. 'She's still laughing' she heard someone say from the front row, then all hell broke loose. The rented crowd whistled shrilly on their keys, surging down from the circles, determination clapping against it. It was a neatly calculated theatre scandal. In the rout everyone fought everyone. Cilly, a bunch of violets in her hand, stood in front of a roaring house. She was pale and kept straight, something in her took a stand.

And because it didn't stop, the racket, it became a matter for the Police. The Police Prefect demanded cuts. The pepper that had been laboriously inserted, must come out again. The weakened play was allowed to go on.

One critic who was familiar with the first script, looked for Cilly on the street, grabbed hold of her by the car that Polly was to drive her out of harm's way in. 'That isn't the play really,' he protested and wanted particulars to be hinted at in his newspaper. 'It is the play,' said Cilly, she didn't stab anyone in the back. She had swallowed it already, she did herself proud.

At the second première there was no scandal. The toolshed didn't move any more and there were no gravestones. She had written 'Space in the Graveyard', for a night-time rendezvous, totally naive. She needed any deserted place. It turned out that onstage the gravestone was directly behind the lovers. Death just behind the deadly sin, the wings gave no chance of missing it. The whole cemetery scene was cut.

The Press reaction was completely out of kilter with the occasion and was aimed even more at the backers. A section of the Press frothed, tore the play to shreds, tore Cilly to even smaller shreds, made false allegations about her person. Everything was allowed, especially where it dealt with a woman. But the papers that thought something of her, didn't hold it against her, neither now nor later.

The big papers had been at war for a long time. Anything that could be read politically they slaughtered with overstatement, from the right or from the left, there was no protection from it, no islands. One side always slaughtered.

The play was not a flop, the play was controversial. And it was not this play, where the former timber merchant lost his money again, the bold man still had a respite. The production ran for quite a stretch, what was interesting was the direction. The poet himself was behind it. Lenja had the greatest theatrical success as never again.

The title was beautiful it was bigger than the play. Cilly noticed too late, the title was an annoucement. The title was beautiful, for the name of the town was beautiful, she loved the name. The town saw it in a different light, saw itself distorted, thinking its wayward child had besmirched the venerable name. The Lord Mayor got into a panic over the widespread publicity that broke over it all of a sudden, but not to good effect. He did something for his town, wanting to protect it.

Not familiar with art, in total ignorance of its danger for the young, he was still young, had still not learnt his trade, the official insinuated what had never been, he ascribed evil intention to her and did exactly what he insinuated to her, he brought her into disrepute. In the presence of the German Federation of Cities he protested against 'the nasty concoction, the abusive play, and the shameful play'. All the German papers reprinted it and most foreign ones.

That voice penetrated far further than her own, trumpeting her shame over all the towns and taking away her reputation. That was serious, and she did not take it lightly. She would not take it lying down, was all she knew, for it demolished her, it was a devastation. The poet had said in passing, you must grow a thick skin for theatre. She was a booming membrane, set in unbearable vibration.

And at home in the little town her sister went to the parade defiantly, let the many glances spear her, jubilant in her complete innocence. And at home the mob ganged up at the street corner, not five stones' throws away from her father's house. A nerve-wracking time, the blokes lurked about, had stones already in their hands. They shoved forwards, were in clumps, only waiting then for the first one to dare. The front rooms were left in favour of the back ones, the house door was bolted. But then the neighbours found a sensible word, however far the cause was from the anger, then they cleared off.

Cilly was a booming membrane, set in unbearable vibration, she did not go up to the poet. She had not yet come to terms with it herself. A single false step could ruin everything. He rang up on his own accord. 'There's a pile of post,' he said in a voice as thin as a whip. For at home she had given the poet's as her long term address, so resolute was her belief that she'd always be there. She was already trembling on her way there. It was too early for her. She was unsure of herself.

She had left him in the lurch – it wasn't over – he let her know. And she had not even spoken to him about his good direction, she didn't even become aware that she failed him in that, she was full to the brim. Like a bailiff he handed the letters to her, stood four steps away and remained aloof from the scandal, that was only her concern, from the start he cut it all off. He stood there out of reach and was totally untouched, he was such a big animal. His pocket watch hung on a string from the ceiling, ticking in her ears as she read. Her father wrote and banned her from his house, this was the first letter she read. 'You are not to come here,' even Nickl wrote, 'they'll do you and me in.' People completely unknown and known to her spat poison at her. Cilly read them for an hour.

A disagreeable flood of foul slime seeped up from the written and printed words, enough to make you ill. On the floor she shredded cuttings from the local newspapers, they had no scruples at all, safe behind their big brothers. She had seen enough, most of it muck-slinging. One newspaper went as far as a murder threat and printed it, her back would be broken if she was seen in the town again. In a tone like the Franconian *Stürmer** kept up, a young person was attacked. There it was nothing but good for each blow to be harder than the last, it toughened you up. Something snapped inside her. She was done with these people.

If she had written half as shamelessly, as their shameless writing about her, she would have understood. For she was astonished and was able to study human nature, people's evil nature.

She did not look at the poet, she put that off intentionally. He didn't move an inch, which was a little weird. What was he doing there, learning from it? What was he thinking? In her something was slowly getting charged. When she was finished with the filth and the pain, she raised her head with resolution and had prepared herself, it hit home at all her expectation.

She looked into a pupil full of satanic sparkle. What was going on? He colluded in her disgrace, didn't he? She didn't know which chief devil was on his back, she was so incensed, not a word escaped her. She knew he needed a cause now to get his hooks into. She wanted to control herself. He should not say he had brought her to tears. Probably he at least accepted that she wasn't his dog.

She had left him in the lurch, but the punishment followed on its heels. He relished it. He was in the supreme position he was so high above, she stood before him so scourged, he spared her nothing, not letting her avoid his stare. He was such a tamer. She ought just to suffer, as it was, you brought such a scandal on yourself.

Not a word escaped her, she gave him not the smallest motive for his outburst, that was already over for him. He was only waiting for that, she saw it in him. Then she was lost in any case, then there was no more defence. She was already lost.

If he followed it up with something that he brought up, if it was not simply desire for

* This was *the* anti-Semitic newspaper of the Nazi years.

evil, then she didn't understand what it boiled down to and obeyed him no more on this. She felt it was unbelievable. The shock had reached her spot-on.

His look was a knife, something in her died at the critical moment. She was especially susceptible to this in him. She lost so much in that moment and through him, without him it would never have been. She came up against it like the virgin to the child. She had given what she imagined people do not give so lightly, and had to get used to the stigma. She could expect a word and if it was only one, could expect it was not a robot standing there, feelings deliberately frigid. He was not now to get on with it. When he did get on with it, he drove her away.

Fury soared high in her, it was no ordinary fury and it had consequences. With the fury she went at her own life, with the fury cut into her own flesh. As the scorpion seeing no way out of the fire turns the sting against itself, she did that to herself. She didn't want anything from him any more, that was over. And she had to drag it like a chain throughout her future.

She risked her skin no longer for him. That you could only feel yourself, how long it went on, if it went at all. But if she stuck to him she was lost. She saw it suddenly, completely sober. She repudiated her obedience to him, completely conscious. She had to be without him, perhaps not empty of him. She had to learn to get by without him, it was a different direction from today. She had her personal life and if not in his sparkle then there'd be no sparkle.

She was marooned near him. You would have to know a great deal more, not to be undamaged by being near him. Or you must have protection through a man who kept watch. He had grabbed hold of her life so deeply there was no way back from it. It would never again be as before. He took from her the little town that she was fond of, he took her reputation, on which she set great store, and when he had taken both from her and when the stigma became familiar to her, she'd be proud. She went out through the door with all the letters, she did not come back in through the door. Neither said a single word to the other.

She had swallowed and swallowed, you could not be squeamish with a man like him, you had to make allowances for him and you did make allowances for him. Nothing helped. She had not deserved that look. If he had done something for her, that look took it back. She did not get away from that look any more. It obstructed the way forward for her, stopped her going forward.

She would have a genius's perception no more. And when every fibre of her wanted to go back, it hit her that she must flee from him. It would not change any more. Something had happened. Perhaps she was too sensitive.

She was her own worst enemy. Something atrocious had got hold of her, she began to go bananas over the play. For a few days she was still around, then she got ill. She vomited her soul from her stomach, she puked out her inner life. If she stood up, everything spun round. If she laid down, anguish crouched in her diaphragm. Her temperature rose, she was delirious. It was all to the best that no one listened to her, she whispered such terrors, she would always be alone with them, the angel had already flown. There was no justice now or ever.

For hours the bed rolled with her, as if she was drunk, but there was not a drop in her stomach. The walls contracted hazily around her, bulging out again hazily. The walls had it in for her. The walls were not fixed, in mockery of her. Everything waved and wobbled. She let it pass over her, what could she do? She dug the back of the head in, as if she had to get into the floor and beyond through the pillow, her throat gaped, stretched. It was as if someone was boxing her there. The bed kept on rolling with the floor, rumbling in loose ellipses, going backwards a bit then forwards again, hanging fire once more. The hanging fire was the worst, hanging fire petrified her.

It crashed over her, what she most wanted was to blot herself out. The fever rose and fell, rose again. It hung onto her. But then it was gone. After weeks she was back on her feet. Just the shivers hung onto her. She forced herself to eat. She would not stay so weak. She had completely forgotten several things. Burnt in the shivering fever. She never touched on them again.

The call came now and it affected her like a farce. She had come to the big city with four typed copies of the original text, during the rehearsal run three got stuck somewhere else, she didn't relinquish the fourth, as it was her own. Now someone also asked for the fourth in his name, it was all the same to her, let it be gone, it left her so cold. The writer didn't have an original any more, perhaps deliberately, she didn't know, perhaps someone had given himself security as a man of the world.

But if it was deliberate and smart, it was planned too worldly-wisely. For it would not have been needed at all. She would have done nothing. She still owed him a lot. She had swallowed it and would swallow it. She wanted nothing more to do with that confounded play, this idea branded her for life.

IV

She had freed herself from the genius. But she could not go back to Nickl, who was completely different. She sent the ring back and made it clear to him he must make headway there in the small town and he'd never be able to, connected with her. If he wanted to come here to see her, to discuss things with her, let him do so. If he asked for a parting, he could have every parting from her he needed, she would give in to that, she would always like him. Just the ring, he must take that.

Over the parting Nickl took her at her word. He came on a Sunday and had time till midday on Monday, no longer. In that time he wanted to jam in what he went without in all innocence, it had to be everything at once. In a single night he would exorcise the parting or have his revenge on her, and yet this revenge would be an act of love.

If he could only fight a man! If he could put his finger on it, this one has taken her from me! He would certainly have done in a normal man. He would do that with his fists. He had not even learnt to box, his arms were trained for something else, but his arms were trained for muscles. He could smash someone like that to pulp with his hands nailed down. If only he was a normal man! And if it had only been about something so normal as taking a woman away. The man he meant did not even hold onto this woman, he knew that from Cilly. It was all far too complicated. Cilly had become an incredible creature.

The poet, this was the superior force. He did not come into contact with the poet. That was an impossibility. It was beyond his power. He just went after the magician. He raised his hand, masses of money rained down. The poet in his frail body was like the Himalayas to him, he had learnt the way from Cilly of seeing things with her eyes, he hadn't unlearnt that yet. He would hold onto Cilly once and for all. He just kept shaking his head. He had to bring Cilly round and had so little time. Tomorrow he would certainly know if it went well or he wouldn't need to know any more, he would take care of that.

He had imagined the Wannsee where there were plenty of rooms to let, and it was to be a special room, the one he had pictured. He looked at rooms till he was sick of it, at last he found something to the purpose that was smouldering within him.

The big room was out of the way at the end of a corridor, it could not be better, no one would hear him. It had a large recess for doing things in you don't do every day. He stood in the doorway, his eyes darting into all the corners, estimating the distance from the street across the front garden, he thought of everything. He did a deal and paid in advance. Then he picked Cilly up from under the tree at the street corner, she didn't go with him inside all these houses. In the evening light they went to a restaurant. 'You must eat,' he encouraged her.

Afterwards he unfolded his expectations. For sure she was rich by now. The people at home worked that out from the high ticket price multiplied by so much. They whispered, all that money is hers, she must have earned a fortune with a play like that, it being in rep. for so long. The fortune made up for a number of things. He for instance wasn't even angry with her over the play.

'You must build the town an indoor swimming-pool, then the town will certainly forgive you, I'll certainly see to that. An indoor swimming-pool is urgently needed, they can never train in winter without one, they get out of practice in winter, then of course others surpass them. An indoor swimming-pool has been wanted there for a long time.'

That was his greatest desire. He himself would certainly be satisfied with a track suit, she promised to send him one as he kept coming back to this track suit. Of course he could buy himself one, but that was not the same, that wouldn't be from her.

As for the future he was ready for a lot. He wanted to move to another town with her, where people were not angry with her and where he would make headway. They had the money for this from the play, the play appeared to him an inexhaustible source, and he worked it out again, every one of the seats, the tickets at so much, an acquaintance had been there, he had specially worked out the seats and recalled the expensive prices. It didn't matter to Nickl if he left it all behind, whatever he had, a grimace cleaved his face. 'Ah, Nickl!'

She took away his illusions about the money, she had only had the publisher's advance up to now which had to be paid back by instalments, that's what she had been living on. That was all she had made, the advance contract carried on. He suddenly looked so forlorn, but did not admit defeat. It was really not so bad. Surely you could draw credit on it, if you had already earned something by writing. Besides he was selling his business. Again the grimace cleaved his face. In reality he was despairing. 'Ah, Nickl!'

He assumed a composure she would not have credited him with, but he was on another tack, he listened, lost. He was going down a train of memory here that he did not betray, sometimes he smiled at her apologetically, he was totally wan today, the little spots were gone. Afterwards he slept with her, he seemed his usual self.

A long while afterwards he was awake, she heard him panting with short breaths, the pause disproportionately long afterwards, as if he was considering something meanwhile, that he still couldn't decide. She stared into the opalescent dusk above the bed and could not help.

A distant street-lamp threw in an oozing light so you could just see, the lamp swaying in the wind. Here in the room there was a faint movement of it, she saw the light swinging. She still kept staring at the ceiling.

He stealthily reached for the table near the bed, he looked about in the still life that he always created there, he was very quiet about it. 'What are you looking for?' she wanted to say, then her heart drummed.

Because he had got it then, she saw it flash then. In a trice he had laid his thigh over her thighs, held her down like a sack of cement, there was nothing she could do. His arm pushed her torso down, she couldn't get up. They both held their breath. Against the light all she could see was his head, not his face. Out of the dark came the voice. 'Are you putting the ring on again?' He put the knife on her naked chest above her heart, the point bored hard, he would pierce the bored hole. She saw from the dark head, he would do it. The power was lying in wait, when would it break loose?

His senses had become cruelly confused, they were in a trap, both of them. In the trap she suddenly had completely clear sight, she must think for two. She knew this was a man stricken by love. She wanted to be frightened, but she held the fright back.

If she had shrunk from him in the least, if she'd made the feeblest attempt, she would be dead. She must think for two. He did not even put his hand over her mouth, why should he? By the time people came everything would be over, stabbing is quick. What came afterwards didn't trouble him, he just didn't want to survive. She didn't even come up with the idea of screaming. This must be negotiated by them alone.

She left her chest exposed to him, as she lay under him like a lamb. Her voice had never been so soft, her body had never succumbed so much. She called him by his name so he'd know himself again. She nestled her face up to his face, as if it was priceless this pitiable thing, as if the pitiable was intimate. She was tender to him, however confused he was he had only her. In truth he had only her to help him. She did him good and peace poured from her.

He put the knife away only when she let the ring be put back on. Her hand didn't jerk away, she let him have his way in silence. He stroked her for that, not saying a word that made her shudder. She repressed her shudder, stopped him reading into it. He had only her to help him. She cheated him of course. Even if she was cheating she needed her protection from the cruel power that would smash his whole life. That must come first now. Besides, she wanted to live.

All night long he said not another word to her. After a while he lay down properly, he could sleep now. The ring was in place again.

In the morning he could not endure it in the room. He had to get out of this room. He wanted to see the huge wine casks in the department store, he knew about them through a representative ('If you ever get there, don't miss it.') She didn't have the first clue, which store they were in. Although he was a new boy in the city he took her straight there, he had remembered the described way so eagerly, and now he fulfilled his wish. On their last morning together they went from cask to cask in the resounding rooms, he took a teeny taste of wine here and there, he turned it round his tongue, he tickled the wine, ate a little bread in between, got himself some cheese. He went about it like an expert and met with respect. After an hour he'd had enough of the casks.

Once more they went up to their room. He took her on his lap, held her in his arm, but he could do nothing else, the excitement was too intense. All at once he had no more faith in the ring. He let her go with his arm, shaking his head furiously, bending over what he could not take for real, and yet it was real, the cleft went through his face. He pulled her towards him, pushed her away again, shook his head in the same mute despair. Then he plucked up courage for his thoughts.

'Well,' he said, 'I've made you a signatory at my bank, if things ever go badly for you, you'll be able to withdraw something then.' He dug out a note from his bank for her to sign, so his bank knew her signature. And then he sobbed out loud, because this was his limit, in truth he could do no more. She listened and wanted to run away. She saw this man was stricken by love. He pulled her back onto his lap and nothing sated him.

I'm sitting on the lap of a would-be murderer occurred to her. He had made her a signatory of his bank before he left home, had come here with a knife, wanting to kill her, he had planned it, otherwise he would not have hidden the knife so well. He had made her a signatory at his bank, at the same time he wanted her money that she really must have earned from this play, he always muddled up mine and yours.

'In any case I'm not going home any more,' he let out, 'I'll throw myself in front of a train here.' – 'No,' she said, 'you are not throwing yourself in front of a train, I'll go with you. I'll stay with you till the last second. As soon as the train starts, I'll jump off.' – 'Yes,' he said, 'that's what you must do.'

All and sundry, she thought, all and sundry! And it wasn't only fear that came upon her, she had to cuddle him. The whole time they sat on this one chair, till he had to leave for the station. And he performed with his ears, grinned at her unexpectedly, it was not manly always just crying.

She still didn't know if it was right, letting him come here, but maybe he would not have believed her otherwise. She went round feeling depressed, she took out his letters, these were the only ones she had taken with her on her trip. She held the letters as if they were objects of value.

His writing slanted more than any she had ever seen, the letters fell over each other on the lines, the tails beneath went on for ever, exclamation marks stood in the middle of sentences, three together, he stressed a word for inexplicable reasons that must have been important to him, lower case was written in capitals, capitals in lower case, he really had not learnt very well at school. All he had done was rolled the casks, rinsed the glasses, remembered the bills, he did that well. He killed himself in the pub, paid too little attention at school, so much confusion was stuck in his head and was nutritious in itself. 'Gifted but retarded' the teacher had noted in his school-report. And he had often bunked off school, secretly going fishing, catching crabs or mucking about in the wood, which he loved, and after supposedly being at school he biked back home at the right time. How else would he have come by what he loved?

She still kept the ring, handled it often, had to hold it as if that helped him, it seemed to her she was a bitch. She could do nothing to change that. She went on fighting for a few weeks, then he would be over the worst, she felt. Once more she sent the ring back to him.

She was fair game in the open season. And yet she had to have a man's protection. Something curious happened. You can't just search for a man straight away, you do have to find him, and as she found one so soon, she soon gave up her freedom again. It was always the same whirlpool and for the very reason, she had to have some reality, she could not go on any more without a soulmate. But she could never be cautious when choosing and had to take the consequences afterwards.

The Jew would have been appalled if he had known, but she no longer went to the Jew, because she no longer went to the poet. He would not have understood her here. He had amputated her from that one, just for her to lose her irrecoverable freedom again to someone else, so her need was obviously overpowering. Without a steady man she apparently could not exist any more. But it was devastating for a woman if she wrote, she was really not allowed to want that.

Besides the man was on the right, this would be difficult for sure, one paper brought it out at once. It announced their engagement with a picture, 'Hugenberg and Ullstein unite' written beneath, and two enormous chimneys sinking towards each other in the form of a cross. Being engaged was devastating for a woman, if she wrote. But how otherwise would she arrive at a life with a plumb-line? She had just to hope she survived it. Yes, she had to hope that.

Early Encounter

Marieluise Fleisser

translated by Tinch Minter

Early Encounter

Rathenau was soon to be murdered, Germany was in turmoil. At this time, in the spring of 1922, I was a frequent visitor at the Georgenstrasse, the Munich flat of Lion Feuchtwanger. Here I heard a lot about a young man from Augsburg, called by Feuchtwanger – and only partly in jest – his house-poet. He became a legendary figure; meanwhile I never came face to face with him, either he had already left or I made no intrusion into the work-room. And Feuchtwanger rushed out for odd moments, still looking intense, because there in the room he was racking his brains over the collaboration with the man from Augsburg. I sensed something special was going on in there.

The poet came irregularly, on the spur of the moment, he didn't have a room of his own in Munich. He came over from Augsburg, where his father's house – number two Bleichstrasse – stood, close to dark waters evoking dreams. Or he came over from Starnberg, where he had tiny weekend digs, writing poety by the lake.

Feuchtwanger had already given me the poet's ballads to read, which I found an uphill struggle. Weird things reached me about this Brecht. He had a horror of pregnancies, he railed against women in that condition when he had put them in that condition as if they were the ones who had got at him. He had nothing against children, on the contrary, 'Let them grow, the little Brechts!' It was just as if Feuchtwanger had to vent what was stirring in him on someone or other. For that Brecht was stirring within him. He could be genial in a flash, as insolent as a young god, the favourite child of the machine age.

He never dug his heels in when he had done something. He was always prepared to make changes; he had a strong sense of what was still unfinished, in flux, he greatly preferred the developing process to the finished article. With the true love of a gardener Feuchtwanger pruned bits off him here and there. Brecht accepted it or not as he chose, maybe enticing him somewhere else, but the elder man still carried more weight. Feuchtwanger might well complain that he had come from Starnberg with something totally bland, and this doesn't suit a Brecht, they would now have to use all their cunning to rough it up, to be by Brecht it must be rugged.

In his novel *Success* Feuchtwanger had a terrifying idea. In the young engineer Pröckl he portrays Brecht as he then was and makes the doppelgänger of this key figure, a controversial painter, live in a lunatic asylum. Feuchtwanger split his understanding of genius.

But Brecht was too much of a dissenter. He fitted in where he had to, and he took the lion's share wherever there was a chance; all this was how he understood staying power, that was the prime duty.

The first productions which had previously evaded him now came to meet him. Falkenberg wanted to produce *Spartacus* in the Augustenstrasse, the play was already called *Drums in the Night*. The Bavarian State Theatre put on *Jungle of the Cities*.

I had read *Baal*, his stroke of genius, within my own four walls, the play made my heart race, and when I saw *Drums* given life on the stage, I was done for. After the curtain came down I ran around for hours on end in the rain-laden October air and knew I wouldn't get this poet out of my system: he offers me something, he undermines me, I can't get away from him throughout my life.

'His writing is childish', said the Frau Hofrat, where I was lodging, 'nobody writes like that.' On the other hand she praised Bruno Frank as the really interesting writer in

Munich, whilst Brecht's writing was really primitive, his writing was childish. 'No, childlike!' I said.

Private affairs with Brecht came to a head. He had to establish a household, and really he was keen to go to Berlin, that was his town. But the Berlin production of *Drums* was to be a disappointment, and he didn't ever forgive Kerr for his review – or at least not for a long time.

He went straight back to Bavaria into the real thick of his writing, once again with Feuchtwanger. He worked on the *Life of Edward II*, at a version of *Gösta Berling* in the style of a morality play and in rhyme. Shortly before the production he rewrote *Jungle*. All that at one go, three things at once, when he hit a block he turned to another.

The bridal couple stayed in Augsburg under the paternal roof, in Munich there were no flats to be found, and when one was found it was too small. Brecht ran away from the screaming child and the matriarchy, he didn't know where to write. He turned up at friends' doors to work. The currency plummeted, Hitler marshalled the masses. Stones were thrown at Feuchtwanger's windows, anti-semitic slogans were shouted at him. Brecht had productions contracted, but the Mark kept falling.

Meanwhile Brecht had read something of mine as Feuchtwanger had given it to him, he told me to meet him at Feuchtwanger's. And as he'd given up the time for me and I saw the lovely cheek-bones in his lean face and how his eyes wandered over people, I was so overwhelmed with emotion I could hardly get out two words. I was already in fear I had spoiled it all but nothing was spoilt. He told me that I just dress the facts sensitively.

I only ever saw him on the go, it seemed to me my life depended on him. I wrote towards the man, as well as I could at that time, I had only fragments. Brecht had formed in me a tabula rasa.

'You must write like a child,' he said to me, 'what is important is naivety, just write naively. Go ahead and make mistakes, that doesn't matter.' Social criticism was not the point then. One mustn't forget, the Brecht we know today didn't exist then. We see the whole of him now. At that time there were the ballads, three plays. I was educated in a convent, a stranger to the world. Brecht talked to me about totally naive things. He was taken with a woodman-song and he sang it to me to prove how persuasive a language could be which used so little. 'We be the merry wood-cutting crew and we do as we please, and we do as we please.' And he got up and took a step as if he were on stage whilst reciting to me: 'He who wants to be a soldier must have a musket, matey, this must be loaded with powder and with a bullet weighty.' And it seemed that a bullet was rolling forward in his hand as he said again: 'and with a bullet weighty', so I noticed what his point was. He gave me such simple examples of a language which is so compressed that nothing can be subtracted and nothing can be added. He was keen on the people's tongue where nothing came by chance. On the tiny sentence 'I dunno' he could talk at length and about the subtle transformation in people when they no longer know a way out of their problems because right then they 'do know'. It was as if he took me right to the source of language, to where it originated.

'He looks like a cyclist,' I said when people asked about the young Bert Brecht, and by that I meant the inconspicuous man in the street, who people are more likely to take for a technician in a factory than a poet, and not before he spoke or made a move was his special quality revealed. Like a masterly line, he made the simplest of gestures, which might lead to a revelation.

And that time he wore leather jackets, in which with his bones as frail as a bird he almost disappeared, and having something tailor-made, he had to have the collar sticking out at the neck, which would be counted a mistake among tailors, Brecht bespoke them like that.

Inflation rocketed, life on an author's fees became impossible. When you did get royalties they weren't worth a postage stamp. In any case Munich at that time was pretty cheerless. Lots of people wanted to leave Munich. The State Theatre removed *Jungle of the Cities* from the programme in response to 'public outrage'. On several occasions Brecht had wanted to retreat to Berlin. But his contract as dramaturg at the Kammerspiele kept his head above water, and also Feuchtwanger became a publisher's reader, which he could work at in his flat. Then there were shots at the Feldherrnhalle, the Putsch, maybe Hitler would come to power. One whole day things were really dangerous, and a cautious Rudolf Bing, man of the theatre, cycled out to Nymphenburg so as not to be found at his flat, and spent the whole night cycling around for fear of the worst. Feuchtwanger stayed in the Georgenstrasse but was uneasy about it.

This time the storm passed over, art could still breathe. The Kammerspiele bought the *Life of Edward*, I was allowed in to the dress rehearsal. Brecht directed, in an understated way, very strange, the actors spoke woodenly on purpose, like puppets, they left things in suspense. It was very unusual, parts were magnificent, with elements of mime, they went straight for the nerve, Brecht was trying something out. Time and again he ran up the little steps to an actor, light-footed and young, carefree as if he'd been doing it all his life. He said it all simply. 'Different lighting,' he said, 'seven o'clock a.m.' He wasn't easily satisfied with the light, wanting subtle colours, not garish, striving for transparency. Too many people were in the auditorium, who weren't always quiet, and when a humming started up, almost a buzz of voices, Brecht said nothing but 'I'll have the hall emptied if it's not quiet.' That helped at once, one noted he was in earnest. It was his second attempt to direct, if I've got it right.

Brecht knew a little story about rehearsals. There was a scene with soldiers before a battle, just a short scene, but it didn't work, it didn't feel that a battle was in the offing. 'How do soldiers behave before a battle?' Brecht asked everyone around, he asked Karl Valentin. 'Soldiers before a battle,' he said, 'are shit scared. White as a sheet.' Brecht put white make-up on their faces for the scene and achieved the atmosphere he was after.

The Mark steadied itself. Brecht set off for Berlin. Before that I had to go back to Ingolstadt. I only saw Brecht again after Seeler's production of *Baal*. He had managed to get my first play on, that was called *The Washing of Feet*. As *Purgatory in Ingolstadt* I witnessed it at the Deutsches Theater, Berlin. Maria Koppenhöfer, Helene Weigel and Matthias Wiemann led the cast, and really Seeler wanted to put on the play of a young man, but Brecht said, 'No, you're not putting on this young man, you're putting on Fleisser.' This was the time of my early strokes of luck.

There was a man in Berlin who could do magic. He invented a mechanism, I mean with very little money. He called it *Junge Bühne*, and the man could do this because he knew the actors, and because he knew the rich people. He ran round them, some performed for him, the others gave him money. With the money he paid for one Sunday morning in a really big theatre, the audience streamed in, and the press took their places. They brought the actors and the writer as well onto people's tongues, the press wrote about them, which was really worth something in Berlin.

Seeler sent me from Berlin seven-page demanding letters, written as if with a match, and *The Washing of Feet* is no title, no one cares a hoot about it, he had already given the press a better title, *Purgatory in Ingolstadt*, and that would be a title that they would care a hoot about, and I must authorise it. I was knocked sideways, but did authorise it.

Seeler took a booking on my next plays, I must promise them all to him. Brecht wrote, don't promise Seeler a thing, he's taking you for a ride. Seeler wrote, why have I still not got a written agreement on your next play, I'll put on all your plays. I just arranged with him the sign for recognising each other at the Anhalter station. His first words were, 'Don't you wear a hat?' I didn't have a single hat. There weren't many rehearsals, the actors had to produce it by a flick of the wrist. I had the money to get there, no more, I only got to the dress rehearsal. The place was wracked with nerves.

Brecht was in the theatre then, I met Helene Weigel. From the moment I stuck close to the couple, Seeler looked grim. Something was in the air, as if two opponents were pulling me apart. They had an old score to settle, Brecht and Seeler, that wouldn't keep, and to my misfortune I was in the middle. I arrived in the middle of a landslide between two men, both obsessed with theatre, opposites in their conception of theatre. Brecht wanted to radically cut out of my play everything atmospheric, only – what would be left if it was cut? Seeler now watched me from afar as if I'd fallen into a snake-pit, no one was going to pull me out of it. Actors raised a storm against cuts. Some had only taken their parts for the sections which were now to be cut. After the dress rehearsal everything was as if thrown up in the air, nobody knew what was going on, what was staying in the text, what wasn't. Overnight the director sat down to it once more, and the actors were smart and came together to another morning rehearsal, and immediately afterwards gave the première.

As usual at premières Seeler was wearing an old bowler hat. 'Someone ought to bore a hole into his hat,' Brecht said scornfully, 'he believes his luck sits in his hat. If he can't wear the hat, the whole man is knocked for six, he is a fetishist, it's that easy for me to do for him.' 'This one's going to open a theatre,' Brecht said menacingly, 'he also knows the rich people', and good actors would be no problem, they were already to a great extent playing the way he pushed them. It was a horrible atmosphere.

After the performance it evaporated in the storm of applause. Seeler still didn't say a word. At lunch in a sunny arcade leading to a garden we all sat together as if we were at a wedding, we said charming things to each other, regretting not a single word. But Brecht felt the landslide and remembered their old score, and having to sit at the long board diagonally opposite Seeler for an hour was more than he could stomach. He grew as red as a turkey, then grabbed hold of the salt cellar that was in front of him, and hurled it across the table at Seeler's face. The salt cellar stemmed from *Baal*, it had been rankling that long but now it erupted; Seeler could no longer count on Brecht. It was not without tragedy for him, as he was in the vanguard of theatrical productions, and he paid for it under Hitler.

The same day Kerr wrote well about me, and Ihering wrote a paean and that these two who were usually opponents were of one mind, was a sensation in Berlin . . .

First it was at 16 Spichernstrasse, then at the dog-leg of Hardenbergstrasse, and always by a lucky chance through friends Brecht came easily by flats. Feuchtwanger was already living in Berlin. Their relationship had already entered into an equally balanced phase. Feuchtwanger pulled his leg that something happened to Brecht at every moment. Brecht sneered because Feuchtwanger had inscribed on *The Life of Edward*, 'I wrote this play with Bert Brecht.' He couldn't understand that Brecht always needed others for his writing, to use as a springboard, on the other hand Brecht found Feuchtwanger's books too voluminous. All this between friends and for that matter between equals. Now Brecht even awarded a prize to a frustrated racing cyclist for a trivial poem. 'Cyclists are ungrateful' was Feuchtwanger's violent reaction, and even the lyric poets took it amiss. But Brecht was on the way towards his didactic poems, he demanded that poetry had a use, wanting it to serve as an example, what he no longer understood by lyrical poetry. For him day-dreams were spray-bubbles.

I was still transfixed by his law of the jungle of his imaginary Chicago; Brecht was already somewhere totally different. Feuchtwanger's influence was on the decline, now Sternfeld became the man of importance, and Korsch. What happened then was not an important time in terms of creativity, but in what he took in, setting the path for his great development. Certainly, he wrote. *Man is Man* he wrote, which was a trailer, showing where he was going; at the same time he demanded *Pioneers in Ingolstadt* from me, as if I worked the same seam with him at a distance.

Sternfeld didn't come accidentally, nor Korsch. Brecht was already on his way, therefore he took them along with him. He wrote songs, the stories of Herr Keuner, *Mahagonny* he wrote but as Feuchtwanger was digging at him, this was the moment of the masterpiece, he wouldn't let himself be harrassed. 'No,' he said deliberately, 'I'll take my time.' With the *Threepenny Opera* he wrote himself into his success, and did that indolently. What sparked were the songs, the whole play Brecht made light-handedly, it was given a tight deadline. 'Let's ask the little book' they said when they hit a block, Weill told me, and they asked the little book, that is *Villon* in Ammer's translation. Brecht responded to the huge success almost cynically, because it hadn't been a great effort. Effort and success are not interdependent. 'Just get on and write,' he told me then. He invested more in *St Joan of the Stockyards*, what at that time was all his skill.

The path beside him was interrupted for me. I had still not experienced reality from A to Z, and not having done that, I lived in the clouds, and then I couldn't write. I just couldn't leap over the steps, I had to take them slowly. And certainly Brecht was the force which had a lasting effect on my personal destiny, time and again it broke through, and brought with it bitter fruit for me.

After he returned from emigration, Brecht sent for me from Ingolstadt, I visited him once or twice, at the rehearsals for *Courage* in Munich, and the last time in Berlin six months before he died. He was very kind to me, though that did nothing to help me in my minefield. He wanted me to write a play for him. It wasn't his fault if the circumstances of my buried life didn't allow me to write. He sat himself down on a chair at a great distance from people, I saw a tragic face.

I wrote a story *Avant-garde* that was published by Carl Hanser. In the beginning I had in mind a young girl beside a genius. From this, quite against my will, it became the young Brecht. But it is a story which has a gradient, of where it's coming from and where it's going to, it can't be the same as a biography. In it a lot is different and from it the whole life experience flows into you, that is a process against my will. Whoever had been forced into the wrong place by Hitler and couldn't free herself in the thirties, has thorns growing round her. That is not the intention. The whole long heavy chain helped itself to the beginning, even dragged me along, a trauma is in the story, for a while it was called *The Trauma*. What is important is Brecht, his immortal figure. He had exploded the story's frame for me and I got something from that.

I do believe that it gives a lively idea of the early Brecht; it's only about this one, not about the mature one. And this one is Baal. 'A hard nut in a rough shell.' This was Brecht's favourite idea of these early years, how he wanted to see himself. I didn't polish it up. When people insinuate that I wanted to attack Brecht, I take up arms. No one has to defend Brecht from me. I belong to the friends of Brecht.

I Wasn't Aware of the Explosive

Marieluise Fleisser

translated by Tinch Minter

I Wasn't Aware of the Explosive

I wrote my first play at number seven Ainmillerstrasse in Munich. It was the year 1924 . . . I was not yet 23-years-old. I wrote it in a large room on the first floor, where I lived with an elderly Hofrätin . . . I was at University reading Theatre Studies, had hardly any money.

My play would centre round young people, I'd known that from the very beginning. I had no title for it, only when completed did it become *Die Fusswaschung (The Washing of Feet)*, but it was never performed under this title. It was a corner house, my wide window opened onto a quiet side street, Ainmillerstrasse. Through this side street I could run a short cut into Georgenstrasse where the writer Lion Feuchtwanger lived with his wife, Martha, on another first floor on a side street corner. After the last war I never found that corner again. The area was flattened here to the point of being unrecognisable and later on was built over.

I showed Feuchtwanger everything I had written, it was only my play that I wrote in secret. I was a true Schwabingerin (from Munich's bohemian quarter) and ran about in a man's rainproof jacket. My friend has given it to me, as he had bought himself a coat. The jacket with its raglan sleeves was too wide on me, but I yanked it in very snugly with a broad belt, it hung down almost to my knees and became my coat, looking outrageous. When I passed that Max Halbe on the corner of Franz-Joseph Street – he was a half Municher, half Danziger and was going along with a companion – Halbe just said: 'To arms! To arms!' and the two of them stopped in their tracks and watched me. He said it very loudly. I took it as evidence that I had grown up differently to the way his generation thought a young girl should, and that satisfied me.

In this jacket I looked at my fellow creatures with strange thoughts. Their faces became revelations to me, they seemed changed from what they had been a year ago. My friend had decamped to Paris, I went on wearing the jacket. He had witnessed Lion writing a dedication to me in one of his plays, before giving it to me. 'To little Lu in good friendship L fullstop F fullstop' stood there in black and white and couldn't be denied, it was in his very own handwriting. In the beginning Lion was so cautious that he didn't even write out his name in full. I was the unknown student, he was already a famous man in Munich. When I was out of the room, my friend found the dedication and, in letters that hopped in anger, put underneath: 'Who's sneaking off with my name?' My friend was the first to give me the Gallic short form, and no one else called me Lu. He was jealous when anyone else called me that.

But it became clear that Lion didn't even like the Gallic shortening. 'Anyone can be called Lu,' he said to me. 'That's no name for a woman who writes, it doesn't come and hit you.' Lion turned my names round and made Marieluise out of them. So he gave me the name I wrote and still write under and under which I was banned as it became a part of me.

And Lion gave me a book and I don't even know what it was called, yet it became an important book for me, the book was his hot tip, he only gave it to the chosen few. 'You must read it carefully,' he said to me, 'it'll get rid of your illusions for you, so you know the world is an evil place.' I read the book carefully, and although I didn't make a note of the author and never heard the name again, the book went right through me. For me it was the book of knowledge. And I quite liked it being there in the darkness and in secret, where it became impregnated. To me thereafter people on the street had their new faces. Some time still passed before I wrote my play.

The book didn't do it on its own. A story preceded it, the very first one of my writings that he didn't fault. Everything before that wasn't factual enough for him. 'No one writes expressionism any more,' he said, 'expressionism is a strait-jacket.' And because I believed him, I burnt it all, even the easy *Is Rebellion a Sin?* which I was really proud of and was really attached to. The story had the title *My Twin Sister Olga* and was the foundation stone of my play, it was the first attempt.

During my childhood, while somewhere else the *Titanic* was sinking, the fatherless son of a tenant publican pestered me, ran after me in the streets, jerked stretched rubberbands off in my unprotected face, lay in wait while I was playing in the baker's yard, took away my handkerchief as a fetish, and returned it to me as a fetish, but only after two days. With his toes he clambered onto the back wall of our house right up to our roof terrace, because we bawled down to him from there, he'd never manage it, and because we goaded him. When he swung himself up over the terrace railing without breaking his neck and nothing had put him off, we weren't protected by the height, so we became frightened at his uncanny deed and ran away. Sometimes I played with him and sometimes I didn't. I went to the better school, he envied me for that. He wanted to break out of his class. He wanted to have a thing going with me, but he didn't have the nerve. This was to do with becoming a man, but it was too early for that.

A breath of yearning for far places hung around him, from his foreign sailors and the carpenters with their wide flared trousers, who came from far away and turned into the pub because it wasn't a genteel one, they let themselves be stared at by the boy of the pub who was running about there, told him their experiences, making them into tall stories. He would have liked to do what they did, hadn't got enough years for that.

His half-knowledge of the things that never happened to the rest of us, allured me. Then he repulsed me again. He threw in the odd blasphemous sentence, not a hint of becoming a saint. They sounded odd from a boy's lips, in fact they came from the godless grown-ups he mixed with. He poured scorn on my first holy communion.

My mother stepped between us and parted us. It was an absolute prohibition, I had to abide by it. But he was booted into an apprenticeship, the escape routes of his fantasy were closed to him. He was leaden in the evenings and worn out, he was gnawed, exploded, rough mates cut him down to size and put him on the lowest rung, the place where he belonged for the time being. And now when I passed him standing in the pub doorway, he blushed because of his speckled overall.

The encounter with him made a lasting impression on me. Nine years later, I spun the story of the twin sister Olga from it. This was the first seedling and it didn't lie dormant there.

I had written it naively and wasn't aware of the explosive hidden within. It could have brought evil upon my head, the story. As it was, a lot later, when his life didn't go the way the boy had dreamt in his fantasies, when a banal narrowness with no way out hung about him, it forged the path ahead. From early days he became one of Hitler's men, in a search for adventure. And as they felt themselves to be special, with special rights, they who'd previously been lepers when they were outlawed, suddenly had the law behind them so they paid off old scores with far-reaching revenge; and as I for some time had not been a blank sheet, mixing with Jews and left-wingers, they talked him into denouncing me because my story about him was criminal. Overnight it became a crime which could propel me into a concentration camp, if he reported me to the right quarters. I had even used his real name from childlike naivety. Anyone could twist that into an evil intent, he didn't have to take it. But he did not denounce me, remained steadfast, refused to do so.

When I wrote the play I didn't know anything about its explosive power, I was only a student and had a mental image within me. The early story had been written, Lion's book had been read, the schoolboy long forgotten, but he broke through again and became the second seedling. New leaf mould had fallen, his way was blocked, he had to go somewhere else now. But once more I was circling round a schoolboy. Meanwhile, to me he had changed, coloured by my monastic boarding school. I was corsetted, girls weren't allowed into boys' grammar-schools then, I couldn't matriculate, I had to go away. His yearning for new places took a new turn and he had to leap over a fissure again.

In the story he was a primary schoolboy, still a minor, in the play he was a few years older, a grammar schoolboy and he was expelled from the school. He functioned within the religious constraints, which were a reflection of that constraint which wanted, but failed, to bury me alive. Although it had sat within me for a long time I hadn't permitted the constraint to surface, but now it raised its head, nudged me and said: 'That's what you might have become.' It did not say: 'That's what you were.' It said: 'That was your danger.'

Purgatory in Ingolstadt grew out of the clash between my convent education and my encounter with Lion Feuchtwanger and the early works of Brecht; these couldn't exist side by side. At that time I didn't know Brecht personally, only through his early plays and the things that Lion told me about him. During this time Feuchtwanger was literally obsessed with him, his tongue ran away with him over his discovery, he called Brecht his pet poet.

Purgatory in Ingolstadt is a play about the pack-law amongst schoolchildren and about non-conformity. The schoolboy and this girl moved me more than male or female teachers moved me, more than schoolfriends moved me. Only my father had moved me like this, only my mother's death had moved me like this and the harsh treatment I experienced which took away my family when I still needed their protection after her death.

My six years of banishment in the convent with its barbed hooks were brought in here. Not being able to go where you wanted to go, not running into the country, not seeing the town when you felt like town, having to sit when you would rather not sit, having to be silent in the long corridors and stairways, having to be silent in the refectory until the matron gave permission to speak, not being able to wash one's feet when they were hurting, not whispering in the dormitory, even when one can't fall asleep for ages. On Sunday hearing about Father travelling over specially on a visit, but not seeing him because of being in quarantine in the sick-bay and although it was only rheumatism, being chased out the following day onto the communal walk, so the prohibition of the previous day revealed itself as nothing but bullying. Being dependent on the moods of women in an enclosed order, not being able to speak one's mind in letters, knowing full well every letter was censored. There was a girl there with me who was kicked out because she told me about Kleist's *Marquise von O* when we were in the crocodile.

The convent was a barracks or a prison to me. There was no escape into the outside world, there were only escape routes into one's head. 'Still waters run deep', as the Mother Superior rebuked me in front of the whole school ticking me off in public, and I didn't even know what for. She must have felt a black sheep was concealed within me, even if I was silent, simply because I was silent, so she tried to curb me, but couldn't. I knew then and learnt from it for later, fetters hurt the more you grapple with them. You had to forget them as an act of will, till the leaving exams exploded a way through to the outside world.

The outer constraint was what I most objected to in the convent, I pushed away the inner constraint from me, or so I made myself believe, and looked for escape routes in my head. And it was all round me like the air you inhale, you breathe it in, for people must breathe, there's nothing amazing about that. So, suddenly and in the hereafter, the religious constraints that I was permeated with broke out of me, without me knowing.

Therefore it became a play about implanted religion, which young people wanted to discharge like a foreign body, even though they drag it around within them the whole time.

I believe that this work was peculiar to me – an unredeemed, Catholic, small town scrutinised through the view from the big city and blown up, as the stage demands. The experience of young people, who have to search and not find for a long time, who err and stray as far as a death-wish – there is no one who can help them, they remain locked in themselves. They push away the assumed helper and have to do so, because they don't believe in the helper, the helper doesn't deliver the goods. This is characteristic of young people: in the play there is no authority. Olga's father thinks first of himself and takes refuge in his ailment. The young Roelle has never known his own father. His mother wants to sit on him, as if on some property, and repels him by this. The young people don't want to be told anything by these older people and rebel against them. They run without knowing where to and provoke the pack against themselves, and one inflicts on another what has been inflicted on him.

The young Roelle is a person who's all too easily damaged and who has to swallow his wrong-headed education. His non-conformity stems from the damage done to his soul. It is just these wounds that keep the unwounded away. The schoolchildren say crude things about him, and when they say 'he's smelly' that means, 'he gets up my nose', and when they rebuke him for his bulging neck, it is heartless exaggeration, they mean the inhibitions which seep out of him. They want to draw the dividing lines, because they feel something distances him from them, he is saturated with the power of imagination, he lives in his own stories.

I believe it's wrong to cast Roelle as an ugly person or as a horror who turns the audience off. Also his model wasn't ugly, he had reddish hair, a freckled face. He was just different. You have to be able to follow his fate, you shouldn't be turned off him. He's got nothing ignoble about him, he isn't a mean type. You must always feel the possibility that it could be different, if his inner shyness didn't outwardly isolate him. He can only shatter his shyness by force, it's got so far with him. He is not in himself evil. He is pushed to the limit so, through nothing but prohibition, he doesn't know what's what any more. If Olga hadn't kept pushing him away he'd never have got the idea of turning the knife on her. The desire to kill her becomes love-making here. This is the only possibility of consummation with her, because she doesn't let him do it any other way. Threats mean contact here. Threats don't mean that Roelle has a criminal tendency.

I only took it to Lion Feuchtwanger when I felt sure I'd completed the play. He read it the same day. I hadn't told a soul that I'd written it. In all those years I didn't change a word. I lost sight of it. It was my only copy I handed over. It was really remiss of me, because it went the rounds between people and could have disappeared, like my convent story, *My Friend, the Beanpole*.

'Shows talent, but rambling,' Lion described it and handed the play on to Bert Brecht, who had returned from a trip and, on the basis of the play, wanted to get to know me. 'If there is a way of putting it on, it's only through Brecht,' Lion said. Brecht on the other hand said: 'You must only get a contract for the play after it's put on in Berlin or you'll be speechless by the kind of contract they give you.' I had to go back to Ingolstadt. I couldn't support myself in Munich any more.

The play lay about in Berlin for the next eighteen months and wasn't even offered to a publisher. But Herbert Ihering read it, Moriz Seeler read it. It was obvious that Brecht would promote his own play *Baal*, which he couldn't place at a commercial theatre, but Moriz Seeler's *Junge Bühne* finally took the risk. In all this Brecht hadn't forgotten my play. After *Baal*, with Ihering behind him, he worked on Moriz Seeler to put on my play.

Seeler didn't want to at first, he had already promised to do the first production of a young man's unknown play. 'No, you're not doing the young man', said Brecht, 'you're doing the Fleisser.' The world collapsed for the young man, he went and shot himself through a lung – one of the things Seeler could never forgive Brecht for. I wasn't told before the production, I only heard about it later. Seeler changed my title. '*The Washing of Feet*, that's no title,' he said, 'no one cares a hoot about it.' So he put Ingolstadt into my title, I got stuck with the town.

I went to Berlin for the first production and lived with the Twardowskis, arranged by Seeler, Twardowski's son was in my play. I was so excited, the bed rolled about with me the whole night. But because mother Twardowski didn't like him playing the role of Gervasius, I bought flowers for her and moved into Helene Weigel's flat who was about to make a guest appearance, in Frankfurt, I think.

Paul Bildt with his strong cast made the first night a success. Maria Koppenhöfer played Olga, Helene Weigel, Clementine and Matthias Wieman the young Roelle, who climbed onto a chair to hang himself at the end. The applause lasted a long time. After those who didn't like it so much had left, it lasted a very long time and the person clapping the longest was the director of Schmiede, a publishing house that Ihering put odds on for me. So on the Monday he took me there with him, because he wanted to settle a contract for my play. Schmiede would have liked my play and me. But Schmiede had no money to pay me a monthly advance, and 'We're not doing it for less than an advance,' Brecht and Ihering agreed between them, 'after all, Fleisser's got to exist.'

I got the advance contract from Julius Elias at Ullstein's and this time Brecht went along with me. It was my very first contract with a publisher. I can still see Elias with his dark mane of hair above his powerful body and the way he haggled with Brecht who was able to flaunt my sensational reviews. Elias invited me to a meal, Brecht had warned me: 'He will want you to get his girlfriend a part in your next play, she's a young actress. Don't do anything about it, he tries it out on everyone, but she's hopeless, she's just an arse of creaking leather.'

I needed the advance urgently, I had no money for the journey home. Like almost all the performances of the *Junge Bühne*, the performance itself was a one off, on a Sunday morning lease in the Deutsches Theater, it brought me no money at all, but it brought notices. The actors, the director, the author, they all had to give their work for nothing at the *Junge Bühne*, it gave you a name in Berlin, because at that time a wide range of newspapers wrote about you. The performance was the starting pistol for me, with one bound I was at the literary heart of Berlin.

The playwright, who'd done the most work on a play, who'd had to hand over something irreplaceable from her very being, gave the most. She had to create it out of herself, all on her own, the difference was she couldn't feed off an existing text. And if I'd failed it would have been a real disaster.

I bought myself a pile of newspapers and carried my notices back up to Babelsberger Strasse. When I got back Helene Weigel was already sitting in the bath on the floor, snipping her own notices out of the same papers with a pair of scissors. Most exciting for me was what the two literary popes of Berlin wrote. Ihering and Kerr were at opposite poles on the left, all Berlin waited for their critical duels, but both had resolutely decided for me.

Brecht had prepared me for a stinker. As I came from the Brecht camp, he was surprised at Kerr's reaction. Although Helene Weigel thought she detected an approach by Kerr towards Brecht and pointed this out to him. Kerr, who first heard of me at this performance, and made my name into an Anna-Luise, wrote as if he didn't totally believe in my existence, or as if a couple had worked on it together, one of whom was Brecht. However, there wasn't a single sentence by Brecht in the whole play, there was nothing that could even connect me with his line of thought. In any case I got to know Brecht only after the play, it was my home-grown play. During the last rehearsals Brecht had, on the contrary, cut several sentences which lent it atmosphere, amongst which was one of the Father's monologues. I still know its ending today: 'One must get up in the night, that's to say in one's chemise, one must go to the window. We don't see God, having no sense for that.'

Brecht took great satisfaction in the ones who wrote badly about me, I couldn't understand that at the time. 'When they write badly, it's good for you, that must be so, because they're on the opposing side. What you've got to learn is, you mustn't please everybody. You've got to become as thick-skinned as an elephant.'

Helene Weigel was away, this was another day. Brecht displayed an inexplicable reaction to my success and deflated me, so the sudden fame didn't go to my head. I didn't understand a thing. He vigorously championed my play, he must have thought something of it. Brecht was a complete riddle to me and I headed straight back to Ingolstadt. I next saw Brecht in Augsburg where he spent the summer and then I followed him back to Berlin.

Brecht now tried to mould me according to his personal plan. That resulted in him taking my very own individuality and wanting to transform me. I was to become his useful tool. He demanded *Pioneers in Ingolstadt* from me, a big leap for me, almost beyond my reach as I knew nothing about soldiers. He confronted me with puzzling problems, gave me no human support. In the long run it wouldn't have worked, it would have snuffed me out if I'd stayed too close to him. I had to tear myself away, however hard I found that and however attached I was to him.

A way out opened up for me, a far too swift way out, that should have made me wary, I was crying out for some support.

A man wanted a close connection with me and threw himself into it with all his energies, whatever he stood to gain. The paradox about him was that he came from the opposing camp. But he was different from the national paper he wrote for. He waltzed off on his own tack too much and couldn't stick to it. Soon, all things financial for the two of us depended on me, my means didn't stretch that far. He was basically anarchic, in himself iridescent, but crossed by reactionary prejudices. My really hard time began with him: he ground me down, and after years of being ground to bits, I had to break away with the resolution of despair. It was a very difficult resolution, Hitler's Germany put the tin lid on it all and annihilated me as a writer, I had only a mouse-hole left. My talent was buried, I was completely cut off from nourishing springs, I was never even left the time to look for them, I was as shackled as a chained dog.

From 1950 on some theatres and publishers made an effort, but it didn't make much of a mark, I was still as shackled as a chained dog, I remained a hot tip. Why did it all head straight at me?

And yet I became an effective power. Much later on some young poets took possession of me, they declared themselves to me, they followed in my wake. They were blown along by it, making it into something new, they gave of their very own individuality along the wash they had learnt from me. They had the great success, a reflected ray fell on me, even when it hurt sometimes, even when I still wasn't allowed to live as a poet.

There was then no suggestion that the arch would stretch over me from my first beginnings to my declining days. The miracle started in December 1970. Suddenly the Wuppertaler Bühnen and its chief dramaturg Horst Laube dug my *Purgatory in Ingolstadt* out of its obscurity. They wanted re-writes in various places, then they would put it on. So the play was put on in Wuppertal, in Ingolstadt, well incidentally, at the Theater am Neumarkt, Zürich, at the Städtische Bühnen, Frankfurt and lastly it was directed by Peter Stein at the Schaubühne in Berlin, where it was also a success at the Theatertreffen. Recklinghausen staged it, Hamburg is in the process of doing it and some other theatres will follow suit.

Suhrkamp Verlag responded to a public proposal by Franz Xaver Kroetz in the *Süddeutsche Zeitung*. They published my collected works in December '72. Everything is now working together and bunching up together and being done at last, it is not too soon.

Marieluise Fleisser was born in Ingolstadt in 1901. Her first play was *Purgatory in Ingolstadt* (1924), at that time called *The Washing of Feet*. Her second play, *Pioneers in Ingolstadt* (1926), brought her into disrepute which made her life under the Nazi period extremely precarious. From 1923 she wrote prose pieces and plays, and Brecht produced *Der Starke Stamm* in Munich, 1950. She constantly revised her work – even though she was totally neglected for many years, if not forgotten. In the late sixties the new young wave 'rediscovered' her, with Fassbinder directing the first production of *Pioneers* for almost forty years – Kroetz played the Sergeant. Kroetz wrote an open letter to the German press which led to Suhrkamp publishing her *Collected Works* in 1971/2 in three volumes. She married in 1935, working in her husband's tobacco shop till his death in 1958. This was a childless marriage but she called Sperr, Fassbinder and Kroetz 'all my sons'. Marieluise Fleisser died in 1974. A fourth volume of posthumous papers followed in 1989.

Tinch Minter worked as a teacher, theatre administrator and recording manager before becoming a full-time writer. Her many translations with Anthony Vivis range from Botho Strauss's *The Tourist Guide* (Almeida, London), and *The Park* (Sheffield) to Manfred Karge's *The Conquest of the South Pole* which transferred from the Traverse, Edinburgh to the Royal Court, London, before being filmed for Channel 4 and published by Methuen. In 1988 she began her fruitful collaboration with Annie Castledine who directed the first play of Gerlind Reinshagen's war trilogy *Sunday's Children* at Derby. She has recently concentrated on new German woman playwrights, Gundi Ellert, Kerstin Specht and Elfriede Jelinek, who might be thought of as Fleisser's granddaughters.

Elisabeth Bond-Pablé, born in Klagenfurt, Austria, studied theatre and music at Vienna University (Dr. Phil.). Theatre and book critic and feature writer for German language periodicals, papers, radio. Writes and edits books and anthologies mainly on theatre, music, cabaret etc. She moved to England in 1970 and married Edward Bond. Apart from the Fleisser plays with Tinch Minter, translations include Kroetz's *Homework* for the Half Moon Theatre, London and, with her husband, Wedekind's *Spring Awakening* for the National Theatre.

Tokens of Affection

Maureen Lawrence

Tokens of Affection was premièred in 1986 by the Northern Studies Theatre touring production, with the following cast:

Annette Rushworth, *the head teacher*	Kate Lynn Evans
Nancy Mattieson, *her deputy*	Laura Cox
Gillian Leiver, *a new teacher, on trial*	Sarah Jane McKechnie
Andrea, *a new girl*	Naomi Wirtner
Debbie, *leader of the girls*	Liz Rothschild
Kelly, *her friend*	Anna Keeling
Liane, *a school-phobic*	Maggi Stratford

Directed by Annie Castledine

All the action takes place in a room in a centre for the education of violent or maladjusted adolescent girls in our time.

Act One

The ground floor of a terrace house has been adapted as a work-room: school desks, a table, chairs, cupboards, a dingy sofa and armchairs. Windows are protected by steel mesh. The scarred walls are bare. At the turn of the stairs a landing, glazed and meshed, serves as an office. There is a door leading upstairs, an outside door and a kitchen door, which is ajar. All doors are well provided with locks. It is a grey day in mid-winter and the main room is half dark.

Annette *is in the office which is brightly lit.*

Annette (*warily*) Andrea?

Andrea *enters from the kitchen.*

I thought you'd got lost. You'll not be on your own long. There'll be some more girls here soon. Then we'll have our dinner. We'll soon get you straightened out, eh? You don't have to wear uniform here. We have a right fashion parade every morning. Make-up. Jewellery. The lot. While we're on our own, just let me give you one word of advice. All you need to do to stay on the right side here is keep your nose clean. Don't be led.

Silence.

I'm just going down in the cellar to look at the boiler. If this lady comes, let her in and give me a shout right away.

Annette *goes.* **Andrea** *investigates the room. A gentle tap at the street door.* **Andrea** *goes back into the kitchen.* **Gillian** *enters.*

Gillian (*with misgiving*) Hello?

Andrea *enters.*

Goodness! You startled me. I am in the right place?

Andrea *goes to the office.* **Gillian** *follows.*

Is anybody else here? I wasn't sure if this was the house. There's no name – no sign outside.

Intimidated by this silence **Gillian** *retreats.*

If Mrs Rushworth comes, would you tell her I was here?

Annette *returns.*

Annette (*relieved*) Come on in.

Gillian I was beginning to wonder . . . You did say around lunch-time?

Annette (*breezily*) That's right. Nippy, isn't it? Here, give me your coat. We generally lock our things in the office. So? You've decided to join us after all.

Gillian I need the work. I ring the office every day, hoping.

Annette Well, you've struck lucky. There are just three of us here and if one goes sick, it's instant crisis. As a matter of fact, it looks as if it'll be a long job – hysterectomy – so maybe you've got your in – for a bit. It could even be for keeps. But I'm not promising anything at this stage, of course. Ever worked with this sort of girl?

Gillian No, not actually – but I must say it appeals to me, working one to one.

Annette (*lightly*) Well, so long as you've made up your mind. I can't do with being pinned down. I have to go to meetings and such – and I can't leave one teacher holding the fort. By the way, just for the record, it isn't always one to one. I mean we might only start with two or three, but every week I've got some headteacher or social worker on the phone pleading for a place. When we've got one broken in, we take another. And so on all through the year.

Gillian How many altogether?

Annette (*smoothly*) On paper a dozen. Luckily the numbers are down just now, so you'll be all right for a bit. This morning we've got two in court and our other one's gone to the hospital with my deputy. Then there's this new one.

Gillian Why is she here?

Annette Basically, it's because nobody else would touch her with a barge-pole.

Andrea Oh? But she looks quite – nice.

Annette You can have a skim through the records later.

Gillian What do you want me to do?

Annette Just play it by ear first.

Gillian The man said: violent?

Annette Don't worry – it's very rare they set about one of us. Just remember: if they start fighting never get in the way. Come on. I'll show you round.

Gillian (*nervously*) What happened to the wall?

Annette That? Oh! They've been picking at the paper.

Gillian It looks as if it's been raked by claws.

Annette Now you know why we keep the other rooms locked up! Here! I've got a bunch of keys for you.

Annette *goes into office for keys.*

(*To* **Andrea**.) How about you going down there and making yourself comfortable on the sofa, while I talk to Mrs Leiver? No? Well, suit yourself.

Andrea *does not respond.* **Annette** *closes the office door.*

Gillian Thanks.

Annette My office, would you believe?

Gillian Maybe she's shy?

Annette You want to bet on that? In a day or two we'll be wishing we could stitch up her lips. I keep my keys on a cord myself

and then there's no danger of them getting lost. We've had a few light-fingered villains here. Now then: this is the cupboards and this big one is the master key. Once they all get here in the morning, we lock up till home-time.

Gillian Is that really necessary?

Annette We never used to bother, but the girls are getting worse. We couldn't do with them screaming in and out all day, pilfering from the local shops and so forth.

Gillian I see.

Annette Any more questions? You might as well get it all off your chest now, before the music starts.

Gillian Is it just a holding operation or is it supposed to be a therapeutic community?

Annette What? (*Glibly.*) Both, I suppose. Come on. I'll show you round the house. It's fully equipped for life-skills. Nice kitchen.

Gillian Very nice.

Annette That's really the whole object of the exercise. Half of them have never known what it is to experience a normal family life. We do washing and ironing and all sorts.

Gillian I see.

Annette Tell you what: we won't fling you in at the deep end. We'll let you work with Liane for a week or two. Supposedly she's not a real nasty, she's a school-phobic. She's the one that's gone to the hospital with my deputy. You'll like Mrs Mattieson. I'm not one for organised religion but she's a proper Christian. She wants to save these girls. No, joking apart, she's got the knack. If you take a leaf out of her book you won't go far wrong.

Gillian A school-phobic?

Annette In plain English she's never been

in bother with the police. (*Chuckling.*) Well, she's never been caught – unless you count skipping school. It's an offence not to go to school, you know.

Gillian I see.

Annette You will do before long. Liane is no saint. Sometimes the cringers can be just as bad as the other sort. But at least she's little. Believe me once or twice I've felt inclined to put her over my knee and give her a good drubbing. Tubbing, more like. One of these days I'm going to get her in the bath-tub – with a scrubbing brush and a good lump of soap. Mind yourself on that step.

Annette *and* **Gillian** *go upstairs.* **Andrea** *heads for the street door but at a noise turns into kitchen.* **Debbie** *and* **Kelly** *erupt into room.*

Debbie They're not here.

Kelly Where are they?

Debbie How do I know, you daft cunt? I've just come in with you. (*Screeching.*) Mattieson? Rushworth?

Kelly That's not Rushworth's coat. Leave the pockets alone. You'll get us done. She must be upstairs.

Debbie They're empty anyway. Bitch! (*Expertly trying doors and drawers.*) Locked! Rushworth! Get your arse in here! We know you're listening.

Kelly I've got gut-ache.

Debbie Shut up about your gut-ache. You're getting on my nerves. This place is getting on my nerves. Where's the bleeding dinner?

Debbie *opens and shuts kitchen door, agog.*

Kelly What's up?

Andrea *enters.*

Debbie That girl!

Kelly What girl?

Debbie I know her. She was in the Assessment Centre last time with me.

Kelly You know everybody, you. You said you knew that lad that was with that Probation Officer, but you never seen him before this morning.

Debbie I go out with his brother.

Kelly You big liar! If you know her, what's her name then?

Debbie How do I know her name? It was ages ago.

Kelly Ask her. Ask her if she's coming here.

Debbie You ask her if you want to know. He was wearing one of them jackets with studs. That's how I know it was his brother.

Kelly Plenty of people have them jackets.

Debbie I'm talking about this particular jacket, thickhead. It had his name on in studs: Bullitt. He's in prison. I'm going to write him a letter and tell him his brother's nicked his jacket.

Debbie *goes into kitchen.*

Kelly (*shouting*) That's right, stir. Always bleeding stirring, you. You, what's your name?

Debbie *wheels in dinner trolley.*

Debbie Hey! Look, Kelly. They've fetched the dinner.

Kelly Let me see then.

Debbie Fuck off! Chips! Here stuff your gob and shut your face. Here, you. (*To* **Andrea**.) She won't miss a few chips. They send loads. We have to scrape the leftovers down the lavatory. Custard and beetroot all mixed up together, like sick, all sloshed together down the lavatory, like sick.

Kelly It's not hygiene. It makes you want to spew.

Debbie Here! Fritters! Catch!

Andrea *ignores* **Debbie** *and* **Kelly**.

Kelly (*outraged*) It stinks! I can't eat that muck! Why can't we have nice bacon sandwiches – instead of that fucking mixed-up muck? Debbie! Shut your mouth when you're chewing, you foul cow. You're sickening me off. I've got a pain in my gut. If that bitch won't give me any aspirin, I'm going to complain to my social worker. I'm off now anyway before they lock the bleeding door.

The office phone rings. **Debbie** *barges past* **Andrea** *and knocks the receiver off its rest.*

Debbie! Leave it alone! Let's go.

Annette *hurries into the office.*

Annette (*yelling*) Ladies!

Debbie *and* **Kelly** *freeze.*

Hello! Jean? How are you?

Debbie (*shouting*) It's me, Debbie.

Kelly Hello, Miss. Are you in hospital?

Debbie Have they cut you open yet?

Annette Get off! Don't be so stupid. She's speaking from a pay phone. I want to hear how she is before the pips go. Yes. Yes. Don't worry. It's all taken care of – we've got somebody. Just you concentrate on getting better.

Debbie I'll send you one of them get-well cards.

Kelly Ta-ra, love. We've got a new girl.

Annette Get off! Yes, I'd better. I'll be in touch.

Debbie She the new girl?

Annette Now then, what you two been up to? At the dinner again, eh?

Kelly Not me. I never touched the pissing

chips. They're all flabby and they've got bits on.

Annette Bits? I'll give you bits. Get those coats hung up. Come on, let's have a bit of order round here. Then you can tell me all about it.

Debbie I never touched no dinner.

Annette Never mind dinner.

Debbie She the new girl?

Annette Never mind new girl. I want to know what happened in court this morning?

Debbie What's her name?

Annette I'm asking the questions. Anyway, she's got a tongue in her head. You don't need me to be the go-between. Come on, love, in here now. Let's be having you.

Andrea *goes back into the office.*

I think somebody must have a bit of wax in their ears.

Kelly Ugh!

Debbie Hey! Deaf-lugs! We're having us dinner now!

Annette Since when have you been in charge of this unit? I hope if you're going to give the orders round here, you're prepared to carry the can?

Kelly What can?

Debbie How do I know what bleeding can? Thickhead!

Annette Never mind can. I want to hear about Kelly's court case.

Debbie What about the new girl? You never let us stop in the office.

Annette My turn to ask the questions. You've had your turn. Kelly?

Kelly Nothing happened.

Annette What does that mean – nothing? Debbie?

Debbie How should I know? They made me wait outside in this corridor.

Annette They didn't let you go in court?

Debbie I've told you once. I didn't fucking care. There was this lad. I go out with his brother.

Kelly It could be his mate. How do you know it was his brother?

Annette Just let's keep to the point a minute.

Debbie (*sullen*) Where's Mrs Mattieson?

Annette Well you may ask!

Debbie I am asking, aren't I? Christ! I'm not stopping here if she's not coming. I only do work for Mrs Mattieson. She's the only good teacher in this dump.

Kelly It is a dump. Look at the walls all peeling. Look at the floor – it's filthy!

Annette If it's a mess, it's a mess you've made, madam.

Kelly It's not me that makes messes. I keep my room good. I don't even wet the bed – like some people.

Debbie Shut up, Kelly. I'm talking. What's she done?

Annette Nothing good that's for sure.

Debbie She got a record?

Annette That's for her to say. How would you like it if I started divulging your secrets?

Kelly That means she has. You! You ever been in court?

Annette Not necessarily. It just means I'm good at minding my own business.

Debbie Fuck off!

Annette (*lightly*) Language!

Debbie I'm sorry, Miss. I haven't done nothing wrong except nicked a few measly chips. I'll set the table for you, if you want.

Annette You know the rule. If you don't get here before ten in the morning, you're not entitled to any dinner – unless I decide to be nice.

Debbie I'm off then if you're not going to give me no dinner.

Annette Fair enough!

Debbie I'm famished to death.

Kelly Shut up, Debbie. She was asking me something important about my business. About my business. But you have to go butting your nose in. We never went in no court.

Debbie 'Course we did – that was the courts where we went. That was where I went when I got done for shop-lifting.

Annette Was your lawyer there?

Kelly I don't know. There was this man there, but I hadn't never seen him before.

Annette Was he wearing a wig?

Kelly No, he was just a man with hair on.

Annette Well? What did he say?

Kelly (*irritable*) I don't know.

Annette Didn't your probation officer explain it to you afterwards?

Kelly Something about evidence. I told her they'd got my knickers, but she said that didn't mean nothing. He was all right with me was this man. He was kind. But he had bad breath. He kept leaning over the desk and breathing.

Annette Then what?

Kelly Nothing. That was the end.

Debbie Her social worker bought us a cup of coffee in this cafe. (*Shrieking.*) Mrs Mattieson. Mrs Mattieson. There's Mrs

Mattieson. She's got her new coat that her husband gave her for her birthday. Isn't she lovely?

Kelly MOVE! Let me see!

Annette Now then, that'll do. Come on. Move yourselves. Let me get locked up.

Nancy *enters, hugged by* **Debbie**.

Nancy How did it go, my love?

Kelly Don't touch me!

Annette Where's Liane?

Nancy I left Liane in the public library.

Debbie Why should you go to the library with that little rat?

Nancy Because I want a private word with you. Now, listen to me: this morning I had to go to the hospital with Liane with that hand. I want you to promise me that from now on you'll leave her alone.

Debbie I never touched her bleeding hand.

Nancy Never mind who did what. I'm just asking you to make a new start from today. Every day is a new day. You know that's how we work here. Put it behind you. Let bygones be bygones. All right? Why haven't you started dinner? Have you waited for me? I hope it's something nice. I'm famished to death.

Debbie (*hugging* **Nancy**) Isn't she lovely?

Nancy Who's this?

Debbie (*jealously*) We've got a new girl.

Nancy (*twinkling*) So I see! Hello!

Andrea *freezes*.

Annette Here. You two. (*Offering cigarettes and lighter.*) Go in the kitchen and have a smoke. Andrea? Smoke?

Squealing **Debbie** *and* **Kelly** *rush into kitchen.* **Andrea** *holds out her hand for cigarette.*

Nancy Come on, lovely.

Annette Just one thing. We only smoke in the kitchen here.

Andrea *pockets the cigarette and stays on the landing.*

Nancy Go on, lovely, with the others. You don't have to be frightened. This is not a nasty place. It's a lot nicer than an ordinary school. I know it's not easy coming to a new place, but you'll be all right in a day or two. There's only us few – we're like a family. Go and give yourself a chance to get to know the others. No? All right then, love.

Andrea *goes into office.*

Annette You'll not crack that nut with kind words.

Nancy Lighter?

Annette My crikey! I must be losing my grip. Lighter, please.

A hand appears round the kitchen door clicking the lighter with a gigantic flame. **Annette** *grasps the hand and prizes out the lighter. Yelps of protest.*

Annette Guess what? We've got a new colleague.

Nancy Really?

Annette Upstairs – reading the records. I'll give her a shout in a minute.

Nancy Well?

Annette She seems nice enough.

Nancy Problems?

Annette Well, no, not really. She's a bit – you know – plum in the mouth, but she seems genuine enough. Mind you, she may have had a few strings to pull. But we've nothing to hide, so we're all right.

Nancy You don't sound very sure.

Annette Well, assuming everything's above-board, the question is: can she cope?

Nancy What do you think?

Annette She must be a bit special or they wouldn't send her to us. I don't want to prejudge the woman. I just want to get things sorted for the next day or two. I'll keep Andrea with me.

Nancy What do you think?

Annette She's – different. Has she still got her head down on my desk?

Nancy I bet she's having a weep, poor thing.

Annette Weep or not, we're going to have our hands full if she decides to throw in her hand with Debbie.

Nancy Debbie's all mouth.

Annette Tell that to Liane. Anyway, for the time being, you go on working with Debbie and Kelly. See if we can keep that pair together. And we'll let this new lady have Liane. There are two more girls in the pipeline. If all goes well – well, we'll see in a day or two.

Nancy Am I reading you right? You're very worried. Go on. Tell me. It's either the new lady or the new girl.

Annette Both, maybe. The last thing we need at the moment is trouble. The Office would snatch at a chance to close this place.

Nancy I don't think so.

Annette I know so. Don't forget I'm the one that goes to the meetings. Cost. Cost. Cost. That's all I ever hear. Think of it from their point of view. You can just see the newspapers having a field day: three salaries to keep three girls off the streets. Look at the cleaning bills. The heating. I've just been down checking the meter. It's astronomical. Look at the decorating they've had to do this year. I reckon we only need one more fire like we had in that back room.

Nancy Money! They always want

something for nothing on the council. Come on. Get it off your chest. We haven't worked together for ten years without me being able to tell when you're not yourself.

Annette Has she got her ears flapping?

Nancy She's just sitting with her head on her arm. Something's going on in there.

Annette Something very nasty, I shouldn't wonder.

Nancy Just tell me from the beginning what's been happening. You know I always like to hear everything from rock-bottom.

Annette Humph! Home liaison. The social worker was supposed to be there at nine o'clock. I was there on the dot. It was a nasty district. These high-rise flats, high up on a hill near where they're doing that demolition. There was that terrific rain this morning and it was a blowing a gale.

Nancy So what happened?

Kelly *enters and slides into a chair.*

Annette Well, after a bit, Muggins decides to go in alone. I knock and she comes to the door in her nightgown. Andrea. On her own. In her nightgown. I ask you. It was a bit awkward.

Kelly What was it like?

Annette It was flimsy.

Kelly I like nice things.

Annette Pink. Yes. It didn't leave anything to the imagination.

Nancy (*lightly*) Little pigs!

Annette Here! Kelly. Go and share that with Debbie! We're just waiting for Liane and then we'll eat. Go on, while we finish.

Kelly *goes.*

Don't ask me what it was like – it was a pigsty. It would have turned your stomach. No mother and father. No social worker.

Nobody else there, just the two of us. Andrea and me. Right off it seemed to put us on a wrong footing.

Nancy (*sagely*) It was knowing what we know –

Annette She never said a word. I walked over to the window. I was up in the clouds. I thought: it's a long way down to the bottom. Anyway, in comes she, dressed quite decent and I think: ready. But no. She stands in front of the mirror. Make-up. I was watching her face in the glass and she was watching me. Behind me was the window. She started rubbing at her face with the back of her hand and lipstick smeared all over her chin. You could see she was getting mad, making a mess on purpose, drawing on big lips, a big red mouth on her face as if it was a mask. It was like a dark purple colour. What with rubbing and smudging her face was all enflamed. It was horrible. Grotesque. I thought: let me get out of here before she does something. I sort of slid round the back of her and I said: I'll wait for you downstairs, love, in case your social worker comes. I bolted down that stairway and I didn't feel safe till I was back in my own little car with the door locked.

Nancy What happened?

Annette Nothing. In the end I came back here on my own and eventually they fetched her, the Dad and the social worker. And she's been mooching about ever since. But when she first came in she looked at me so vindictive: it went right through me.

Nancy And she's said nothing?

Annette Not a dicky-bird.

Nancy It's only a question of time.

Annette This girl's not for our unit.

Nancy She's a nice-looking girl. Well, you've got to give them a bit of credit when they manage to crawl out of those places looking decent.

Debbie *bursts in.*

Annette (*fiercely*) Out!

Surprised **Debbie** *retreats.*

Nancy We'd better eat. They're getting hungry.

Annette All right. I'll tell you what, though. We could do with losing Debbie for a week or so, till we get this lot sorted. (*Mischievously.*) I shall have to see what I can do!

Nancy I hope you're only pulling my leg.

Debbie (*returns*) When are we having us dinner, Miss? It's time.

Annette Nay, Debbie. When is it not time with you lot?

Kelly (*entering*) They're too busy yattering, lazy bitches.

Nancy Shush, Kelly! Patience is a virtue. Table ready?

Debbie What's she doing in the office?

Annette I've given her a test to do.

Debbie Hey! You! Cloth-ears! We're having us dinner now. Is she fuck doing a test! She's a big fat liar.

Kelly You can always tell when people are telling lies. I always know when you're lying, Debbie. It shows on your face.

Debbie Do I go red?

Kelly No, but you bat your eyelids, somehow. I can just tell.

Debbie Is she eating?

Nancy Shall I give our other new lady a shout?

Debbie You what?

Nancy Surprise. Surprise.

Kelly What's she on about?

Annette Yes, just give them both a shout, Nancy. Wait a minute, Debbie. Keep your mitts off the plates. Come on. Hand it over.

Nancy Dinner, Andrea! (*Out by stairs door.*) Dinner!

Debbie What?

Kelly She wants your dinner money, you silly cow.

Debbie I must have lost it.

Annette Wonder of wonders. You know the rule: no money, no food.

Debbie Please. I'm starving. Just this once. I'll bring it tomorrow.

Kelly You're always fucking hungry, you.

Annette I think she must have worms. It'll do you good to fast, the size you are. No. I'm sorry. How can you learn to be responsible if I keep chopping and changing the rules every time you decide to pull a fast one? Come on.

Debbie *hands over money.*

That's better. Now look who's here.

Nancy *enters with* **Gillian**. **Annette** *doles out food.*

Annette This is Mrs Leiver. Debbie. Kelly.

Gillian (*smiling*) Hello.

Both girls burst into forced laughter.

Annette Take no notice, Mrs Leiver. Right. Let's eat.

Debbie What's your name?

Gillian Mrs Leiver.

Debbie I heard that the first time, stupid. Your Christian name.

Gillian (*glancing at other teachers for guidance*) Gillian Leiver.

Debbie You a social worker or a teacher? You look more like a social worker?

Gillian What's the difference?

Kelly Social workers are kind. Teachers treat you like shit.

Nancy That's a compliment, Mrs Leiver.

Gillian I'm afraid I'm a teacher.

Debbie You're not working with me. I only do work for Mrs Mattieson.

Nancy Debbie!

Debbie You married?

Gillian Divorced actually.

Debbie Actually.

Kelly Actually.

Gillian I've been at home for a long time with my own family, but now I'm divorced I've come back to work.

Debbie Your old man run off, did he? (*To* **Kelly**.) I don't blame him, do you?

Gillian It wasn't quite that simple . . .

Annette You're not eating, Kelly.

Kelly I'm not hungry.

Debbie Give it to me: I'll eat it. Here! You! Funeral-face! Don't you want your chips?

Gillian Go ahead. If that's all right?

The door bell rings. **Annette** *admits* **Liane**, *her arm in a sling.*

Liane (*shouting*) She fractured my hand she did, when she hit me with that mop. If she ever touches me again, my Mam's fetching the police.

Annette That's enough.

Liane All that yellow pus stuff was oozing out!

Kelly Shut up, Liane. Mucky cow, when we're having us dinner.

Annette Your Mother should have taken you to the hospital herself when she saw that hand.

Liane My mother was paralysed this morning.

Annette You mean she was having a nice long lie-in.

Liane She was having one of her attacks. She could only move her head.

Nancy (*joking*) Could she move her mouth, though? That's the main thing.

Liane It's not funny!

Annette Get on, now. I hope you're grateful to Mrs Mattieson. We'll know you're worth the effort if you learn to mend your mouth. Look, this is Mrs Leiver. She's going to work with you.

Gillian Hello!

Liane (*glib*) Hello, Miss.

Gillian (*kindly*) Is the hand really broken?

Debbie What you looking at me for, darling? I never broke her bleeding hand. I only gave her a little tap. She was getting too mouthy.

Annette Now you see where it can lead. It was six of one and half a dozen of the other. Let's have no more. Subject closed.

Liane (*accusingly to* **Nancy**) You said we'd sort something out. You said we'd talk.

Debbie Talk! You never stop gobbing it you. (*Grabbing* **Liane** *by hair and threatening with fork.*) Do you want me to stick a plug in it?

Nancy (*calmly*) Debbie, my love, haven't you learned your lesson? I was only saying to my hubby last night: my Debbie, she's a lovely girl. I wouldn't mind taking her anywhere and she'd do me credit. If it wasn't for the one big failing.

Debbie (*letting go*) What failing?

Nancy The mouth. Just think before you open it. Count ten before you say a word.

Liane But if you did that you'd never have time to get a word in edgeways.

Debbie That's the whole point, turnip-head. Anyway, it wouldn't work for you because you can't count up to ten.

Liane 'Course I can.

Debbie Go on, then. Count.

Liane I'm not stupid.

Debbie Who are you calling stupid? (*Grabbing hair again.*) Go on: count.

Liane One, two, three . . . Miss – she's murdering me – four –

Nancy (*very loud*) Debbie! Leave Liane alone.

Liane (*released, shrieking*) Me Mam's fetching the police!

Kelly Shut up about your bleeding mother! Some people haven't got no mothers, but they're not always squealing like you are. Anyway who wants a bleeding Mother? You never get nothing. You're miles better off in care. You get more things. You always look dead scruffy. You look like one of them tramps, you do. Like one of them idiots. Look at her feet – they're filthy.

Gillian (*softly*) That wasn't very kind.

Debbie Keep your pissing pipe shut, you!

Annette (*impervious*) That's enough. Settle down, Debbie. And you, Liane. Stop being such a moaning Minnie.

Kelly Don't you ever get washed at home?

Nancy Kelly!

Gillian Kelly's not eating.

Kelly I've got gut-ache.

Debbie Why isn't she (*Indicating* **Andrea**.) eating?

Liane Who's she?

Annette She? Who's she? The cat's mother? People do have names round here, even if they've got nothing else.

Debbie The new girl. She was in the Assessment Centre with me.

Annette Friend of yours, is she? Want to go and see if she's made up her mind to come and get some dinner?

Debbie No way.

Liane I'll go, Miss.

Annette No, you won't, Madam. If you go, you're liable to get the other hand broken. She's been told it's dinner time. (*To* **Debbie**.) You should make a right match by all accounts. You see Mrs Leiver, Debbie only likes fighting little people that are too feeble to fight back.

Debbie Ha! Ha! She better steer clear of me, that's all.

Annette How many big brothers has Andrea got in and out of jug? All very fond of their little sister by all accounts.

Nancy (*on cue*) Not so little, Mrs Rushworth.

Annette I should be surprised if she couldn't give you an inch or two, Debbie, though you're probably carrying more weight.

Debbie So?

Annette So think on. She's no little weakling. She could make mincemeat out of you, madam.

Nancy I'm still waiting to hear what happened in court this morning.

Gillian You were in court?

Kelly It's my business. I don't want no strangers pushing their big noses into my business, leaving their snotty trails.

Debbie Yes, it is a bit like a snail.

Nancy Kelly! Come on – eat up now.

Kelly (*pushing dinner on floor*) I can't eat this muck. I've told you: it's got bits in it.

Annette (*clearing up*) What bits? There are no bits. No wonder you've no energy, my girl, you eat nothing. Nancy, just serve the pudding for me, while I get a cloth.

Nancy Kelly, just a little bit of this nice milk pudding. Then you can tell us about this morning.

Kelly Nothing happened – if you must know, carrot-nose.

Liane (*spilling on sling*) Oops! I'm always having accidents, me.

Kelly We know that, darling. We can see what you have for your tea on your dress next day.

Debbie Is that your party-dress, Liane? I bet she goes to loads of parties. She's so popular.

Liane I like this pudding. We never have nowt to eat in our house except bread and beans and cornflakes.

Annette I'll tell you what we'll do this afternoon. We'll get Debbie to make us some nice chocolate crispies to have with a cup of coffee – on the house.

Debbie What? Me? Baking? I'm not doing no bleeding work in the afternoon.

Nancy Debbie!

Annette Fair enough. That's your choice.

Debbie What do you mean?

Annette No work: no tokens.

Debbie Fuck the tokens!

Nancy (*on cue*) Who's the boss? You or my friend?

Annette There's no boss about it, Nancy. It's cold walking home three miles in winter with no proper shoes on your feet. It could even snow this afternoon. Just remember: it'll be too late to come whining to me at home time.

Gillian Tokens?

Nancy If they behave themselves they get tokens for the bus.

Debbie Don't you even know what tokens are? Fuck me!

Gillian Of course I do, in general. I just didn't know about these particular tokens.

Debbie (*as to an idiot*) Little round tin things with a hole in the middle.

Kelly (*shrieking*) A hole in the middle. Shut up, Debbie, you filthy thing.

Nancy That's enough now. Before we start work I want to have a private talk with Kelly – about this morning.

Kelly Leave me alone.

Debbie Go on. You can trust Mrs Mattieson with your secrets. (*Quoting.*) She knows what it's like with her daughters and their problems.

Annette My goodness! I should hope Mrs Mattieson's daughters haven't got the same problems Kelly's got. By golly!

Kelly You tell her, if you're so interested.

Annette Who? Me? I'm to be the mouthpiece, am I? Too lazy to tell her own tale now. They dropped the case, didn't they? They decided they can't prove a thing.

Nancy But she was telling the truth.

Annette Truth!

Nancy She was telling the truth.

Annette They don't know that, do they? With her record?

Gillian What happened?

Kelly I must have told them about five times.

Liane (*pensively*) A girl on our estate got raped.

Debbie Keep your mouth out of it, you. It's got nothing to do with you. Did you tell them his name?

Kelly They knew his name. It was written down in a book.

Debbie (*excited*) Go on. What did you say first?

Kelly I said I got chatting to this lad down the Exchange.

Nancy He was a grown man. Twenty-five years old.

Debbie She knew him by sight. She'd seen him, anyway. He said she could listen to his tapes, so she went back to his flat.

Nancy Kelly, my little Kelly, you were playing with fire. What is the first thing a Mother tells her child: never trust a stranger. Haven't I tried to din it to you that you must have nothing to do with strange men?

Kelly I knew one of his mates. I thought: we'd just have a cup of coffee and listen to some tapes and then I'd go home. How was I supposed to know he was an animal? I wasn't scared. He was kind at first. It wasn't a very nice place. Dead rough. He didn't even have any coffee. No cups or nothing. He didn't have no proper furniture – just one of them big stereos. He let me look at his tapes. Then he told me to get down on the bed. It didn't have no legs or nothing – like his mattress was just on the floor covered with all these rags. I said I was all right standing up. Then all of a sudden he locked the door and he knocked me down and he put a pillow over my head and he tried to stick it up the front and then he turned me over and he stuck it up my backside and he made his nasty mess all over me like a dog on a lamp-post.

Debbie (*avidly*) Which was worst – back or front?

Kelly Which was worst? The pillow over my head, you daft cunt. How would you like to be half-suffocated? I thought he was going to kill me.

Debbie I bet he thought you wanted it. He couldn't be expected to know you'd never had it.

Kelly Well, I didn't want it. I'm a good girl, me. You'd take your knickers off for anybody for a packet of fags, but I'm a good girl – not mucky like you.

Annette Right, ladies. We'll have five minutes to let our dinner settle and then we'll start.

Kelly I'm too tired to do any work.

Annette Well, go and get rested then, while you've got the chance.

Kelly If you were decent, you'd put the kettle on and make us all a cup of coffee now, but you're a mean cow, you.

Debbie and **Kelly** *lie on sofa.*

Nancy It makes my heart bleed.

Liane (*chattily*) Have you ever been raped, Miss?

Annette Go on over there with the others, you.

Liane I'd sooner stop on my own. I'm not allowed to go with anybody that nicks.

Nancy Sh! Liane, remember what you promised?

Debbie What's she saying about us? Creep! Get your arse over here, Liane.

Liane No!

Annette Go! (**Liane** *hovers.*) Come on, Nancy. Cheer up! There's no point looking on the black side. Go, I said. If you start thinking about what goes on outside these four walls you'd drive yourself round the bend.

Liane Miss? I want to start work.

Nancy Two more minutes.

Debbie I'm dying for a drag.

Kelly I'm dying for a piss. Unlock us the door.

Nancy Please.

Debbie Only snobby people keep saying please and thank you.

Annette Kelly? Please?

Debbie Piss in the bin! Serve them right. Everthing's locked up – even the bleeding lavatory. They must be frightened we'll nick the bleeding paper. Nick. Nick. Nick. Let her go, you mean cow.

Kelly Please! Satisfied?

Annette (*unlocking.*) Make it quick. We're starting now.

Debbie As if anybody'd want to hang about in there. It's filthy. There's been shit on the back of that lavatory ever since we first got here. Somebody couldn't aim straight. It must be you, Kelly. You're the only one that's been here all the time except me and it's not me.

Kelly Don't be disgusting, Debbie. Come on then, if you're coming.

Annette Only one at a time.

Kelly I'm not going up there on my own.

Debbie (*wailing*) I am the ghost. I am the dead nun.

Nancy Come along, both of you, with me.

You know very well there's nothing to be frightened of up there.

Nancy *goes with* **Kelly** *and* **Debbie**. **Liane** *takes cards out of her bag and plays Patience.*

Annette Now it'll be half an hour while they comb their hair and mess about with the make-up. You might as well take your weight off your legs again.

Gillian What about the new girl?

Annette I'll keep her with me in the office for a day or two.

Gillian Isn't she allowed to mix with the other girls?

Annette Of course. But she's playing hard to get.

Gillian I see.

Annette She'll soon get tired of that game. Then she'll try something else.

Gillian (*intent*) Like what?

Annette Nervous, are you?

Gillian I'm not brave.

Annette You needn't worry. If they ever did start any rough stuff, we'd hit the alarm bell straight away. The police would be here in two minutes.

Gillian But –

Annette Our job is to get them to play the game – off their own bat. We've got a few sanctions and that's all. The tokens. The food. We use rewards – cigarettes, sweets. Even one to one we haven't the strength to start getting physical.

Gillian I was going to say: couldn't we try talking? Could I try? I just thought, my being new. It puts us in the same boat – a bit.

Annette Go ahead. Have a talk. Just don't go taking any chances. We're not paid danger money.

Annette *goes in kitchen with trolley.*

Gillian Andrea? Hello!

Gillian *enters the office.* **Andrea** *promptly goes out onto landing.* **Gillian** *follows.*

It's a strange place, isn't it? A school in a house. I'm not sure myself whether I'm going to like being here, but I'm hoping to make a go of it. I expect you think it's not the same for me, being new. And you're right, of course, but it's not that easy. You see: I haven't worked for a long time. I've been at home with my family. I've got two children, a bit younger than you – a girl and a boy. How old are your brothers? What are they called? You're looking at my ring? You like jewellery? I made it myself. I used to teach art and craft – we might make something similar, if Mrs Rushworth agrees? Would you like to try it on? No? Andrea? Why don't you come with me and meet the other girls?

Andrea *walks slowly downstairs. Since she is walking away from* **Gillian** *we cannot tell whether this indicates compliance.*

Annette (*returning*) Right! Let's get sorted. You can put your coat on one of those hooks by the door and you can use this desk.

Andrea *lifts the desk lid.* **Liane** *retreats.* **Nancy** *enters with* **Debbie** *and* **Kelly**.

Nancy (*pleased*) Hello! Andrea. Is she too late for dinner, Mrs Rushworth?

Annette 'Fraid so. Pity about the dinner. We don't deal in second chances here. No means no and a promise is a promise. It's very simple. Isn't that right, Mrs Mattieson.

Nancy That's right.

Liane Ask her if you can go to the shop to get something to eat. I'll come with you if you like.

Andrea *turns to* **Liane**. **Liane** *recoils.*

Debbie Look at Liane – she's shit-scared.

Kelly Look at Mrs Leiver – she's spastic.

Gillian I think chocolate buns were mentioned.

Debbie Pipe down, gas-guts.

Nancy Shush a minute. You see, Andrea, my love, you have to do as you're told here. That's the first lesson of the day. It's that or else.

Liane Or else what?

Annette Debbie knows.

Debbie Debbie knows what?

Kelly What's she bleeding on about?

Debbie How should I know?

Nancy I think you'd better spell it out, Mrs Rushworth.

Annette Yes, I think I better had. Right, Andrea. This is the end of the line. There is nowhere else to go – except a proper lock-up twenty-four hours round the clock. We have a nice carry-on here. We ask no questions. You've all got on the wrong side of life. Well, we don't go raking up the past. Everybody here is in the same predicament, so there's no need for calling names. There's no nicking because everything's locked up. You won't find a pencil out of place and everything broken is paid for in hard cash. So it's nice and simple. All you have to do is do as you're told and then you get your tokens to come and go on the bus and your free meal ticket – if you're on frees. Do you understand?

Andrea *goes to door.*

Debbie It's locked!

Liane (*wailing*) I've never been nicking like this lot!

Kelly It's no good shaking the door. It's got three bleeding locks.

Debbie She's forgotten the key-word.

Kelly What you on about?

Debbie (*striking a pose*) Open Sesame!

Kelly Put the boot in! I nearly broke my big toe. I couldn't walk for a week.

Andrea *tries the window.*

Liane She's going to smash the window.

Annette It's none too warm in winter without the glass, is it, Debbie?

Debbie Big joke!

Kelly We're all splitting our faces laughing.

Annette Well, ladies. Shall we start?

Andrea *faces the others, trapped.*

Debbie Start what?

Nancy (*on cue*) How about letting them have a bit longer to get to know each other? Then we'll start. All right, my love? Don't let me down, you two. Be nice girls. (*To* **Andrea**.) You'll be happy with us. Nobody ever wants to leave us in the end. We do interesting things. We have lots of treats and outings. You can smoke if you smoke and I expect you do. You know it's ruining your health, don't you? But our philosophy is this: it's in your own hands. You're not children any more. You're young women – old enough to have babies yourselves. Come on, Gillian. I want to get set up in the kitchen. I'll show you where I keep everything.

Liane No-o-o.

The three teachers go into the kitchen. **Liane** *squats on the threshold.* **Andrea** *stays by the window.*

Debbie I'm gagging for a fag. Liane, lend us your bag.

Liane No-o-o.

Debbie You got any money?

Liane No.

Debbie Go on. Lend us your bag.

Liane No.

Debbie (*to* **Andrea**) Got any fags?

Kelly Shut up about fucking fags. We're supposed to be getting friendly. You! Andrea! She says you've got three brothers. I've got a brother, but I've never seen him. He's been adopted by somebody. Me and Debbie live in this hostel in care. (*Pat.*) She's out of control and I've got nobody.

Debbie I used to live with my granny. The old rat-bag.

Liane Miss . . .

Debbie Shut up, Liane. We don't want to do no work. She went to the hospital. I smashed her hand. She went to the library. The pissing library. She can't even bleeding read. I gave her such a crack on the back of the hand. Now she can't bleeding write either.

Kelly When she eats, she dribbles. It drips on her chin and she wipes it down her dress. She's got bits on her skirt. Like bed bits. I bet she goes to bed in her clothes. Like little white balls stuck on her skirt.

Debbie Shut up about bits, you. You've got bits on the brain. They think she's so fucking innocent because she's never nicked. But she's a mucky bitch. I bet she's had it with loads of lads. I bet it's big enough to get a bus-load up. I bet she'd love that. She'd be begging for it.

Kelly You would, you mean. Look at you now! Look at her now, crossing her legs! You want to try keeping them crossed at night for a change.

Debbie *grabs* **Kelly** *and pulls her onto floor. They roll over, play-fighting.* **Kelly** *breaks free.*

Liane Miss . . .

Kelly (*breathlessly to* **Andrea**) That's a nice blouse. I like nice things. Did you buy it or

did you get it given or did you nick it? You can come with us round the shops if you like. Can't she, Debbie?

Debbie I'm not going nicking. If I get caught again I won't get fostered. I've got my review board coming up next week.

Kelly Will you still come here when you get fostered?

Debbie 'Course.

Kelly It's supposed to be a school, but it's all right really because they don't teach you nothing –

Debbie Lazy cunts! Stick a plug in it, Kelly. I'm tired.

Andrea *lights a cigarette.*

Kelly Two's up?

Liane You've got to go in the kitchen if you want to smoke.

Debbie Shut-up, Liane. Can you do that arm-wrestling? I'll arm-wrestle you for a fag. If I win, you give me a fag. If you win, I bring you one tomorrow. Agreed?

Liane Miss?

Gillian (*at door*) Liane?

Liane I'm lonely.

Gillian Try and join in with the others.

Liane No.

Gillian Just try and get friendly.

Liane Tell Debbie she's got to leave me alone.

Annette (*off*) Leave Mrs Leiver alone.

Liane Let's start.

Gillian Soon.

Liane (*shrilling*) She's got a lighter!

All three teachers surge into the room.

Nancy Tale-telling slit the cat's tongue.

Annette Come along now, ladies. It's time. What's this? Lighter, please?

Debbie *and* **Andrea** *arm-wrestle. Neither wins.*

Annette Right. It's a fair fight. I'm going to count to three and when I get to three, you break. Ready? One . . . Two . . . Three . . . Break!

The girls break. **Debbie** *grabs the cigarette packet only to find it is empty.*

Kelly Empty! You didn't beat her, anyway. She was winning.

Liane She's bigger than you!

Debbie Shut it, mouthy, or you'll get what's coming to you. We was only having a laugh, wasn't we, Andrea? Mates, we was, at the Assessment Centre. Isn't that right, Andrea? (*Shrugging.*) Suit yourself. (*To* **Annette**.) If we're good this afternoon, can we have a fag with our coffee?

Nancy Now, Debbie. You know better than that. We don't strike that kind of bargain.

Annette I might decide to be nice.

Kelly She means yes. Come on, Debbie. Let's get stuck in.

Nancy, **Debbie** *and* **Kelly** *go into the kitchen.* **Gillian** *starts unlocking cupboards.*

Annette Andrea, you're with me this afternoon.

Annette *goes into her office.* **Andrea** *remains standing.*

Gillian Let's see what we've got, shall we?

Liane *tumbles stuff out of cupboards: cloth, knitting wool, paints, paper.*

Liane (*agog*) Look at all this stuff!

Gillian (*politely to* **Andrea**) I think Mrs Rushworth is waiting for you.

Liane Let's clean out the cupboards!

Gillian Another day perhaps. Andrea? Andrea? If I were you, I'd go up and see what happened. I'm sure if you want to get out, the best way is to fit in – if you see what I mean. Believe me, I know how you feel.

Liane (*pulling at* **Gillian***'s face*) Miss? Talk to me!

Gillian Just a minute. It's your first day in a new place. Give it a chance. See how it goes. That's the best way.

Andrea *goes into the office and sits at the desk with her head on her arms.* **Annette** *works at the same desk.*

Liane You like her better than me!

Gillian Of course not. I don't know either of you. Tell me: what do you like doing?

Liane (*ardently*) I like cleaning out the cupboards.

Gillian Look at this mess. We'd better put some of these things back. Suppose you read to me from one of those books you fetched from the library?

Liane I don't want to read.

Gillian Please.

Liane No.

Gillian Suppose you read to me for a little while and then I read to you. How would that be?

Liane Uh uh!

Gillian Do you know how to read, Liane?

Liane Uh uh!

Gillian I see. Show me your book. (*Nonplussed.*) *Goldilocks?* Is this what you chose this morning?

Liane Go on, then: read.

Gillian 'Once upon a time there were three little bears . . .'

Liane *Goldilocks.* It's good. (*Archly.*) Do you think it's a true story?

Gillian What do you think?

Liane (*scathingly*) It's a fairy story. I'm only having you on. I'm not mental. Go on: read.

Gillian Why don't I find something more suitable?

Liane No.

Gillian 'Once upon a time there were three little bears. A Daddy bear, a Mummy bear and a baby bear – '

Liane (*snuggling*) Here, let's see the pictures.

Gillian All right.

Liane (*head to head*) It's all right. I haven't got no nits.

Debbie *enters, licking a spoon. Unseen by* **Gillian**, *she steals to the open cupboard and takes out a craft knife.* **Liane** *watches,* **Debbie** *mimes cutting her throat. She drops the knife into her own desk.*

Nancy (*off*) Debbie!

Debbie What?

Nancy (*at door*) Haven't I told you I've got eyes in the back of my head. Please?

Debbie What?

Nancy (*jokily*) My spoon, please.

Debbie I was only having a lick.

Nancy Get a clean teaspoon and then just pop a dollop in each case, please. Come along, my love.

Nancy *steers* **Debbie** *back into kitchen.* **Gillian** *uneasily checks cupboards, takes out paper and felt markers and starts cartoon.*

Liane Miss?

Gillian Mmm?

Liane Can I have a lift home in your car?

Gillian I'll see.

Liane That means no.

Gillian No, it doesn't. It means I'll find out if it's allowed.

Liane Can't you do nothing off your own bat! Please? She'll say no because she's a mean cow. And they're going to get me on the way home.

Gillian Listen. If you stop fussing, they'll stop too. It takes two to make an argument. Do you understand?

Liane I'm not daft.

Gillian Then why do you act daft?

Liane Everybody hates me.

Gillian Nonsense. I don't – for a start.

Liane Debbie put piss in my cup of coffee. She made me spew. She put that cold cream in my pockets. She squirted ink on my coat. She broke my flask. She stuffed my sandwiches down the pipes. (*Screaming.*) But if she ever – if she ever touches me again, my Mother's fetching the police!

Debbie *flings open kitchen door.* **Liane** *instantly subsides. Again* **Nancy** *steers* **Debbie** *away and shuts door.*

Gillian Liane? Liane, are you listening?

Liane No!

Gillian I'm making you a poster. See?

Liane They're going to kill me on the way home.

Liane *crouches in a knot.* **Annette** *leaves the office carrying letters and coats. She mimes posting, holds up a hand to show five minutes and taps her watch. She goes out locking door.* **Nancy** *enters at once.*

Nancy (*annoyed*) Where's the boss?

Gillian Gone to the post, I think.

Nancy Andrea? Do you want to come in the kitchen and give us a hand? I bet you're a genius at washing up with three brothers? No? (*Seeing open cupboards.*) Gillian, I should shut those cupboards if I were you. We won't be long now, before we have our little treat.

Nancy *goes.* **Gillian** *begins to tidy.* **Debbie** *enters.*

Gillian Come and help.

Liane (*sulking*) No.

Debbie (*disarmingly*) Here. Here. I'll help.

Gillian (*nervously bundling things back*) Thanks. Look at all this nice material. Do you like sewing?

Debbie (*offhand*) Give us your keys.

Gillian Keys? My keys!

Debbie (*snatching bunch in triumph*) Keys!

Debbie *flourishes keys, dancing about the room.*

Gillian (*pleasantly*) Keys, please.

Debbie You'll have to catch.

Gillian Come on then.

Kelly *enters.*

Debbie Here, Kelly, catch.

Kelly (*throwing keys*) Debbie!

Gillian (*nervously joining game*) Come on, Debbie.

Debbie (*taunting*) Catch!

Kelly Here, me, Debbie!

Gillian (*piggy-in-the-middle*) Here. (*Jumping in vain.*) Me.

Debbie You'll have to do better than that!

Gillian (*tremulously*) Debbie!

Kelly (*tosses keys to* **Liane**) Liane!

Liane *clutches keys, dithering, then with an*

imploring glance at **Gillian** *she flings the keys back to* **Kelly**.

Liane Kelly!

Debbie (*wildly*) Jump, Gillian.

Gillian End of game. My keys, please.

There is a lull. **Debbie** *has the ascendancy but does not know how to use her power.*

Debbie What's it worth?

Gillian (*grabbing*) No bargains!

Debbie Just you try!

Gillian Please?

Debbie (*throwing keys*) Andrea! Here!

Andrea *ignores the keys.* **Gillian** *goes on her knees to retrieve the keys but* **Debbie** *is too fast. She pushes* **Gillian**, *securing the keys again. Then she seizes a tube of red paint, taking aim.*

Debbie Ack-ack-ack-ack!

Gillian Don't, Debbie, please. That's enough. Just stop now. Please.

Debbie Please!

Kelly Please!

Debbie You going to stop me?

Gillian Stop it now!

Debbie Who's going to stop me?

Gillian Mrs Mattieson!

Debbie Feeble! Can't fight your own battles. Like Little Miss Muck-Mouth!

Nancy *enters as* **Debbie** *squirts red paint onto* **Liane**'s *white sling.*

Kelly Ugh! You know what that looks like? Jammy rags! It's disgusting. Liane! You've been a dirty girl. What have you been doing? Your fingers must have slipped in, you bad girl.

Gillian (*to* **Nancy**) Sorry.

Liane Sorry, Miss.

Annette *enters.*

Annette What's this? Liane? You been messing?

Liane No!

Annette Mrs Leiver?

Gillian (*caught*) I'm sorry –

Liane I never did nothing.

Annette Well if I can't get a straight answer. Let's not bother with the treats, Nancy.

Debbie (*seizing* **Liane**) Creep! Now look what you've done! Creepy, creepy crawly. Crawl then.

She seizes **Liane** *by the wounded hand forcing her to her knees.* **Liane** *faints.*

Annette Out of the way! Let me see!

Debbie Fuck me! She's paralysed – like her bleeding Mother.

Gillian (*very angrily*) She's hurt!

Debbie She's faking!

Nancy Let's get her on the sofa. I think it's a faint. She's freezing cold. Get something to wrap her up.

Nancy *and* **Gillian** *carry* **Liane** *to sofa.*

Annette Now what have you got to say for yourself?

Debbie It was only a bit of fun.

Kelly Don't look at me, darling. I've been good.

Gillian A bit of fun!

Annette Mrs Leiver? Who started this monkey business?

Gillian It happened so quickly –

Liane (*faraway*) Miss?

Nancy Shush! Just lie still a minute.

Annette Debbie?

Debbie That's right, blame me. We was just fooling about. She starts screeching if you look at her, that one. I want me Mam. Me-Mam-me-Mam-me-Mam. It was an accident.

Annette Right, Debbie. You've made up my mind for me. I was just wondering how you were going to frame yourself in the next few days. You need a change. When's your Review Board coming up?

Debbie Next week.

Liane Miss?

Annette Just a bit, Liane. Don't come wheedling round Miss. I'm taking you home in a minute and having a word with your mother.

Liane (*shooting upright*) I'll get battered if I go home early!

Nancy You should have thought of that before you started creating.

Liane *burrows and whimpers.*

Debbie What do you mean change?

Annette What do you think, Nancy?

Nancy (*on cue*) You're the boss. I shall be sorry to lose my Debbie.

Debbie What do you mean?

Annette Have they cleared up in the kitchen? Kelly?

Kelly It's got nothing to do with me. I've been bleeding good all day.

Nancy Just go and put those few pots in the sink.

Kelly *goes and comes back at once.*

Annette Now, Miss. Tokens, I think. Move out of the way, Andrea, while I get in my office.

Andrea *watches.*

Debbie I'll clear up if you like?

Nancy It's too late for that, Debbie. You've gone too far.

Debbie I never did nothing. It was an accident – sort of – accidentally on purpose –

Gillian Is it so funny hurting people?

Debbie It depends who's doing the hurting.

Gillian You knew she'd fractured her hand.

Annette *returns with a large jar of tokens.*

Annette Leave it alone, Gillian. Words won't work. We'll have to try a bit of hurt. We'll have to see how she likes it when the boot's on the other foot.

Debbie What do you mean?

Annette All in good time. Tokens, first. Liane, I'm taking you home, so you only need for the morning. Kelly, there. Andrea? Has she been behaving herself, Gillian?

Gillian Yes.

Annette Well, that's something. So? How many? Come on down here and work out your bus-fare.

Andrea *remains on the landing.*

Still no word. What can we do, Nancy, if she won't help herself?

Nancy (*on cue*) If she lives where I'm thinking, she'll need one-twenty.

Annette I know what she needs! All right. I'll be nice. One-twenty. You can thank your lucky stars Mrs Mattieson is a kind lady. Come on down here, blossom. I'm not running after you. You want your tokens, you come and get them.

Andrea *does not respond. After a longish wait*

Annette *drops the tokens back in the bottle and screws on the lid.*

It's no skin off my nose.

Debbie What about me? Please.

Annette (*giving tokens*) There!

Debbie But you've only given me enough to go home.

Annette And that's more than you deserve. I'm giving you a rest.

Debbie You mean you're suspending me? What about my review? Please. If I don't pass the Review Board, I won't get considered for fostering.

Annette It's too late. I never change my mind.

Debbie Please. I won't get a family. Mrs Mattieson. Please?

Nancy What can I do? How many times have I told you? Your life is in your own hands – to make or break for good or ill. That's the lesson you've got to learn, my love, regardless of what else.

Debbie Please?

Annette Nancy? I think it's about knocking on for home time?

Nancy Three minutes. (*Deferentially.*) I think we should spend these few minutes talking. Listen! How can we give you a good report at the next meeting if you constantly make trouble in the unit?

Debbie It was an accident.

Nancy But Liane keeps on getting hurt. Do you realise it's very serious? Her mother could decide to fetch the police. You have to think about the consequences of your actions.

Annette (*impatiently*) And I'm giving you time to think. (*Unlocking door.*) Off you go now, you two. You stop there, Liane, till I'm ready. Andrea, the door's open. Walk!

Nobody moves.

Kelly Come on, Debbie, love. Let's go.

Debbie (*desperate*) I'm sorry, Miss. I'll say I'm sorry to Liane. Don't make me go. I swear to God if you suspend me now, you'll never see me again. I'll go on the run. I'll go back on the game. Don't make me go. Please. Please. Please.

Annette Crocodile tears!

Debbie I'm not pretending. I swear to God I'm not pretending. It's my last chance to get a family.

Gillian (*moved*) Mrs Rushworth . . .

Debbie (*catching at straws*) You, tell her we was only having a game.

Gillian (*torn*) But you see – you were being a bully. If we hurt weak people . . .

Debbie (*fiercely*) Tell her it was only a game.

Gillian But I can't if it's not true. I'm sorry . . . It was a game to begin with but when you grabbed hold of her hand, you knew you were hurting. I can't condone bullying.

Annette That's right, Mrs Leiver. It's bully, bully, bully – all the way along the line. I've seen you on the buses – knocking old ladies out of the way. Spitting at the bus conductor. You're lucky to get tokens at all. You're not fit to go on public transport. You behave like an animal. Come on. Let's have no more of this play-acting. Stop this snivelling. I'll believe you mean it when you show me you can treat other people like human beings. Off you go now.

Debbie *stands her ground.*

Gillian (*low*) Debbie, you've still got my keys.

Debbie (*fuming*) You never said nothing when we was on our own. You daredn't do

nothing without them two other bitches to back you up, you old Granny!

Nancy Debbie, I'm disappointed –

Debbie Bitch! Get out of my way. It's all right. I'm going.

Nancy Wait –

Debbie *goes to door. She flings the keys down.*

Debbie I'm going to get you, Liane. If I fail my Review Board, I'm going to kill you. You won't know where I am. I might be anywhere. I might be waiting outside. I might be behind your door. But I'll get you in the end. Come on, Kelly. Let's go. Andrea? Are you coming with us or are you stopping in this dump all night?

Nancy *tries to prevent* **Debbie** *from going but* **Debbie** *knocks her aside and goes.* **Kelly** *follows.* **Andrea** *walks slowly after the other two girls.*

Annette Let her go, Nancy. Well, that's your first day's pay. (*Laughing.*) I think you've earned it today just for staying the course!

Gillian I feel terribly guilty –

Liane *tries to climb on* **Gillian**'s *knee.*

Nancy Little pigs! Later.

Annette Here. Go and get in the car, you. And don't be fiddling with knobs. Go on. It's all clear.

Liane *goes.*

Annette If I'd had my wits about me just now, I'd have staggered that parting. Never mind. With any luck Debbie'll keep her word and we'll be shut of her for a bit longer than a week! The game indeed!

Nancy You know it's true.

Annette Well then, she's got nothing left to lose. Nancy believes in redemption. I only believe in original sin. Anyway, I'm off! See you in the morning.

Gillian (*shaken*) I'm sorry. It happened so quickly –

Annette Oh! Fiddle-faddle! It's all in the day's work. We'll talk about it tomorrow.

Annette *goes.*

Gillian If Debbie really does run away, it's my fault.

Nancy No. The boss was just looking for a pretext. To give us a chance with this new girl. It'll give us a few days' grace. She's all on edge – the boss.

Gillian Why?

Nancy She thinks the office want to close us down – to save on the budget. She thinks this new girl is a test case – not just an ordinary naughty girl, but a real head-case. If we can't cope, we don't deserve to survive, so it's our jobs on the line. She doesn't really care about the girls. There! I've said it and I feel a right traitor. Because she's a good boss – she looks after our interests, but she only goes by the book. There's nothing in here. No feeling. I've just been keeping my fingers crossed, hoping and praying they'd send us somebody good.

Gillian But I've no qualifications for this kind of work.

Nancy Qualifications! It's what you've got inside here that counts. Just let me give you one little tip. Try to use their language. Get down to their level.

Gillian Down?

Nancy Now you're twisting my words. I know your heart's in the right place. I believe in my woman's intuition. You care. It's the caring that does the trick with these girls. If we could work it together, we could introduce some proper counselling. We need new blood. I think you'll be very good with the girls.

Gillian You really think so? I'm desperate for work and that's the truth.

Nancy I believe in this work. If I could have a few girls of my own, living together round the clock, I know I could work miracles. Are we ready?

Gillian *goes to door.*

Gillian She's still out there!

Nancy Who? Andrea! (*Calling.*) Andrea!

Gillian Why doesn't she go home?

Nancy Andrea? I wonder if she knows her way home?

Gillian Maybe if you gave her some tokens?

Nancy I can't go against the boss.

Gillian Shall I take her in my car?

Nancy No, it's not allowed. It's too risky.

Andrea *enters.*

Gillian Andrea, do you know your way home?

Nancy It's a long way on foot. Do you know where to get the bus? The number forty-two?

Gillian (*getting purse*) How much does she need?

Nancy No, wait.

Nancy *fetches the token jar.*

Gillian Enough for two journeys – today and tomorrow?

Nancy (*holding out tokens*) What about the magic word?

Gillian (*exploding*) Bugger the magic word! Andrea, it's home time. Here. Now go home. We'll see you tomorrow. Go home.

Andrea *goes. The two women look at each other.* **Nancy** *switches out lights and they leave. Quick fade to blackout.*

Act Two

Mid-morning in the same unit two weeks later.

Kelly *is sewing with* **Gillian**. **Liane** *is helping* **Nancy** *to make a chart.* **Andrea** *is in the office with* **Annette**.

Kelly (*yelling*) Mrs Rushworth! Come and look at what I've done good.

Annette Just you get on. I'll see it when we have a break.

Kelly Am I good at sewing?

Gillian Yes, you are good at sewing.

Kelly I'm good at sewing, me.

Gillian Maybe we could find you a job sewing, when you leave?

Kelly No.

Gillian Why not?

Kelly I'm happy when I'm sewing. It's nice and peaceful, sewing.

Gillian Yes.

Kelly (*musingly*) It's nice and peaceful without Debbie.

Nancy Have you seen Debbie?

Kelly No.

Nancy Kelly, don't you care about your friend? It's been two whole weeks she's been on the run. You must have heard something?

Kelly No! If I had, I wouldn't tell you. Shut up about Debbie! (*To* **Gillian**.) You do a bit now. I'm tired.

Gillian All right.

Kelly *continues to sew.*

Kelly I've done that good.

Gillian We could go down to the Job Centre and arrange an interview.

Kelly Shut up about jobs. Anyway, it's pissing it down. It's nice and warm in here. I'm not going out, getting me socks wet, stupid cow.

Gillian We could try getting you on a course.

Kelly You mean them schemes. That's slave labour. I'm no fucking dope. I'd sooner go on the dole. Anyway, I'm too tired. I'm going to lie down when I've just done this bit.

Annette (*at office door*) Is it time, ladies?

Nancy (*principled*) Another five minutes.

Balked **Annette** *retires. The radio plays. Peace.*

Kelly (*softly*) Miss?

Gillian Mmm?

Kelly Am I ugly?

Gillian Ugly?

Kelly (*earnestly*) Could a lad like me? Debbie says I'm too ugly. I don't think that's fair. I didn't make my own body, did I? It's not my fault. No. But I mean: could a lad, a lad that was decent, like anybody that was like me? I mean: I don't go fucking around like Debbie – except that one time and that doesn't count because I was raped – see? I didn't enjoy it or nothing like you're supposed to. What I mean is: does that count against me or can he say I'm just a slag.

Gillian Of course you're not –

Kelly No, but this lad – I mean if there was a lad. I mean to say: could anybody like anybody that was like me?

Gillian *reaches out a hand.*

Don't touch me! (*Roaring.*) Liane! Two's up! I'm gagging for a sodding fag! I'm tired. I want to lie down. Move! Liane!

Liane (*merrily*) Let me just finish sticking this! (*Archly.*) Me friend wants me.

Nancy Just finish that bit.

Liane I'm dying for a smoke.

Nancy I hope you're not going to get hooked.

Liane You're worse than me Mam. Whenever I try and cadge one of hers she says: you can smoke your bleeding head off if you like but you're not killing yourself with my cancer sticks. She's too stingy.

Nancy Liane! How can you say that about your poor Mother with all she's got to do with her bit of money? I know if you were my daughter, it would be a very different kettle of fish. You wouldn't wheedle round me, my love.

Kelly Liane!

Liane She won't let me!

Nancy Here's the glue. Just a dot. Then nothing oozes out on the paper. That's right. You're learning. (*Pleasantly.*) We'll lick you into shape.

Kelly Come on, you miserable cow. Let her have a break.

Gillian (*softly*) Kelly!

Kelly Kelly!

Gillian Just another minute.

Kelly Just another minute! Shit-house!

Nancy All right! That's quite enough. We'll have a short break now because it's time on my watch. Mrs Rushworth! Break! Go on then, you two. Make up your minds.

Kelly and **Liane** *go into the kitchen.* **Annette** *emerges from office with newspaper.*

Annette Come on, Andrea. In the kitchen with the others. You can give up writing now.

Andrea *goes on writing.*

All right. Stop there then. (*Closes office door.*) I've got some news for you, ladies.

Nancy Oh?

Annette We've got a visitor.

Nancy Debbie!

Annette She's round the back. In the shed. I've just caught sight of her out of the window. She dodged back under, but she's just waiting to be seen. She looked like a drowned rat.

Nancy Thank goodness! Shall I go?

Annette Let's keep her on pins for a bit.

Nancy In this weather – ?

Annette It's not our funeral if she catches her death!

Gillian (*anxious*) What happens now?

Annette Let's just hold on a minute. Nancy, what are we going to do about this other one?

Nancy What's she doing?

Annette English language. She's filled that book.

Nancy I'm not happy. It's not right to be keeping her on her own.

Annette It's not my doing.

Nancy I know that. I wasn't casting nasturtiums.

Annette I should hope not. Everything all right down here?

Nancy Liane's been a little angel.

Annette (*shortly*) I always maintained Liane was no bother on her own.

Nancy Do you feel you're making any headway at all?

Annette It's like talking to a blank wall. Two weeks she's had me pinned down and we're getting nowhere fast.

Nancy This is not my boss talking.

Annette I'm going to have to ring the

office. There are two more girls in the pipe-line, but I can't accept anybody else till we've got this one sorted.

Nancy You'll just have to play for time.

Annette We need the numbers. How can we justify our existence if we can't cope with what we've got? It's diabolical. Have you seen last night's paper? Here! Debbie!

Nancy I thought they weren't allowed to advertise for minors?

Annette Well, there she is – large as life, hair like a haystack. If the girls see that, they'll all be wanting to get their faces in the paper. Fame! By crikey! That's what's flushed her out of hiding.

Gillian How do you mean?

Nancy Somebody'll have threatened to shop her to the police.

Annette Next thing we know we'll have the press sniffing round here for a story. Well, Nancy, what are we going to do about Andrea? Do I get rid or what?

Gillian But she hasn't actually done anything.

Annette Would you want her in the room with you on your own? Take next week when I've got a Head-Teachers' meeting. Nancy might want to go out shopping with the others. Every time you turned your back you'd be wondering. Isn't that right, Nancy?

Nancy If only we knew what she was thinking!

Annette She knows she's keeping us guessing.

Gillian But suppose she's just desperately unhappy?

Nancy It's not as if she's shown us any aggro.

Annette It depends on what you mean by aggro. Dumb insolence is what I'd call it if I was looking for a word.

Gillian But there must be a reason.

Annette There might be fifty good reasons but that's not our department. (*Strategically.*) All right. We'll just have to play this one by ear. Nancy, you go and see if you can catch sight of Debbie out of the kitchen window and you keep an eye on the other two, Gillian, while I see what I can do.

Nancy and Gillian go. Annette goes to office. Andrea goes onto landing. Annette follows.

Annette Just a minute, Andrea. By the end of this day I want you to tell me whether you want in or out – in your own words. Listen, love. If it was just you and me, it wouldn't matter. You'd have something to say to me in the end. You wouldn't get the better of me. But it's not that simple. There are other girls here and they all need help. It's no good filling that book with beautiful writing. You've had your chance to do beautiful work in school and you've blown it. This is the real nitty-gritty, Andrea. This is what it's all about underneath all the trimmings. It's about toeing the line. Am I making myself plain?

*Silence. Thwarted, **Annette** is interrupted by a thundering knock at the street door. Everbody crowds round except **Andrea**.*

Nancy Calm down, everybody!

Kelly It's the police!

Annette (*Unlocking*) Mind!

Liane Nobody there.

Kelly Let me see!

Annette Go and have a look round the back, Nancy. She's more likely to come in for you.

Kelly It's Debbie!

Nancy *goes.*

Annette Gillian, keep them in the kitchen a minute. (*Giving cigarettes.*) Here, you two. Just go and keep out of the way while we're busy.

Gillian *and the two girls go.* **Debbie** *is ushered in by* **Nancy**.

Debbie (*shivering*) I'm perished.

Annette At last! Look what the tide's washed up. Now before you go flying off the handle, let me ask you one question: have you had enough freedom?

Debbie *shrugs.*

Have you come to talk to Kelly?

Debbie Nothing to do so I thought I'd come and cadge a cup of coffee.

Nancy No money?

Debbie No.

Annette Just let's get one thing straight. You do realise I'll have to tip off the police you've been seen?

Debbie Suit yourself.

Annette I have go to by the book.

Debbie So?

Annette Just so long as that doesn't make me the nasty in five minutes time. I'll do it now, Nancy.

Nancy Can we find her some dry clothes somewhere?

Andrea *watches from the landing.*

Annette In that big cupboard. Not much fun being on the run in winter, is it, Debbie? Just stop there a minute, Andrea, while I use the phone.

Debbie What's she looking at?

Nancy (*peeling off wet clothes*) Don't start before you've even got your foot in the door. What's this? A new coat and shoes, ruined in the rain. Did you nick them?

Debbie (*lying*) I swapped them with this lass. My corns are killing me.

Nancy Where've you been sleeping?

Debbie This lass till last night. (*Proudly.*) Did you see my picture?

Nancy You look terrible. Who's been messing with your hair?

Debbie It's that spray stuff that washes out easy. What happened about my Review?

Nancy (*drying hair*) Debbie! Debbie! Debbie! That's gone up the spout now, hasn't it? You've no chance of a nice family taking you on, if you can't prove yourself worthy. If you go on the run every time you have a little tiff. Every time you've got a grudge. Every time you get a bit bored. Can you just imagine a nice lady, a nice kind motherly lady – sitting there on the edge of her chair at midnight waiting for the phone to ring wondering whether you've been knocked down or strangled or just done a bunk? Why did you do it, if you wanted a placement?

Debbie I don't know. I went to this lass's flat and it got late and I missed the bus so I set off walking and I just didn't fancy it at that time of night on my own so I went back again.

Nancy You could have phoned. Somebody would have fetched you.

Debbie There was no phone.

Nancy There's always a phone somewhere.

Debbie I was too tired to find a fucking phone.

Nancy What about the next morning? You weren't too tired then. And the next. And the next . . .

Debbie Can I go in there and talk to Kelly?

Nancy (*disappointed*) Ask my boss.

Annette (*offering clothes*) You're not using me as a convenience, Debbie. If you stop, you stop for good and I hand you over at the end of the day. Is that understood? Gillian! We'll sit in the office. Go on, Andrea. Down!

Andrea *still stands on the landing.* **Annette** *and* **Nancy** *go into the office.* **Gillian** *enters with* **Liane** *and* **Kelly**.

Debbie (*dressing*) I might just as well be in a bleeding cell. There's nowhere else to go.

Gillian (*nervously*) Hello, Debbie.

Debbie What you doing here?

Gillian I'm very pleased to see you still in one piece.

Debbie I bet.

Gillian I was very worried.

Debbie So? What do you expect me to do about it? Cut my throat?

Gillian I felt responsible after that afternoon.

Debbie What's she on about?

Gillian I hope that now you've come back we'll be able to start afresh . . .

Debbie (*at large*) What's she wittering on about? We don't need a sermon, darling. If we want a preacher we can go to church. Hey! Kelly! I nearly did go to bleeding church but the fucking front door was locked.

Kelly (*jealous*) I thought you was staying with that Angie.

Debbie She chucked me out last night, didn't she? For knocking off her old man. I thought morning was never going to get here.

Gillian Debbie –

Debbie Look! Scram, will you? I want to talk to my friend. I haven't seen her for a fortnight. Go on.

Debbie *stamps and* **Gillian** *recoils.* **Debbie** *cackles.*

Liane (*confidingly to* **Kelly**) She sounds like a laughing hyena.

Debbie (*whirling to face* **Liane**) Come again?

Liane My mother's got a laugh like that when she's had a few drinks.

Kelly (*reluctantly curious*) What was his name?

Debbie (*concentrating on* **Liane**) Who?

Kelly This chap that you knocked off.

Debbie Oh! Him. He was nobody. (*To* **Andrea**.) Got any fags?

Liane (*nudging* **Kelly**) Let's go in the kitchen and have a smoke.

Debbie What you doing smoking?

Liane (*proudly*) I smoke now. Miss gives us fags. I haven't got none of my own.

Debbie (*reaching*) Two's up.

Kelly (*implacably*) I'm two's up with Liane.

Balked **Debbie** *goes to sofa and looks at her feet.*

Debbie (*to* **Andrea**) What are you staring at, darling? Haven't you never seen feet before? Is she deaf and dumb – or just daft?

Liane She never says nothing all day.

Debbie What does she do?

Kelly She stops in the office.

Debbie Why?

Kelly How should I know? Did you go nicking with that Angie?

Debbie What if I did?

Kelly Where did you get them shoes?

Debbie They're too tight. Hey, you, Andrea! I'll swap you these slip-ons for a fag.

Kelly (*drawn*) We thought you wasn't coming back no more.

Debbie Nothing else to do is there? Nowhere else to go. Anyway I got fed up. They never had nowt to eat, did they?

Kelly How should I know? She never invited me to stop at her flat. I thought you was my mate.

Debbie I am your mate.

Kelly Very funny! How can we be bleeding mates if we're not together?

Debbie Anyway, believe what you want. It's your lookout.

Kelly (*tempted*) What did you do?

Debbie Stopped in bed.

Kelly I know. Dossed in the morning. Nicked in the afternoon. And fucked at night. No different from normal. You might as well come back home – at least you get nice bacon sandwiches.

Debbie I could just eat a great big plate of stew with loads of carrots and gravy and them dumplings.

Liane (*fervently*) I hope it's not fish fingers. I hate fish fingers. They never give us enough.

Debbie Who asked you for your opinion?

Kelly (*reminiscent*) The cops came asking. Carrot-nose went to the door and said to this lad: you can't come in here, lovely. He flipped open his wallet and he said: Vice Squad. Vice Squad! She looked really surprised. She said she thought he was one of my boy-friends – he looked so young. He was fit.

Liane (*echoing*) He was fit.

Debbie What did you tell him?

Kelly I never told him nothing. I'm no grass. It's been nice here. Nice and quiet without you. Mrs Leiver is teaching me to sew. I'm making a blouse out of some white stuff out of that cupboard.

Debbie (*recalling*) Fuck me! What happened to my desk? My things in my desk.

Debbie *barges across and investigates her desk. She takes out the craft knife and begins to pare her corns.*

Kelly Ugh! Look at your toes all twisted. Ugh!

Debbie (*contentedly*) Shut up, Kelly. I'm trying to see what I'm doing. Ouch! Now I've cut the top off that corn. (*She scratches on the desk top with the knife.*)

Kelly She's nice is Mrs Leiver. She's got a nice quiet voice. We've been good without you.

Liane (*whispering*) Have we to get on with us work? Come on. Let's do it. Tell Miss. Miss?

Liane *makes for office, veering away from* **Debbie** *but* **Debbie** *causes her to stumble. She recovers and freezes.*

Kelly Leave her alone. She's not doing anything to you, you big thing.

Debbie I never tripped her up. Did I do anything?

Liane *hangs her head, tugging at* **Kelly**.

Kelly Don't touch me! I can't stand being touched. Leave her alone.

Liane Come on. Never mind.

Kelly All right. But I stick up for my mates.

Debbie Just look. She's shit-scared. Go on. Boo!

Kelly Leave her alone, Debbie.

Debbie Who's going to make me? You? That's a joke!

Liane (*whimpering*) Miss . . .

Debbie *lunges at* **Liane**, *but instantly* **Kelly** *hurls herself at* **Debbie**. **Debbie** *and* **Kelly** *fight. The three women rush to the scene but do not intervene. At last* **Kelly** *wriggles free and rushes for cover. It takes all three women to hold* **Debbie**.

Debbie (*shrieking*) I'll kill her. I'll kill her. I'll kill her.

Andrea *slowly moves down the stairs from the office.*

Annette (*breathlessly*) Andrea – get back in that office. Gillian, see if Kelly's hurt.

Liane Of course she's hurt. That bitch!

Annette That's right, mouthy. Why didn't you stick up for her, then?

Gillian Get up, Kelly. Let me look.

Debbie Don't let her come near me again. I'll kill her.

Annette That's enough!

Debbie She started it. Nobody picks on me. Nobody falls out with me for that stinking little rat. (*To* **Liane**.) You stink, you do! You stink! You! Kelly! I bet you made it up about that rape. Who would want to rape you, you ugly little cunt.

Kelly (*seizing a chair*) Say that again!

Nancy Kelly. Put down that chair. Debbie's not going to say that again. She's not going to hurt you.

Annette Kelly. Put down that chair. Unless you want another fight.

Kelly *hangs on to the chair.*

All right, Mrs Mattieson. Let Debbie go. We're not putting ourselves out for somebody that doesn't know how to do as she's told. We'll soon see who's boss.

Kelly (*hurling down chair*) Give me my tokens. I'm not stopping here now. I'm finished.

Annette No tokens for bad behaviour. I don't know who started this but I do know who is going to have the last word. You can all simmer down. Right! That's better. Now we can hear ourselves think. Decisions. Decisions. We try to give you some time to yourselves but each time you blow it, so there'll be no more breaks for a while. It's got to be nose to the grindstone. Liane! We may as well get one thing straight, now it's come out in the open. You do smell. I recommend soap and water for openers, so you may as well get started on that right now. (*She unlocks stairs door.*) You, too, Kelly. Mrs Leiver is going to bathe that eye – touch or not – before it swells up and makes you look a sight. (*They go.*) Andrea? Andrea's still not talking but she's on the prowl. All right then. Prowl, but just keep your hands to yourself and your mind on your own business. Just remember: you've got some thinking to do because you've got something to tell me before you leave here today. Now. Let Debbie go, Nancy. I want a word with her in private.

Debbie (*opening fist*) Hair! Look! Christ Almighty!

Annette Proud of yourself, are you? Still full of fight? Already forgotten we did you a big favour letting you come in out of the cold? Don't like the smell of dirty knickers, eh? Well, I've got some news for you. News, yes. In my office, lady. Lucky we didn't take that attitude to dirt when you came scratching at the door. We might have been frightened of catching something, but we decided to be charitable, didn't we, Mrs Mattieson?

Nancy We did.

Debbie What's she on about?

Annette We try to play fair. We try not to

show girls up, humiliating them in front of other girls. People in glass houses, Debbie. Postcard came for you a few days ago. No wonder we got the wind up. Come on. We've got some telephoning to do, you and me.

Nancy It's serious this time, lovey. It could be a matter of life and death.

Debbie (*frustrated*) What you both on about?

Annette Life and death, Debbie. It just says: Debbie and the name of the unit. No second name but you're the only Debbie we've got around here, so somebody has done you a big favour that doesn't even know your name.

Debbie *goes into the office.*

Nancy, just you try having a word with our other lady. I'm getting nowhere in a hurry. I must be losing my grip. I'm going to have to ring the office.

Nancy I'm not happy. We need to talk first.

Annette We'll talk about it later when we're on our own. Just have a quiet word for now. (*Slyly.*) You know you've got the knack.

Annette *goes with* **Debbie** *into the office.* **Nancy** *goes to* **Andrea** *who shifts at each approach.*

Nancy Andrea? There you are. I'm glad you've decided to come out of your shell a bit. I don't like to see you stuck in the office on your own all the time. Let's make a really special effort from now on to help each other. That's how we work here. Debbie's had a rough time and she's going to need a lot of support from us all. I wish you'd say something. At the back of my mind I've got an idea you might just be having us on – you know – taking us for a ride, laughing at us up your sleeve. Well, it's not funny, lovey. It's very serious. You've got to join in with us, otherwise it's

a no-go area. There's nothing we can do without you. It's in your hands. I wish I could make you understand. You see: I believe we were put on this earth to help other people. There are no good people and bad people. There's good and bad in every single person. And we all make mistakes. We all fall. Life is a struggle, my love. It's so easy to fall. So many temptations. So much danger. So many pitfalls. We're not trying to make things hard on you, but you're making it hard on yourself. You're punishing yourself. I wish you could talk about whatever it is that's eating you. Because that's what's happening: and the longer you keep it to yourself the more eaten up you're going to be. Do you understand me, Andrea? Am I making sense to you at all? (*Disappointed.*) Look! It's your choice. I'm going in the kitchen and I'm going to make us all a drink and I want you to come to me and give me a hand. All right?

Nancy *goes.* **Andrea** *prowls. She finds the craft knife, tests the blade and with one or two swift strokes mutilates* **Kelly** '*s sewing. She is still holding the knife when* **Liane** *enters.*

Liane (*involuntarily*) Debbie nicked that knife off Mrs Leiver. It goes in the cupboard. Now she's come, she'll try and get Kelly back. I'll be on my own again. I never had a mate of my own. Even at home. They all pick on me. It's because I look like my Dad. When they sent me away to that school, my Mother never meant for me to come back. She burned my bed. She took it out in the yard and burned everything. You can see where she did it – the bits that wouldn't burn just got left there. I said: you expect me to fucking sleep in the yard on a bunch of burnt rags and she hit me across the mouth. I don't care. I lie on the sofa and watch telly all night till it wakes me up with that whining it makes. (*Pause.*) Debbie won't touch you: you're big. You've got brothers. Do you talk to your brothers? My Mam gets like, paralysed. Stiff as a board. We have to lug her onto the lavatory, me and our June. It was all right here without Debbie. Better than stopping in the house. Are you miserable? Why don't you say nothing? My Mother says I never stop yapping. How do you stop yourself yapping? My Mother says she's going to put tape on my lips. Andrea? It's miles better here than at school. I'm never going back to no school. If them in schools knew what it was like when you get expelled they'd all be getting expelled. Schools would be empty. Teachers would be out of work. You won't get me nowhere near. You think when you hear that word expelled it means something terrible, but it's a big con. Me, first of all I had a holiday for seven weeks and then I ended up in this place. Our June, that's my sister, the one that's pregnant, our June says: trust you to fall on your feet. My Mother says: better to fall on your feet, our June, than flat on your back with your legs wide open. Andrea? Can you hear me? If Debbie gets Kelly back, you could ask Mrs Rushworth if you could be with me? Andrea?

Nancy *enters with a tray of cups. She offers a cup to* **Andrea** *who takes the cup and drinks.*

Nancy (*pleased*) Come along now. That's right. Sit down.

Andrea *sits.*

Let's all have a drink. Stop fiddling with your bag, Liane. You know you're liable to spill if you try to do two things at once.

Liane I'm just getting my cards. (*To* **Andrea**.) Play patience?

Nancy I know: let's all play a game, while we have our break. (*Unlocking cupboard.*) You choose a game.

Liane *pulls out games.* **Gillian** *and* **Kelly** *enter.* **Kelly** *hides her face.*

Gillian (*softly*) Now what?

Nancy (*warningly*) Sh! Later. I've had a word.

Gillian (*eagerly*) And?

Nancy (*unhappily*) I've told her I'm not happy.

Gillian What did she say?

Nancy Nothing. She knows we've been talking. (*Defending.*) But when it comes to the crunch somebody's got to draw the line. They need that control. Would you like to be in her shoes?

Liane Whose shoes?

Nancy I thought you were finding us a game?

Liane (*archly*) I'm going to tell Miss you're talking about her behind her back. (*Singing out.*) Miss! Only joking, Miss. Can we play Ludo?

Nancy (*resolutely*) Ludo. Come on, Kelly. We're going to be together now.

Kelly I want to sew my blouse.

Gillian *rises.*

Nancy Sit down, Mrs Leiver. She's not sewing now.

Kelly I'm not playing no fucking babies games.

Liane Don't be mardy. Just because you can't have your own way.

Nancy Pearls of wisdom.

Gillian We need four players.

Nancy Andrea? Come on, love.

Andrea *hides her head on her arms.*

Gillian Choose a colour.

Kelly You haven't told us what to do yet.

Gillian (*unwarily*) You don't know how to play Ludo?

Nancy (*hastily*) Tell us all.

Gillian It's a game for four players. You each choose a colour. See, this is your base, Kelly. Andrea, you want red or blue?

Gillian *dishes out counters.*

You have to throw a six to start. Let's play and I'll show you as we go along. There, Kelly. No good. Now, Nancy. Then me. And then Liane. Now Kelly again. Keep trying.

The dice passes from hand to hand. **Andrea** *watches.* **Nancy** *puts an arm round her shoulders.*

Kelly I want to do my blouse really. This is boring. Why don't we just start? What do we have to wait for sixes for? It's a waste of time. Here. Stop a minute. Just let me look to see if there is a six on this bleeding dice.

Nancy Andrea, don't you want to play?

Gillian Do you want to take my place?

Nancy I think she wants a cuddle. Let's be partners and share this corner. Come on. Hutch up your chair near me. That's better.

The dice circulates. **Nancy** *cuddles* **Andrea**.

Kelly (*shrieking*) Six! I've got a six!

Gillian Right, you can start, Kelly. Shake again. Five. Now count carefully and move. There. That's a good start.

Kelly Come on, you lot. Don't be taking all day. It's like being at a funeral, this.

Nancy Come on. Play. Your shake again. Speed it up. I believe in playing to win. See? Six. Now I'm in the game you'll all have to watch out. One two three and you're off. Back to base, Kelly.

Kelly (*outraged*) What? What you done that for?

Liane She can knock you off if she lands on the same spot.

Kelly Then what? Do I have to wait for sixes again? Not bleeding likely.

Gillian That's the rule of the game.

Kelly Well, I'm not playing then. You've had that. Just when I got round somebody else could get on my spot and knock me back again. It's stupid. What's the bleeding point of it all?

Gillian (*drily*) Good sportsmanship.

Kelly What?

Gillian The point of the game –

Kelly What you on about – wittering? My turn!

Gillian All right. But if you shake any more sixes get some more counters out, then you won't be kept waiting.

Kelly What? I'm not playing no more. This is bleeding daft. You mean I've got to go right round from start to finish four times and I might be knocked off every fucking time? Bleeding hell! It's no joke! What you laughing at, Liane? She's happy, Miss. She likes getting knocked back. I'll let you fight your own battles next time.

Annette *and* **Debbie** *emerge from office.*

My head still hurts where fucking Debbie helped herself to a handful of my hair. Look! Have I got a bald spot? There? Just there!

Debbie (*muttering*) Sorry.

Nancy What was that little word?

Debbie I said sorry.

Nancy Well done, my love. Now then, shush! Let bygones be bygones. Do you want to take my corner and join the game?

Annette I don't think Debbie's feeling much like playing games.

Nancy Did you ring the clinic?

Debbie No, she didn't. There was no need. (*Jealous.*) What's she doing on your knee?

Nancy (*sing-song*) Peace and quiet.

Debbie *shows* **Kelly** *a postcard.*

Debbie Look what somebody sent me. This card!

Kelly What does it say?

Debbie It's from that VD clinic. Somebody must have given them my name – for a joke.

Nancy (*kindly*) The clinic ask them to name their contacts. Each person gets given a few cards – just in case . . .

Annette Funny calling cards!

Debbie I thought you said it was supposed to be private?

Annette I'm not the one that mentioned the subject out here.

Debbie How come you talked to the clinic then, big boots? If it's supposed to be my private business.

Annette If a piece of correspondence comes to my unit, buttercup, I assume it is my business.

Nancy Debbie! It's not the disease you should be ashamed of, it's what you do to get the disease.

Debbie (*raging*) There's nothing wrong with me!

Kelly You've got like a few little spots on your neck. (*Grabbing dice.*) My turn!

Debbie Where? That's nothing. There's nothing wrong with me. I haven't got no disease.

Annette You'll soon know if it gets round your system.

Debbie What does it do to you, anyway?

Nancy It's a terrible sickness. It could

have permanent effects if you don't go for treatment. If the poison gets into your bloodstream, it could be carried to all your glands. There'd be no babies.

Debbie I don't want no bleeding babies! Bastards! I'm not going to no clinic. I don't care if it kills me. I'd be better off dead.

Nancy That's a sinful thing to say.

Debbie Shut your face, you silly old cow. Leave me alone.

Kelly (*shaking*) Let it be a two. Two. Two. Yes, it is. I told you I was winning.

Liane You need another six now.

Kelly I don't. I'm already out, see? Come on. Come on. Hurry. Hurry. You're putting me off. Six. Six. And a two! What did I tell you? I'm winning.

Nancy Sorry, Kelly. You're off. Back to base.

Kelly I'm not playing no more.

Nancy Finish the game.

Kelly (*overturning board*) I said, NO.

Nancy Kelly, we were playing by the rules.

Kelly (*screaming with frustration*) Well, I'm changing the fucking rules!

Annette All right, ladies. We'll get back to work. The fun's over.

Nancy (*cradling* **Andrea**) What do I do? She's sleeping.

Annette Let her sleep for now. I sometimes think we could do with a nice big bumper bottle of tranquillisers. Kelly, get your sewing. Liane, you're with Mrs Mattieson.

Liane Mrs Leiver, I want a private word.

Nancy Come on, Liane. Let's wash these cups in the kitchen.

Liane No-o-o. Leave me alone. I don't like

you. I want to talk to Mrs Leiver. It's private. Get your hands off me!

Gillian Later, Liane. Come on, Kelly. Get your sewing. Debbie, would you like me to show you some patterns?

Andrea *remains at the table.* **Kelly** *inspects her sewing.*

Kelly (*critically*) It's got like little dots on the right side.

Debbie Let's have a see. That's only the stitches showing.

Kelly I never wanted no dots on the right side.

Debbie The needle's got to come through else the back and front wouldn't stick together. Daft-head!

Kelly (*cheerfully*) Don't be calling me no names.

Kelly *proudly holds up her sewing. Gradually realising her face registers total outrage.*

Debbie What you done?

Kelly It's been vandalised!

Andrea *lifts her head.*

Annette Let's have a look. It'll be right with a bit of lace.

Kelly Lace! Lace! I'm not having any fucking lace! What do I want with fucking laces? Get away from me, you fat old cow! And you! Leiver. You're stupid you are. Leave me alone. I don't want it any more. It's no good now. It's useless. It's rubbish. It's rags. I'm not wearing no rags. I'm no bleeding scarecrow. Give it to one of them tramps. They were jealous because I'd done it good. Well, when I find out who it was done it, I'm going to tie it round their necks and strangle them till they're dead.

Annette It's no good carrying on, Kelly. You've only yourself to blame. Fighting.

Let's get down to work and stop this caterwauling.

Gillian But, surely –

Annette What?

Gillian Surely we ought to find out how this happened?

Annette What's done is done. That work should have been locked up, not just left lying on the table.

Gillian Locking everything up isn't the answer. We need to talk –

Annette Talk! We can talk till we're blue in the face but it won't alter the facts. Nancy, I'd like a word with you in the office, when they've got settled down.

Nancy (*awkwardly*) No. Gillian is right. For once I think we should all sit together and talk about this problem. Come on, everybody, make a circle. Annette? Aren't you going to join us in the circle.

Annette (*annoyed*) I'm right like this.

Nancy What about Andrea? I think we should all join in.

Annette If she chooses to opt out, we can draw our own conclusions. I've got some work to do in my office.

Nancy Shall I begin?

Annette You begin by all means.

Nancy I'm not happy –

Annette (*aloof*) Now what?

Nancy (*sotto voce*) It's no good without you. You're the boss.

Annette *stands on the edge of the circle.*

Annette (*grudgingly*) I'm ready.

Nancy Right. You tell us first, Mrs Rushworth, what you know about Kelly's blouse.

Annette The first I heard was when Kelly starts creating.

Nancy Debbie?

Debbie It's got nothing to do with me. Kelly's my mate.

Nancy You did have a fight this morning. All right. Now Kelly?

Kelly Oh! Yes. I would muck up my own things. Stupid cunt.

Annette I think we're onto a loser. This is for your benefit, madam.

Kelly I'm no bleeding grass. Even if I knew – which I don't – I'm not telling nobody nothing.

Nancy Liane?

Liane *looks imploringly at* **Gillian**, *shrinks and shakes head.*

Listen. We just want the truth. We have to be straight with each other. We don't want to punish anybody, so you don't have to be afraid. Liane? Did you see somebody damage Kelly's sewing?

Liane (*scared*) No-o-o. I'm not frightened of you, Miss.

Gillian Liane, there's safety in numbers. Don't you see? If you all tell the truth, you would all be together, helping each other.

Liane I'm sorry, Miss. I can't.

Silence.

Annette (*accusingly*) Did you leave your shears on the table?

Gillian No. And the cupboard's locked.

Annette (*inspecting blouse*) Well, it's not been torn. That's a definite cut. That's been done with a blade.

Gillian There is a craft knife missing from one of the boxes in the cupboard.

Annette Now we're getting somewhere. So

where is it? We're going to have to have a search now. We're going to have to start turning out pockets when we come in in a morning. We're going to have to go through all the desks. It's come to a pretty pass with girls when we've got to start checking for deadly weapons.

Debbie (*deflecting*) You haven't asked her yet.

Nancy Yes, I know. Andrea. You last of all. Have you got a knife? Did you spoil Kelly's blouse? Listen to me, my love. You've got to start talking to us. Otherwise we're never going to get anywhere. We've got to be open with one another. We've had a better morning, haven't we? Take a minute and think. Andrea, this is very serious. I'm talking to you like a mother now.

A long silence. Then **Andrea** *gets up and leaves the circle.*

Annette (*breathing deeply*) Right! That's that little charade. We've had enough messing. We've a job to do. We're going to have to find that article. And if we don't find it in the next few minutes there'll be no dinner. You know the rule: any funny business and you don't get fed.

Debbie (*leaving circle*) That's not fair!

Annette Fair? You don't know the meaning of the word.

Gillian (*helplessly*) This is not how it's meant to be. (*Appealing to* **Nancy**.) We can't expect to work things out in a moment.

Nancy (*torn*) Be sensible, girls.

Annette (*enraged*) Sensible girls? They're not like girls. In fact, I'm not one for animals, but I'd sooner have a dog. It wouldn't turn round and bite you, like these would. After the treats and the privileges. Go on, Liane. Start turning out that desk. You're going to have to club together and pay for that blouse. Look well when you ask your mother for fifty pence. She'll be paralysed for a week.

Liane Bitch!

Annette Thank you. I've got a long memory. I don't forget. Come along, ladies. We'll sit in my office. When you're ready, we'll be at your service.

The three women sit in the office.

Liane If that bitch asks my mother for money, I'm going to kill myself. I swear to God I am.

Debbie Get on with it, then. We're fed up of hearing about your bleeding mother. It's only fifty pence.

Kelly Fifty pence is fifty pence when you haven't got nothing.

Liane I'm on frees. It's got nothing to do with me. I'm not paying nothing. I'm not saying nothing neither.

Debbie Keep your trap shut then. I never touched no blouse.

Liane It was that knife –

Debbie Did she do it with that knife?

Liane I never saw nothing.

Debbie Where's it gone?

Kelly (*shouting*) It's your fault, Debbie. You was the one that nicked the knife in the first place. You was the one that left it lying around. You was scratching with it on the desk. Look, you daft cow! Where it says your name. Debbie. Bullit. Bullit your fat arse. That's evidence.

Debbie *puts a hand over her mouth.*

Don't touch me. Get your hands off my face. (*Indignantly.*) We're supposed to be finding it, not fighting.

Debbie *begins to ransack drawers creating chaos.*

Kelly *joins. The search becomes an act of sabotage, watched by* **Liane** *and* **Andrea**.

Debbie Listen!

Kelly (*scrawling on walls*) I hate this dump.

Debbie Shut up, I said. Listen!

Annette *is using the telephone.*

Liane (*panicking*) It's the police.

Kelly (*matter-of-fact*) She's only cancelling the bleeding dinner. You know the rule: no food for naughty girls. I don't care. Tastes like pig-shit.

Debbie Bleeding hell! I'm famished. I've never had nothing to eat for two days. What's she saying?

Liane I've got good ears, me. Everybody in our family has got good ears. It comes of listening through them thin walls.

Debbie Listen then!

Kelly Keep your big trap shut. God!

Debbie Well?

Liane I can't hear nothing. They're whispering.

Debbie You get in there and find out what they're going to do. But don't you say nothing. Don't you go telling them I nicked that knife.

Liane No. I'm not going in there. They'll twist it out of me.

Debbie What you holding your belly for?

Liane I want to go real bad. I've got gut-ache. I daredn't go in there in case they force me to say something.

Debbie Just tell them you want to go to the bog. And find out what's up.

Andrea *moves to stairs. She tests the knife against her thumb.*

Liane No!

Debbie Let her go, Andrea. Let her go to the bog. She's pissing herself. She won't say nothing. She knows what she'll get if she starts grassing. Let her go!

Andrea *moves and* **Liane** *scrambles up the stairs.* **Andrea** *goes into the kitchen.*

Annette (*at door*) Well! Look what's here. Are you the errand boy?

Liane No, Miss. I want to wee.

Nancy (*at door*) Just come in here and talk to us a minute.

Debbie (*chanting*) Liane! Liane! Liane!

Debbie *and* **Kelly** *write* **Liane**'s *name on the walls as they sing.*

Liane I can't, Miss. I'm pissing myself.

Gillian Liane, calm down. Mrs Rushworth, please can I unlock the door so that she can go to the lavatory?

Debbie (*chanting*) Liane! Liane! Liane!

Liane Let me go. I beg you. I've got to go to the lavatory. They'll think I'm grassing. Oh! God.

Nancy Control yourself, Liane.

Gillian For God's sake, let her go!

Nancy (*holding* **Liane**) Just tell us what happened with Kelly's blouse. Kelly's your friend.

Kelly (*chanting*) Liane. Liane. Liane.

Liane (*babbling*) Andrea's got a knife. It's your little knife. The one that Debbie nicked out of your cupboard. They're going to kill me on the way home.

Gillian (*raging*) Let her go, I said! (*Unlocking.*) Here. The door's open. Go.

Liane (*sinking*) It's too late. I've done it. I've wet myself. I couldn't help it. Please don't tell my mother. She'll kill me. She hates me. She burned my bed. Oh! Fucking Christ!

Liane *crouches in tears.*

Annette Nancy, we've no option now. (*Snapping.*) Pull yourself together, Liane. This has nothing to do with you. Stop trying to get in the middle. Gillian, get her upstairs.

Gillian *tries to raise* **Liane** *in vain.*

I've tried the parents. I've tried the social worker. If she's got a knife, I'm going to have to get the police.

Gillian (*stunned*) But she needs a doctor.

Nancy We've got to think about the other girls. She's in the kitchen. I'm going to see if I can get her out the back door.

Annette (*commandingly*) Stop here, Nancy. We're not paid danger money. So Debbie? Now what have you got to say for yourself? Look at this mess!

Debbie (*with bravado*) Are you going to get us nicked for nothing?

Annette That depends on you. How you behave in the next few minutes. If I wanted to be really nasty I could say: you let Andrea get hold of this knife, so it's up to you to get it off her and put it back where it belongs – in Mrs Leiver's cupboard.

Debbie (*whimpering*) No.

Nancy What can they do to redeem the situation, Mrs Rushworth?

Annette Listen, girls. Nobody's interested in you three. Give us a chance to get things sorted and then we'll see about dinner.

Gillian What are you going to do?

Nancy Once she touches that alarm, it'll be three minutes.

Debbie (*excited*) The police!

Nancy Gillian, just keep the girls occupied. Get that Ludo. Be partners. Two by two. Liane, you play with Mrs Leiver, there's a little love. Debbie, word of honour. Gillian,

we're relying on you to stay with the girls.
We'll talk later.

The girls sit at the game but do not play.

Annette (*passionately*) I hate the idea of
people coming into this unit and seeing the
state it's in right now and thinking we can't
cope. Let's try and get her outside. Gillian?
If we manage to wangle her outside, you
hit the bell. Right?

Gillian The police?

Nancy Help us sort this one out and then
we'll talk. We've got to be a team.

Liane Miss, I'm scared –

Gillian I'm frightened too. But I can't – I
can't let this happen. (*Appealing to* **Nancy**.)
We can't let them take her away as if she
was some sort of criminal.

Nancy We've got to think about the other
girls.

Gillian Please – let them go. Then we can
try to deal with her on her own.

Nancy (*to* **Annette**) What do you think?

Annette *hits the alarm.*

Annette (*exasperated*) There! That's what I
think – she needs locking up! Think,
Nancy. What happens next time? Next
time we get somebody in that thinks they
can rule the roost? And the next? And the
next? We don't want the police seeing this
mess. They'll think we can't do our job.
Gillian, see if you can wheedle her outside.
She seems to listen to you.

Gillian I can't –

Annette What's come over the woman?
(*Threatening.*) If you won't cooperate I'm
going to have to ring the office and tell
them you can't cope!

Gillian If you do that I shall have a story
to tell too! I'm no little Liane that you can
browbeat into the ground.

Nancy This is not the time –

Gillian When is the time? They've been
battered and abused and humiliated and
denied and then you tell them to be nice?
You're a hypocrite. You think it would be
nice if Andrea chatted to you? It would be
an obscenity. You think she's mad? This is
the real madness – this pretence of decency.

Annette So you think you know all the
answers after two weeks?

Gillian. No. I don't know what to do. How
could I? But I do know one thing. We're
buying their silence and it's cheap at the
price. You keep talking about money.
Doing your little calculations. The petty
cash. The tokens. The wages bill. Of course
it costs a lot of money. These few girls –
only four or five out of the thousands in this
city – they're probably the most important
people in the whole place. Because nobody
wants to be in their shoes – with nothing to
lose. If it wasn't possible to keep them
quiet – my God, girls – we'd all be at each
other's throats. Shut up and sit down – and
be grateful for what's handed out. Isn't
that the whole idea? All she's done till now
is keep her mouth shut! Why, she's our
greatest success of all. She ought to be
given a gold star.

Annette Nancy, you have a go – just angle
her towards the door. One push and she'll
be out.

Gillian Nancy, I thought you cared?

Nancy (*stung*) I do care!

Annette Who cares what happens to the
rubbish they dump?

Debbie (*rising*) Don't be calling me names,
darling.

Annette If the cap fits –

Debbie Just don't be calling me no names!

Debbie *and* **Annette** *stand face to face. At this*

moment **Andrea** *returns. Her clothes are in shreds.*

Annette (*at large*) Don't tell me I couldn't see it coming!

Gillian Andrea? I'm not asking you to talk to me, but I am asking you to give me the knife. Remember the first day? My first day and yours. I was so nervous that day. Debbie took that little knife from the cupboard because I left the door unlocked. I didn't want to make a fuss. It was wrong of me. And now if somebody gets hurt, it will be my fault. Please? Give it to me.

Holding the knife **Andrea** *steals towards* **Gillian** *but as* **Andrea** *advances* **Gillian** *retreats, still reaching out her hand.*

Nancy (*wooingly*) Andrea?

Andrea *turns to look.*

Gillian Andrea? Please.

Andrea *turns back to* **Gillian**.

Nancy (*softly*) Come on, love. Look at us when we're talking to you. We know you've been a naughty girl, but we're not cross.

Annette (*quietly*) The car's here.

Gillian (*urgently*) Andrea! It's the police.

Annette Come with me, blossom. You've had a good run for your money, but the fun's over now. Let's be having you. You try, Nancy!

Nancy Andrea, it's for your own good.

Annette *makes a lunge for* **Andrea**'s *wrist.* **Andrea** *recoils and* **Annette**'s *hand falls on the table.* **Andrea** *stabs the knife again and again into the table around the hand, deliberately missing until the blade becomes embedded in the wood.*

Annette Nancy! Her arms! Gillian! The chair! The door!

Andrea *screams and struggles as she is carried out. The girls crowd to the window.*

Debbie Andrea! Tarraa, love.

Kelly Quiet, Debbie. You'll get us all done!

Debbie Duck down, dickhead, so they won't see.

Liane Two men in a car!

Debbie She's struggling to get free.

Liane She's in the back.

Kelly (*yelling*) Open the other door, you idiot. Get running!

Debbie He's got the engine going. The one in the back, he's fit.

Liane Her mouth was bleeding.

Debbie Quick! Back to the table. Give me the dice, Liane. My move.

The women return. The girls play.

Gillian She never had a chance.

Annette Nonsense. She had the same chance every other girl gets in this unit. These things happen.

Gillian We make things happen.

Debbie Can we have us dinner, Miss? We've been good.

Annette Finish the game first. In a minute or two we'll set up and I'll send across to the shop for some fish and chips out of the petty cash. In fact I'll nip across myself. I could do with stretching my legs.

Debbie What will we do for pudding?

Annette (*crisply*) No pudding today.

Debbie Bleeding hell! No fucking pudding and I'm starving.

Kelly It's us own fault for being stupid this morning.

Nancy Pearls of wisdom!

Liane I'm no good at this game.

Gillian I'll take your place.

Liane Two men took Andrea away in a car.

Kelly My shake. Has she gone to a lock-up?

Debbie I told you she was a psycho. If you try and knock me off on this last corner, Miss, I warn you, don't try. You'll be dead.

Kelly That chap that raped me, he was a psycho. (*To* **Gillian**.) You! What does it mean – psycho?

Gillian A lost person, I suppose.

Nancy A lost soul.

The girls play. **Annette** *tidies. Lights begins to fail.*

Annette Come along, ladies. My stomach is telling me it's time. We'll have a lot of work to do this afternoon. Don't be giving me dirty looks, Debbie. Lucky I don't bear grudges. You can't go taking things too much to heart, Gillian, or you'd end up nowhere. And let me tell you something else: you get nothing in this life by wishful thinking. If you want to do things your way, you have to be prepared to put in the graft. And you can't go sitting on the fence. If you're in, you're in. And you are in, because there's nowhere else to go. You feel sorry for these girls? But sorry isn't going to feed their faces and keep them clean. And you know what? Even the girls know I'm right. If they had their way, they'd strip the flesh off your bones, even our little one there. That's right, Liane, I'm watching you. Bring your cards to me and I'll give you a quick game of Chinese Patience while we're at a loose end. It's been a long morning. But we'll get by. We'll hang on by the skin of our teeth. Right. Lay out the cards where I can see them, Madam. And no cheating.

The light fades to blackout.

Tokens of Affection

Tokens began its life as notes towards a novel, a kind of diary kept by me during a spell as a worker in a unit similar to the one represented in the play. During that time my working days were spent trying to get through to girls whose capacity to communicate had been severely damaged. The play does little in the way of examining the individual histories that led to this state of alienation. A few hints – together with our common knowledge of social and emotional deprivation – are enough to tell that story. No, what concerned me was the fact that my own position as communicator was deeply suspect. I was there to earn my living. But what exactly was I supposed to be doing? This was the question the girls asked in no uncertain terms. Their attitude to the staff was a constant challenge. It led me directly to the moral and social problems that I eventually tried to anatomise in the play. But first and foremost it was felt as a direct threat. Violence was part of the atmosphere of the place and it became the keynote in the play.

Essentially the unit was a container. A derisory term for such a unit was 'sin-bin', since most of the girls were juvenile offenders. The official policy was a different matter: its aims and ideals would be written into the educational policy of the time – invoking familiar notions of personal fulfilment and social utility, leading to a balance between the needs of the individual and the group. But actually, the aim put crudely was to 'keep the lid on things'. However prettily dressed and disguised this aim might be, it was, stripped of its pretence, a repressive process, designed to neutralise the volcanic energy of the clients in order to render them harmless to other people.

In this situation my own position was uncomfortable. In the immediate I too wanted to keep the lid on things – not just because I needed the job, but also quite literally because I did not want to get hurt or to see others hurt. But to me the rage of the girls seemed justified. The girls were often cruel to each other. But the punishments and deprivations they suffered were out of all proportion to the offence given. The notion of fair play was invoked in a context where the very ideas of justice and equity seemed meaningless. I tried to find a way of reconciling these conflicts in my own head simply because I needed practical solutions. Eventually when I came to write the play I offered no overall solution: the problem was too big. First of all it needed understanding.

At the point when I was still making notes these impressions were diffuse and uncertain. A chance meeting with Annie Castledine led to her suggestion that this material would lend itself to theatre. She suggested setting up a workshop with Northern Studio Theatre and this we undertook to do within a matter of weeks of our first meeting. As a novelist I had no experience of working with a group of performers and was nervous of the process. I immediately went home and turned my notes into dialogue. Buttressed with 250 pages of dialogue I went bravely to the first session. Only in retrospect do I appreciate the tact and good humour of those performers and – not least – Annie herself. The first *Tokens* took a whole day to read! The group endured my lines with much fortitude and some hilarity. I like to think this is partly because the characters are funny at times and not just because in those early days my every stage direction was a short story.

The first week of workshops was followed by a month of writing followed by a further week of workshops. This was my initiation into theatre. Under Annie Castledine's direction my lines were squeezed into shape. Every performer participated in the fullest sense in this work. There was reading of the text, further research, discussion, improvisation, informal conversation, debate, observation, voice exercise, movement.

Every effort was made during those workshops to deploy the skills and insights of the participants in the interests of the playwright, during which the cry was ever and again: what does the playwright want?

This was not a simple question. Theatre was not my starting point. I had to learn everything from the beginning. I learned for instance the simple things that will be obvious to most theatre-workers: that a page can become a paragraph, a paragraph a line, a line a word, a word a silence, and that each tiny movement carries a meaning. But to what end? What does the playwright want? Because *Tokens* was rooted in an actual experience I kept going back to life. The problem for me in the unit had been pragmatic: what to do on any given day. In the play the problem went through several evolutions. In the first version I simply tried to record what actually happened. But as more than one member of Northern Studio Theatre pointed out, a record of events is not a play. I found myself asking the most basic question: what is a play? I asked many people and one at least replied: a play can be whatever you want it to be. My abstractions were eventually cut short by Annie's clarity of mind: what is it that you yourself want to say.

In the end the answer is quite simple. I wanted to say a lot of things. I wanted people to hear the language and listen to the lies, the evasions, the false promises, the inconsistencies, the hypocrisies that are enshrined within the common phrases. I wanted people to be angry. I wanted people to be ashamed. I wanted to celebrate the extraordinary vitality that survives the repression and the destitution, which is still there in spite of everything. But most of all – always – I have wanted to give voice to the silent ones. The silent girl in the play is a symbol for me of all the voices that are simply not heard. And for me this is inevitably connected with class and culture in this country.

I am old enough to remember the beginnings of Coronation Street on television. I remember the astonished delight of people in our street at seeing people in our street on television! So, we were fit subjects after all. That was good news. It gave an uplift to cobble-stones and slate roofs. It was a good laugh. When, years later, I came to write myself, I wanted to write the things that seemed to be missing in those popular versions – what I think of as the inside story – the reality that runs like a thick seam underneath the surface prattle. But now it is not just a question of record and recognition. I want to see change. This brings me to the end of the play. Many people have said, nothing changes. There are no easy answers in *Tokens* but there are answers. On the face of it the play comes full circle, but this is an illusion: only we can make change.

Stage History: The play was first commissioned in 1985 by Northern Studio Theatre, under the direction of Annie Castledine, who had a commitment to supporting new work by women writers, particularly in the north. With the generous backing of Yorkshire Arts, Northern Studio were able to workshop the play, which was given a rehearsed reading at the Ilkley Literature Festival that year and subsequently it was rehearsed and toured in the north of England for thirteen weeks. A year later Michael Attenborough and Alan Drury at Hampstead Theatre Club commissioned a rewrite, but the play had to wait for its next exposure until 1990 at Derby Playhouse, brilliantly directed once again by Annie Castledine, whose faith in the play has been unwavering.

Maureen Lawrence was born and educated in Leeds, read English at Nottingham University, taught for a while and then went to America, where she studied at Michigan University and began writing. Her first novel – *The Tunnel* – was published in both Britain and America in 1969; a second novel – *Shadow on the Wall* – followed two years later. A third book – *A Telling and a Keeping* – was published by The Women's Press in 1990. The long gaps between books has been filled by raising a family, teaching, writing, and, latterly, learning to become a playwright. *Tokens of Affection* is almost the first play. Since its production in 1986 there have been three more adult plays – *Black Ice*, commissioned by Northern Studio, *The Pergola* for Derby Playhouse and *Dream Lover* for the Raving Beauties. She has also written several plays for Lancaster TIE (Duke's Theatre) and Derby Playhouse and a translation of Sophocles' *Antigone* for Communicado Theatre Company.

Variations on a Theme by Clara Schumann

Sheila Yeger

Characters

Louise Frampton *biographer*
Clara Schumann *composer, pianist (1819–1896)*
Friedrich Wieck *Clara's father*
Johannes Brahms *composer*
Richard Last *psychotherapist*
Vera Frampton *Louise's mother*
Rhea
Anna K ⎫
Laura ⎬ *travellers*
Marilyn ⎭
Hotel Porter (*Johannes*)
Polythene Woman
Young Guard
Older Guard

This play may be performed by a cast of five women and two men.

Suggested Doubling
1. **Anna, Rhea**
2. **Laura, Vera**
3. **Marilyn, Young Clara**
4. **Older Clara, Polythene Woman**
5. **Richard Last, Friedrich Wieck, Older Guard**.
6. **Young Guard, Brahms, Porter**.

In the *coda*, when we briefly see both **Anna** and **Rhea**, **Anna** may be played by the actress playing **Marilyn**.

Costumes

The costumes of **Rhea**, **Laura**, **Vera**, **Marilyn**, **Anna K** and **Polythene Woman**, whilst being distinctive to each character, should also unmistakeably echo that of **Louise**, to the extent that we should be able to imagine that, given different circumstances, any of them could be **Louise**.

Note

Fugue: Contrapuntal piece of music derived from a theme. All fugues have a definite number of parts, whether for voice or instrument. They are: soprano, alto, bass or soprano, alto, tenor and bass.

Fugue: Term used in psychiatry to describe a flight into infantile behaviour, escape from acute psychological pressure, withdrawal.

The Fugue referred to in the text is by Clara Schumann, Opus 16 in G minor.

Prelude

Light **Louise Frampton**. *She sits on a couch, legs drawn up under her. She is in her late thirties, sensibly well dressed. Her clothes are neutral in tone, her hair is well cut but unbecoming.*

Louise I'm standing in a corner with this man. It's very dark. He's got blond hair, really shiny like . . . like a shiny helmet. We're making love . . . it's very passionate . . . violent almost. But all the time I can hear myself saying, 'I don't want to do this. I don't want to do this.' Afterwards I seem to be examining myself that it didn't . . . that he didn't . . .

Light **Richard Last**. *He is* **Louise**'s *psychotherapist, an urbane, relaxed and humorous man in his late forties. He sits in an armchair, holds a notebook and pencil.*

Last Yes . . .?

Louise That nothing actually . . .

Last Yes . . .?

Louise Then suddenly I hear the church bell ringing. I'm standing with my mother outside the church. She seems to be showing a group of Japanese around . . . students or something. None of them speaks English. (*Laughs.*) Not a word.

Last Why is that so funny?

Louise Well, isn't it? My mother's rabbiting on the way she does and nobody can understand a word she's saying. The church bell's ringing and my mother says it's time for Evensong. But I say I'm too tired. (*Laughs.*) Well, I suppose I *would* be, wouldn't I? Then I'm trying on this very tight black skirt . . . oh . . . and a red top . . .

Last What sort of top?

Louise Rather . . . revealing actually.

Last *nods.*

And I'm stuffing myself . . . God, I'm absolutely *stuffing* myself with all this food that's laid out on the tables under the trees . . . cakes and biscuits . . . oh and blancmanges, red jellies and green jellies and . . .

Last Did you recognise the man?

Louise What man? Oh him . . . no . . . at least . . . (*Laughs.*) Yes . . . of course . . . it was what's his name . . . used to work in the University bookshop. Rather good-looking. But everyone said he was gay. (*Laughs.*) Just my luck!

Last Your luck? In what way? Do you think you have bad luck?

Louise I . . . I don't know. (*She touches her neck.*)

Last What about your neck?

Louise Neck?

Last You touched your neck.

Louise Yes. (*She touches it again.*)

Last Does it hurt?

Louise A bit.

Last Only a bit?

Louise Yes.

Last Why?

Louise How the hell should I know?

Blackout.

Lights come up again on the same scene. Now **Louise** *sits on the floor, leaning against the couch. She hugs herself.*

Louise I'm working in the library. I go out to my car. There's a body under a blanket on the back seat. Stiff, obviously dead. It's a child. A girl. I don't seem surprised. Perhaps I knew it was there. An elderly woman appears. Very ragged . . . a bit like a tramp. She starts shouting at me: 'I live here. This is where I live.' I drive off quickly. I'm looking for somewhere to bury the child. An arm sticks out of the blanket. Someone looks in through the window. I'm frightened it'll be discovered . . .

Last Who put the child in the car?

Louise I don't know.

Last Don't you?

Pause.

Louise I did.

Blackout.

Then light **Louise** *again. She lies on the couch, eyes closed.*

I'm on a mountain . . . very high. It's really beautiful . . . amazing . . . you can see for miles. I'm with you. We're lying together under a blanket. Embracing. Naked. It's very . . . very special. I feel very special. Like a princess or a queen. There is nobody like me . . . nobody in the whole world. Then I wrap myself in the blanket and I come down the mountain. I'm carrying a pitcher. Perhaps I'm going to fetch some water. I open a door and find the water. Later I climb the mountain again. You are waiting for me. Waiting.

Blackout.

Light **Louise**. *She sits on the couch.*

Louise I'm on a railway station. I've got loads of luggage. *Loads*. It's ridiculous. I'm talking to a young man wearing glasses. He's really kind. The train is going. He says we can't travel unless we have a ticket. I don't want to travel without him. Meanwhile all my luggage has been put on the train. I run along the bank, shouting for them to throw it out. They throw out

two bags. One is my briefcase. The strap is hanging off. I go to pick it up. Then I see it's a snake . . . It clings to my hand and I can't get it off . . .

Last How do you feel about that?

Louise How do you think I feel? I've got a snake clinging to my bloody hand. How would *you* feel?

Last What happened to the man? The one who seemed kind.

Louise He pissed off I suppose. They usually do.

Long pause.

Last Why are you so angry?

Louise I'm not angry. I'm just . . . just . . .

Last Yes?

Louise Just so bloody tired.

She sinks her head in her hands. He waits. After a while she stands up.

Louise I won't be coming next week.

Last Oh?

Louise I'm going away.

Last I see.

Louise No, not for ever. Just for a week. You won't get rid of me that easily. (*Pause.*) Don't you even want to know where I'm going?

Last Only if you want to tell me.

Louise I'm going to Berlin. To do some research on my book.

Last Clara Schumann, isn't it?

Louise You remembered!

Last *smiles*.

There's a museum of memorabilia, musical autographs, that sort of thing.

Last Sounds fascinating.

Louise Does it?

Last I'll see you in a fortnight then, shall I?

Louise If I'm not lost at sea . . .

Blackout.

Then light a television and video recorder, placed next to a bed. The TV is switched on. It shows the film Some Like It Hot. *On the bed, a number of video tapes and a tray containing the remains of an assortment of junk food: popcorn, coke, crisps, etc.*

Enter **Louise** *eating from a heaped bowl of Rice Krispies. She wears pyjamas. She sits on the bed, follows the film, eats. She evidently knows the film off by heart, speaks some of Monroe's lines aloud. After a while she gets up, goes to the telephone, picks it up, hesitates, replaces the receiver. She goes to the mirror, studies her face for a long while, then speaks to her reflection with a sort of vicious self-parody.*

Louise Some people have blackheads. Some people have spots. I have what I call my 'Mother' days. Days when I look even more like my mother than usual. Something around the eyes . . . a particularly strong hint of her in the lower lip. As if she'd entered my body by stealth, occupied me under cover of darkness, then surreptitiously worked her way up my neck into my face and out again. Like a great oozing boil . . . or one of those alien masses . . . all green slime and pulsating pupils. I suppose I could always dye my hair black, or grow it down to here. (*Indicates.*) Mother doesn't believe in long hair. She considers it unhygienic. Like public lavatories. My mother would probably wet her knickers rather than enter a public lavatory.

She sings in a parody of Monroe.

Louise
Running wild
Lost control . . .
Don't love nobody
It's not worthwhile

All alone . . .
Running wild.

Light **Last**. *He sits at a desk. He is reading a paperback collection of the writings of Jung.* **Louise** *watches. He looks up, reads aloud.*

Last 'In many cases in psychiatry, the patient who comes to us has a story that is not told, and which, as a rule, no one knows of. It's the patient's secret, the rock against which he is shattered.'

Louise (*quietly*) She. She is shattered.

Last *looks towards her.*

Last Louise Frampton. Thirty-nine. University lecturer. Born, Uley in Gloucestershire. Father, Church of England vicar. Mother, housewife. No siblings. High achiever. Complaining of severe headaches. Is frequently tearful. Chronic insomniac.

Louise Don't forget the eating.

Last Compulsive eater. Presenting to the world a picture of a highly organised, perfectly ordered individual, whilst battling with an incredible anger and a growing sense of . . .

Louise Desperation.

She smiles bleakly. Crosses to turn off the TV and pick up the tray. Exits. The light stays on **Last** *for a moment. Blackout.*

In the blackout, the sound of very young children singing the hymn All Things Bright and Beautiful. *The singing is ragged but spontaneous. They sing one verse.* **Last**'s *voice, very emphatic in the blackout.*

Last Some of you aren't singing at all. I want to hear *every* word. *Every* word, do you understand? No mumbling, no bumbling . . . clear as a bell . . .

They sing the verse again, more self-consciously, with great emphasis, as requested.

Act One

The singing continues.

Lights come up slowly. A sign indicates Platform 3. A railway station in Germany. Night, the present. A train whistle, the sound of a train pulling out slowly, then gathering speed. A **Young Guard** *notes the time of its departure in a log book. He is in his mid-twenties, blond-haired. He turns to a trolley piled high with cases and bags. He begins to trundle it offstage.*

Enter **Louise**, *walking very briskly. She wears a good beige raincoat, sensible shoes, carries a leather suitcase, a briefcase and a small German phrasebook with markers in it.*

Louise Excuse me . . . the 21:49 to Berlin?

Guard Berlin . . . ja. Ein und zwanzig neun und dreissig nach. Berlin. (Twenty-one: thirty-nine to Berlin.) Schon gefahren. (It's already gone.)

Louise 'Schon gefahren'. What's that? (*To* **Guard**.) Berlin . . . train. (*Looks in phrase book.*) Er . . . Zug. (Train.)

Guard Zug. Ja. (*Taps watch.*) Ein und zwanzig neun und dreissig. Schon gefahren. (*He whistles and mimes the departure of a train.*)

Louise This *is* Platform 3 isn't it? (*Looks up at sign.*) Yes . . . 3 . . . I thought so. Well, according to my itinerary . . .

She puts down her case, opens her briefcase, takes out a Filofax, and opens it to reveal a sheet with times and places typed on it.

Louise (*reading from this*) 'Arrive Aachen 21:00 hours. Depart Aachen 21:49 hours. Train number 217. Sleeper to Berlin.'

She snaps the Filofax shut, speaks rapidly, ostensibly to the **Guard**.

I had forty-nine minutes to spare, so I went for a cup of coffee. Hot chocolate actually. Oh and a croissant. I'd *intended* to order coffee, but I changed my mind. The chocolate was surprisingly good. A little sweet, but rather, what shall I say . . . comforting.

She stops suddenly, picks up her case. It springs open and some of its contents fall out. They include a number of well-pressed and folded clothes in good fabrics and pale colours. **Louise**, *embarrassed, hurriedly begins to pack everything back in again.*

I must have forgotten to lock it. When I took my cardigan out at Ostend. I suddenly felt *incredibly* cold. So I took out my cardigan and put it on under my jacket. (*Suddenly to* **Guard**.) You don't understand a single word I'm saying.

The **Guard** *has picked up a small battered rag-doll which was also in the case. He looks at it with amusement.* **Louise** *snatches it from him, thrusts it amongst the clothes, locks the case, stands up.*

Train Number 217. Twenty-one forty-nine. Aachen to Berlin. I've booked a sleeper. (*Pause.*)

The sound of the children singing. A brief snatch. She suddenly puts down the suitcase, opens her briefcase, gets out the Filofax, opens it. The guard looks too.

(*Reads.*) Arrive Aachen 21:00 hours. Depart Aachen 21:49 hours.

The **Guard** *points something out. Pause.*

Asterisk. (*Pause.*) I didn't notice the asterisk. (*Looks.*) Sundays . . . depart 21:39 hours. (*Pause.*) It's gone. The train's gone. That's impossible. I typed out the itinerary myself. (*To the* **Guard**.) The Booking Clerk at Victoria Station assured me there would be no problem. He obviously did not see fit to remark that there is a completely different timetable on Sundays. Hence the asterisk. I *must* be in the library in Berlin by 10 o'clock tomorrow morning. I have a very tight schedule. This really is *most* inconvenient. Doesn't anyone round here speak English?

Blackout. A few bars of the Prelude.

Several hours later. Lights come up slowly on the station platform. **Louise** *sits on a luggage trolley. She holds a book. She is dozing. She loses her grip on the book. It falls to the floor. At the same time, enter* **Rhea**. *She is about twenty, wears a trailing skirt, carries a large, shabby back-pack. She looks as if she has been sleeping in her clothes. Her hair is untidy, her manner relaxed, easy. She takes off the back-pack, bends to pick up the book, looks at the cover.* **Louise** *opens her eyes.* **Rhea** *hands* **Louise** *the book.*

Louise I must have dozed off. (*Jumps.*) I hope I haven't missed . . .

Rhea The train to Berlin? No. That's the one I'm catching. (*She sits comfortably on the trolley.*) Unless I decide to go to Zurich.

Louise That's in completely the opposite direction.

Rhea I know.

Louise *is disorientated. She opens the book, as if it might contain the answer, closes it, puts it down on the trolley, then stands, straightens her clothes, tucking in her skirt.* **Rhea** *watches. A pause.*

I suppose you couldn't buy me a cup of tea?

Louise *jumps.*

And a sandwich . . . baguette . . . whatever they call them round here.

Louise I took the precaution of changing fifty pounds into Deutschmark before I left London. Though I'm not sure the rate of exchange was particularly favourable. I got . . . (*Quotes current rate.*) I decided it would be rather embarrassing to arrive in Berlin in the early hours of the morning with absolutely *no* German money. Which is, I presume, your . . . er . . . difficulty.

Rhea (*completely matter-of-fact*) No. I'm just broke. Skint. Haven't eaten since Thursday.

A pause. Then **Louise** *opens her bag, takes out her wallet, takes out a small amount of money, hands it to* **Rhea**.

Thanks.

She gets up and exits rapidly. The opening bars of the Prelude are repeated. **Louise** *stands, looking after* **Rhea**.

After a while, enter **Laura**, *a soberly-dressed woman of about forty. She wears a good suit (1940's in style), a hat, high-heeled shoes. She looks around nervously, consults her watch, stops near* **Louise**, *looks at her briefly, looks away, looks at her watch again.*

Enter an older woman, dressed almost entirely in polythene. She carries a number of small bundles, wrapped in newspaper and polythene, her feet are wrapped up like parcels, which gives her a peculiar rustling, shuffling gait. She goes up to **Louise**, *stops, stares at her long enough to make her feel uncomfortable, then goes to a large waste bin, rummages amongst its contents. Finds an old newspaper, takes it out, examines it, then shuffles it into one of her bundles, walks upstage left.*

Enter **Anna K**. *A woman in her thirties, dark, elegant. She wears a cloak, with a hood edged with real fur, which half covers her face. She carries an old-fashioned valise. She walks up to* **Louise**, *stops. Their eyes meet very briefly. Then* **Anna** *hurries downstage left.*

The sound of a train whistle in the distance. A whirl of grey smoke.

Enter **Marilyn**. *She walks quickly, and with a definite wiggle. She is improbably blonde, undeniably glamorous. She wears a straight black coat, with fur around the bottom, a little cloche hat and carries a ukelele in a case and a small bag. She walks past* **Louise** *and disappears into the smoke, re-emerging downstage right.*

All the women stand on the platform. The smoke swirls around them.

Louise (*sings sotto voce tunelessly*)
'He gave us eyes to see them
And lips that we might tell . . .

How great is God Almighty . . .'

*The sound of the train whistle is repeated. We
hear a train approaching.* **Louise** *picks up her
case, looks at* **Rhea***'s backpack, looks at*
Marilyn *departing, goes as if to follow, realises
she's forgotten her book, returns to pick it up. She
stands for a moment, the train whistle is repeated.
She picks up the book, looks at the cover as if it's
the first time she's seen it. The lights fade to
blackout.*

*The sound of a train, travelling at speed. Several
hours later. The lights come up slowly on the
interior of a railway carriage. It is night, there are
blinds at the windows. The carriage is lit by small
lamps; these are not switched on.* **Louise** *sits
writing in a large Oxford pad. A file with an
index is open next to her, the book on Clara
Schumann is also in evidence. She has removed her
jacket and folded it neatly on the seat beside her.
She is totally absorbed.*

After a while, enter **Laura***, dressed as before. She
sits down, gazes into space, then takes a women's
magazine (e.g. 'Woman and Home') out of
her bag and begins to read.* **Louise** *notes the
magazine, but continues with her book.* **Laura**
*puts the magazine down, takes a small powder
compact out of her bag, opens it, looks at herself
in the mirror, closes it, returns it to her bag.*
Louise *looks up, then away.* **Laura** *then takes a
crumpled envelope out of her handbag, opens it,
reads the letter, evidently not for the first time. She
folds the letter carefully, returns it to the envelope,
looks at it, makes a decision, neatly tears it up,
screws up the pieces, drops them into the ashtray.*
Louise *looks up, then away.* **Laura** *takes out a
cigarette lighter, cigarettes.* **Louise** *looks up
sharply.*

Louise I'm sorry . . . this is a non-smoker
(*Reaches for the phrase book.*)

Laura (*very well-bred voice*) I'm so sorry.

Louise Oh . . . you're English. One rather
tends to assume . . .

Laura Please excuse me.

Laura *opens the magazine, begins to read.*
Louise *shrugs, returns to her work.*

After a while, enter **Marilyn***.* **Louise** *looks up.*
Marilyn *is much younger than she at first
appeared – probably only about twenty. She still
carries the bag and the ukelele in its case. She
reaches up to put the ukelele on the rack. Her coat
rides up around her thighs. She giggles, tugs at it
without success.*

Marilyn Oops!

*She has a breathy voice, with just a hint of
acquired American laid over the Midlands. She
'dips' amongst the seats.*

Eeny, meeny, miny, mo, catch a fishy by
the toe. If he hollers, let him go, eeny,
meeny, miny, mo.

The 'dip' decrees that she sit opposite **Louise**.
Louise *looks less than pleased.* **Marilyn** *sits
down, then immediately jumps up again, removes
her coat to reveal a skin-tight, impossibly short
dress.* **Louise** *looks, looks away.* **Marilyn**
subsides into her seat, sighs with enjoyment.

I *love* trains, don't you! 'Specially at night.
There you go, speeding through the
darkness, and out there all the little people
in their little houses, watching telly,
drinking tea, and you cut through it all like
an arrow, like a knife through butter, and
you wake up and it's Paris, Rome, Madrid,
Berlin . . . Not disturbing you, am I?

Louise *shakes her head, continues working.*

You writing a book? You *must* be clever. I
always wanted to write a book but there's
not enough up here. (*Taps head.*) My
name's Marilyn.

She extends her hand. **Louise** *doesn't respond.*

Tell you the truth it's my *stage* name. I was
christened Susan Diedre. (*Laughs. She
reaches across and picks up the Clara Schumann
biography, reads the title aloud in a 'posh' voice.*)
'Clara Schumann . . . the artist and the
woman'. He went round the twist, didn't

he, her husband? I saw a film on the telly (*Mimes mad pianist.*) They have any kids?

Louise There were eight children of the marriage, yes.

Marilyn Fancy having *eight* kids! Once you've got kids you've had it. Life's not your own.

Laura *looks up sharply, looks away.*

Louise She *did* travel all over Europe as a concert pianist . . .

Marilyn *loses interest, hands back the book, looks out of the window. Starts to sing under her breath, in a passable and pleasing imitation of Marilyn Monroe.*

'I wanna be loved by you, by you and nobody else but you, I wanna be loved by you alo--ne . . .'

Louise *looks up sharply.*

Marilyn Sorry . . . (*Slaps own hand.*) Keep your gob shut, Susan!

A long pause. **Marilyn** *opens her bag, takes out a toilet bag, pulls out two bottles of nail varnish. She holds them out to* **Louise**.

What do you reckon? This one's called Tropical Sunrise . . . and *this* one's called Venetian Mystery. (*Pause.*) You bite yours, don't you? (*Pause, examines the nail varnish.*) Think I'll go for the Venetian Sunrise.

She puts away the other varnish and begins to paint her nails. A brief lull.

You ever been to Venice?

Louise *shakes her head.*

I heard it stinks. You going to Berlin?

Louise Yes.

Marilyn On your holidays?

Louise I . . . well . . . actually I'm going to do some research. There are some manuscripts in the State Library . . . I hope to . . .

Marilyn I've got a gig in this club in Hamburg. Did it last year too. The money's good and the men don't paw you about too much. Sprechen Sie Deutsch?

Louise No . . . actually I . . .

Marilyn Nor do I much. Only 'Ich liebe dich'. (I love you.)

She laughs. **Laura** *looks up, smiles faintly, looks away.*

Last year I met this *fantastic* bloke. Kurt. He had on a little bomber jacket and one ear-ring and . . .

Louise *suddenly stands up.* **Marilyn** *instantly understands.*

The train's full . . . I looked. This is the only empty carriage. I wouldn't have got in here otherwise.

Louise, *embarrassed, sits down. An awkward pause.*

Louise I'm sorry, I . . .

Marilyn Forget it.

She opens her bag, takes out her toilet bag, gets out a mirror, cream and tissues and proceeds to vigorously clean her face. **Louise** *watches. Stripped of make-up,* **Marilyn** *looks much younger, more vulnerable.* **Louise** *reaches into her case, pulls out a bar of chocolate.*

Louise Would you like some chocolate?

Marilyn I said forget it.

Louise *replaces the chocolate, returns to her work. After a while,* **Marilyn** *starts to roll up her hair into little ringlets, ready for the night.* **Louise** *watches her covertly.*

Enter the **Guard** *with* **Anna K**, *dressed as before. He carries her case.* **Laura** *looks up, looks away.*

Guard Hier gibt es Platz. (There's room here.)

Anna Vielen Dank. (Thank you very much.)

He places her case on the rack. She tips him. He bows, exits. **Louise** *watches as* **Anna** *sits down, removes her hood. She is very still, very pale, withdrawn. After a while she begins to cry, silent desolate.* **Marilyn** *jumps up, goes to sit next to her, offers a grubby tissue.*

Marilyn Here . . .

Anna *takes it, dabs at her eyes.*

Go on . . . have a bloody good blow.

Anna *mops her face.*

Anna You must think me so terribly foolish.

She speaks with a heavy Russian accent. **Louise** *looks up, surprised. Quickly looks away.*

Marilyn Where did you get that *fantastic* accent?

Anna I am Russian. But my husband is English. We live now where he has his practice. Flask Walk . . . it is in Hampstead. Before that we have a house in Vienna.

Marilyn Ooh, how cosmopolitan!

Louise (*looking up*) What sort of practice is that?

Anna My husband is a very eminent psychotherapist. (*She begins to cry again.*)

Marilyn So . . . Clara's bloke went off his rocker; *her* old man's an eminent psycho-whatsit, and our friend over there's (*Indicates* **Louise**.) an incurable nail-biter. (*Pause.*) Looks like you're the only sane one round here Susan. (*Pause.*) Tell you what, why don't I give you a tune? Music always cheers people up.

She stands, pulls down ukelele from the rack, takes it out of its case, begins to sing in the style of Monroe, accompanying herself.

'I wanna be loved by you, by you and nobody else but you, I wanna be loved by you alo--ne . . .'

Anna *cries.* **Marilyn** *stops dead, puts the ukelele down.*

Look . . . if you want to talk to someone.

Anna *looks down.*

But you know I'm here, OK?

A long pause.

Louise I only started biting my nails last year. I never did it as a child. Well, only for a very short while. My father put bitter aloes on my fingers. That soon put a stop to it.

Marilyn Bitter haloes?

Louise Aloes. I think it's a sort of plant.

Marilyn *puts the ukelele back in its case. She sits down. After a while, enter the* **Young Guard**. *He carries three small blankets and three small white pillows. He puts them down on the seat. He pulls down the blinds, switches on the wall lamps. He takes one pillow, places it courteously behind* **Anna**'s *head, then spreads the blanket over her knees.*

Anna Danke.

He bows. He takes a blanket and pillow, coughs discreetly. **Louise** *looks up briefly, gestures to him to place them next to her. He does so. He glances at* **Marilyn**. *She smiles. He picks up the third blanket, sits down next to* **Marilyn**, *opens out the blanket, tucks it round both of them, pretends to snuggle down. Both laugh. He gets up, tucks it around her as if she were a baby. She sticks her thumb in her mouth, speaks in a 'baby' voice.*

Marilyn 'Night, 'Night.'

Guard (*mimics*) 'Night, 'Night.

Marilyn *laughs.*

Marilyn Aren't you going to give me a kiss? Küss.

He blows her several. Exits.

Gorgeous, isn't he! Reminds me of James Dean. (*Sighs.*) Oh well – suppose it's bedtime!

Louise *continues working.* **Marilyn** *stands, puts the ukelele on the rack, sits down. Covers herself with the blanket. She puts her thumb in her mouth.* **Louise** *puts down her pen, runs her fingers through her hair, rubs her eyes, her neck. Then she begins to pack up her books etc into her briefcase.* **Marilyn** *watches, sucking her thumb.*

Anna He wouldn't let me see the child. I travelled all the way to London and when I got there, the door was shut in my face.

Laura *looks up sharply, looks away.*

Marilyn No wonder you were crying your bloody eyes out.

Laura (*softly*) Unimaginable despair.

Marilyn (*to* **Louise**) What did you say?

Louise Nothing. I didn't say anything.

Laura (*to herself*) Doomed to unimaginable bliss or unimaginable despair. (*She closes her eyes.*)

Marilyn (*whispering to* **Anna**) You ought to see a solicitor.

Anna I have already taken much advice. But, alas, it is I who is considered to be in the wrong.

Marilyn Says who?

Anna There are certain rules which must not be broken. That is what he told me. My husband. He was trying to warn me, I suppose.

Laura (*quietly, suddenly*) But it was already too late. Overwhelmed with an emotion so strong that there was no room for reason.

Anna Not to think . . . only to live . . . only to feel.

Laura I should have known we'd be punished for being so happy.

Anna/Laura And yet . . . and yet . . .

Anna I do not reject one minute of it . . .

Laura Because it made me feel more alive than I had ever felt . . .

Anna My blood pulsing at the very tips of my fingers . . .

Laura My body shot through by electricity . . .

Anna For *that* I was willing to give up everything. Everything.

Marilyn Even your kid?

Anna Yes.

Marilyn What an amazing story! Just like in a film!

Louise (*clears her throat*) I don't want to be a spoil-sport . . . but I really *must* get some sleep. I do have a very . . .

Marilyn Tight schedule.

Anna (*to* **Louise**) I am so sorry.

Laura (*to* **Louise**) You must forgive me.

Marilyn There's been blokes I've fancied and blokes I've done it with. Sometimes it's been great and sometimes it's been, let's face it, nothing much to write home about. But that's something else. (*Sighs.*) I reckon that's beautiful. I reckon that's fucking beautiful!

Louise Look, it *is* a quarter to one . . .

Marilyn Is it? Fuck me! Come on . . . I'll sing you all to sleep. (*She sings very softly, sweetly.*) 'Running wild, lost control, don't love nobody, it's not worthwhile. All alone, running wild . . .' etc.

The lights fade slowly, till we see only **Louise** *asleep. The song gradually dies away.*

Light **Friedrich Wieck** *sitting in a corner seat. He is a self-assured, bearded man with a pleasantly deep voice and an authoritative manner. He is quite obviously played by the actor who plays* **Richard Last**. *He is dressed soberly in the fashion of the 1820s. He reads from a manuscript, speaking with a German accent.*

Wieck 'Make it your central aim to train the child to become a good man, for this is the highest goal of humanity. Is it not better to bind the tree while it is still young, to guide the heart and teach the right while it is still tender and pure.'

As he reads, the sound of scales being played on a piano by a child, softly at first, then more loudly. **Wieck** *listens. The player falters, begins again.*

Clara . . . my little Clara.

He picks up a newspaper of the 1820s, reads.

'It was with particular pleasure that we listened to the performance of the very talented nine-year-old, Clara Wieck. Under the guidance of her experienced father, who is especially distinguished by his knowledge of the art of piano playing and the enthusiasm with which he devotes himself to its furtherance, the future may be anticipated with the highest hopes.'

The pianist goes on to five finger exercises, major and minor scales. Light **Clara Schumann** *as a child, at the piano. She wears a frilly organza dress, her hair in ringlets. She is very grave, wooden, unchildlike, almost grotesque. We have no difficulty seeing that she is played by the actress who plays* **Marilyn**.

The correct position of the hands. This is our first consideration. After that, correct movement, precision, Clara. Practice, Clara. And, above all, perseverance. With these three, we can achieve anything. Anything.

Clara *continues to play scales. The light slowly fades on* **Wieck**. **Clara** *looks up from the piano. She does not speak with a German accent.*

Clara My diary, begun by my father May 7th, 1827 and to be continued by Clara Josephine Wieck. (*She quotes.*) 'My father, who has vainly hoped for a change of mood on my part, remarked again today that I am still so idle, negligent, unmethodical, self-willed etc, especially in piano playing and practising that he tore the copy in pieces before my eyes and from today he will not give me another lesson.' (*She plays, sings, plaintively, simply.*) 'I wanna be loved by you, by you and nobody else but you, I wanna be loved by you alone . . .'

Louise (*opening her eyes*) They used this apparatus to teach the piano. It was called a chiroplast. It held the fingers and hand in check to make sure they were always in the correct position. A bit like foot binding, I suppose. *My* father made me eat my crusts. He said it would make my hair curl. (*Pause.*) He slapped my fingers when he caught me biting my nails. It hurt. (*Pause.*) I don't know whether he used the chiroplast or not. Wieck. (**Wieck** *now speaks as* **Richard Last**.)

Last But you *hope* he did. Because it suits your thesis admirably.

Louise Richard?

Last Who else?

Louise You piss me off, turning up all over the place. Piss me off. Piss me off.

Last *nods.*

And stop nodding. You look like one of those stupid little dogs in the backs of cars.

Last That's good. That's very good.

Louise You know I hate you.

Last I see. Can you tell me why?

Louise Because you make me feel like a naughty child. As if I can't do anything right.

Last Could you be with that for a minute.

Describe the *tone* of that . . . you say I make you feel like a child . . . what does that mean to you?

Pause.

Louise I want him to touch me . . . every part of me. I want to feel his tongue in my mouth. I want him to reach out and stroke my breast. See, if I touch my breast, the nipples grow hard . . . (*Demonstrates.*)

Last Him? Who is *him*?

Louise Friedrich Wieck, 1785 to 1873.

Last *gets up, goes to* **Louise**, *pulls her to her feet, kisses her very passionately on the mouth. The piano playing starts up again. He breaks away at once.*

Last Clara . . . my little Clara.

He exits quickly. **Louise** *falls back into her seat.*

Louise Don't go. Not yet . . . please . . . oh please. (*She looks around, trying to get her bearings, struggles awake.*) Not again, not again. 'All part of the process.' All part of the bloody process! I am trying to work, damn you. In case you hadn't noticed. I have to earn my living. Which I do by writing and teaching. This is my work. 'Clara Schumann . . . a new perspective.' Not that it matters to you . . . not that you give a damn . . .

She angrily begins to pull on her cardigan and her jacket. Light **Rhea**, *sitting watching, her backpack beside her.*

I'm . . . I'm sorry. I didn't realise. Oh . . . it's you.

Rhea Must have been one hell of a dream.

Louise *is startled.*

Who's Richard?

Louise I don't know any . . . he's my therapist. My therapist is called Richard. Richard Last.

Long pause. **Rhea** *looks at* **Louise**'s *files etc.*

Rhea You a writer?

Louise Not exactly. I suppose I'd describe myself as an academic. My special subject is feminist studies. Undiscovered women of the nineteenth century.

Rhea *laughs.*

Is that funny?

Rhea *shakes her head, still smiling.*

Louise What do *you* do?

Rhea Nothing. (*She smiles. A long pause. She puts her feet up.*) Tell me a story.

Louise A *story*? What about?

Rhea Anything.

A pause. **Louise** *prepares to deliver a lecture.*

Louise OK. Well . . . as you may know, Clara Schumann had a lifelong relationship with the composer, Brahms, who was, incidentally, fourteen years her junior. When she heard that Schumann was dying, instead of going straight to his bedside, she and Brahms went to Ostend, no one seems to know why. Actually that's one of the reasons I'm going to Berlin. I'm in pursuit of certain letters I believe will be *most* . . .

Rhea I meant, about *you*.

Louise *Me?*

Rhea Who you love, who you hate, what you believe in, whether you ever killed anyone or wanted to. What you'd be prepared to die for. That sort of thing.

Louise *is fazed.*

Louise I . . . well . . . I come from Uley. It's a little village in Gloucestershire. My father was the vicar.

Rhea Is he dead?

Louise Good heavens, no! He retired two years ago. But he likes to keep busy. He's just set himself the task of going through the complete works of Mozart and *Fifty*

Favourite Walks in Gloucestershire. He does one of each a day.

Rhea *laughs.*

Why do you keep laughing?

Rhea Why not? (*Pause.*) You look tired. (*Pause.*) Especially round the eyes.

Louise *touches her left eye.*

Louise She wouldn't let me sleep.

Rhea Who?

Louise A girl who did Marilyn Monroe impersonations. She was sitting where you are. (*Pause.*) In the same seat actually.

Rhea *bursts out laughing, controls herself with difficulty.*

I wanted to learn the piano, but my father said it would be a waste of money. 'A *wicked* waste' were his actual words. 'It's not as if you're intending to take it up professionally,' he said, 'Only messing about.' Messing about was something my father simply would *not* tolerate.

Rhea Where was your mother during all this?

Louise Probably arranging flowers. She seems to have spent most of her life arranging flowers.

Long pause. **Louise** *is thoughtful.*

There was another woman . . . she was crying.

Rhea Was this in your dream too?

Louise *pauses, uncertain.*

Louise No . . . at least . . .

Enter the **Young Guard**. *He pulls up the blind, switches off the lamps, collects up the blankets, etc.*

Guard Gut geschlafen?

Louise What did he say?

Rhea He asked if you slept well.

Guard Berlin . . . fünf Minuten. (*He holds up five fingers, points to his watch, exits.*)

Rhea We're nearly there.

Louise Are we? Goodness!

She jumps up, begins to organise herself to leave. **Rhea** *watches, then calmly picks up her backpack, goes to exit.* **Louise** *stops what she is doing.*

Have a good trip.

Rhea *smiles. Exits.* **Louise** *stands stock still.*

Goodbye.

Just a few notes of the Fugue, played rather suddenly on the piano, then the sounds of the train drawing into the station. The lights fade to blackout.

Lights come up slowly on a small hotel room. The space is very orderly, with a desk, a chest of drawers, a mirror, a tightly made single bed. **Louise** *is methodically unpacking, putting her clothes away. After this she arranges all her notes, paper, books in neat piles on the bed. She then picks up a notebook and a pen and sits down at the desk. A long pause, a struggle. She reaches for her address book. She picks up the phone, hesitates, puts it down again, picks it up, consults address book, plucks up courage, dials. The phone rings. She looks at her watch. The phone is answered on answerphone.*

Last (*answerphone*) '071 794 6151 I'm afraid there is nobody here to take your call . . .'

Louise *replaces the phone. She is distressed. A long pause.*

Louise I could have left a message. I could have said: 'Hello Richard. This is Louise calling you from Berlin. Just to tell you I've started seeing things. Well, *people* actually. Is this to be expected? Is this what I'm paying you for?' I was perfectly all right, you know. Before. *Perfectly* all right. Apart from the occasional headache. I'm

beginning to wish I'd never . . . I'm
beginning to wish . . . Actually I'm glad he
wasn't there. He might have been angry. I
don't like it when he's angry. (*Pause.*)
You've got to stop this. You've got to stop
this right away.

*She stands, composes herself, goes to her briefcase,
takes out a number of index cards bound with an
elastic band, looks through them, takes one out.
Returns to the phone, dials. It rings, is answered.*

Yes . . . ah . . . Guten Tag. May . . . may I
speak in English? Thank you. (*Speaks
slowly.*) I am engaged in . . . engaged . . . er
. . . I am a student. I am writing a
biography . . . *hoping* to write a biography
of Clara Schumann. Schumann. That's
right. Clara. Thank you. (*Pause. She taps
fingers impatiently.*) Guten Tag. I am
interested in . . . I hope to be commissioned
to . . . I am *writing* a biography of Clara
Schumann. Schumann, Clara. Wife of
Robert, yes. (*Sighs.*) I understand that you
have certain manuscripts. Original
manuscripts. Letters and so forth. Thank
you. (*Sighs, long pause. She looks around the
room, starts to bite a nail, stops.*) You *do* have
them? That's excellent. (*Checks index card.*)
Letters from Brahms and other
correspondents – particularly around 1854.
Musical autographs, programmes . . .
tapes, yes . . . Lieder. Excellent. Excellent.
And your opening hours? (*Pause.*) Thank
you so much . . . thank you.

(*She replaces phone. Reads as she writes in
notebook.*) Monday: Collate notes and
outline research plan. Tuesday: 10–5:
Library. Wednesday: 10–5: Library.
Thursday: Query Düsseldorf. (*She closes the
notebook, catches sight of herself in the mirror.
Lampooning her reflection.*) Query Düsseldorf.

*Finding the elastic band from the index cards, she
suddenly separates a little bunch of her hair and
binds it with the elastic band. She stares,
surprised, at the result in the mirror. There is a
loud knock at the door.* **Louise** *is puzzled. The
knock is repeated.*

Come in.

The door opens. A young **Porter** *(Johannes)
stands in the doorway, dressed in uniform but with
his jacket unbuttoned. His similarity to the*
Guard *in the previous sequence should be
obvious. He carries a tray with hot chocolate in a
silver jug. A cup and saucer.*

Porter Schokolade.

Louise I didn't order . . . (*She looks up,
startled, half recognising him.*)

Porter Nummer zwei hundert siebzehn.
(Number two hundred and seventeen.) (*He
points to the number on the bill.*)

Louise There must be some mistake.

Porter Schokolade. You don't like?

Louise Yes . . . yes I do. But I didn't order
any.

The **Porter** *moves slightly into the room. He
glances at the books on the bed.*

Porter Schumann. You like?

Louise I'm researching a book on the life
of . . .

Porter You know this?

*He sings a few bars of something by Robert
Schumann. His voice is very pleasant.*

Louise Of course.

Porter Also this?

He sings something else. **Louise** *suddenly realises
her hair is still caught up in the little bunch.
Embarrassed, she removes the elastic band. The*
Porter *sees this.*

Don't take away. Is looking nice.

Louise I was only . . . I was only playing.

Porter So play . . . here, maybe I can help.

*He puts down the tray with the hot chocolate,
looks around, sees two rubber bands, picks them
up – holds them out to her. She shakes her head.*

I may?

*He approaches her from behind. Very gently
gathers her hair into two bunches, then leads her to
the mirror.*

See.

*He stands behind her, looking in the mirror, his
hands resting on her shoulders. She looks at their
reflection. A strange moment. Then she turns
quickly, pulling the bands out of her hair quite
viciously.*

Louise Hot chocolate. It's a drink for
children. Bonfire night. Thunderstorms. I
didn't order hot chocolate . . . or tea . . . or
coffee. I didn't order anything.

Porter Bitte? (I beg your pardon?)

Louise I have come here to work. That is
the purpose of my visit. Provided that I
adhere strictly to my timetable, there is no
reason why I should not achieve the results
that I am looking for. So, kindly go away,
and take that ridiculous drink with you. Do
you understand?

*A brief pause. He looks at her very levelly, then
picks up the tray. Another pause. Then he exits
with great dignity. The lights fade to blackout. A
few notes of the Fugue, in the bass.*

Lights up on a table in a reference library.
Louise *surrounded by old books, manuscripts,
copying from one of the books, she reads aloud in a
clipped, precise tone, as she writes.*

Louise 'Two years and a half of Wieck's
skilful and prudent training of fingers and
brain produced definite signs that promised
well for the future . . . Her ear has
considerably developed in its perception of
pitch, whilst her knowledge of keys and
chords not only extended from the
principal triads – tonic, dominant and sub-
dominant – to the diminished sevens of
every key, but allowed her to modulate
from one key to another as she desired.
Such good progress was rewarded by

outward and visible signs of her father's
approbation.'

*She sighs, puts down the pencil, runs her fingers
through her hair. Closes the book, pushes it away
from her. A man sits opposite her, head bowed.
He switches on a reading light. We see that it is*
Richard Last. **Louise** *looks up wearily.*

Hello Richard.

Last And how are you?

Louise I'm fine. Really. Everything's going
according to plan. I'll be finished by
Christmas. I mean the book . . . the book
will be finished.

Last *nods.*

Why do you always nod?

Last What would you prefer me to do?

Louise Nothing. I don't want you to do
anything.

Long pause. **Louise** *looks up at the ceiling.*

My father took me to the planetarium. I
must have been about eight or nine.
Spring. I remember because there were
tulips. When we got there it was closed till
2 o'clock. I cried.

Last Why?

Louise Because he wouldn't let me in.

Last *He*?

Louise I meant 'they'.

Richard *nods.*

Anyway . . . we walked and walked the
whole length of Baker Street. I remember
being terribly warm. My mother always
made me wrap up whatever the weather.
Then I saw this picture of a Knickerbocker
Glory. It's a sort of ice-cream. Lots of fruit
and whipped cream and cherries on top. Of
course, I wasn't allowed to have one. My
father said they were astronomically
expensive. Astronomically. (*Laughs.*)

Last And the planetarium?

Louise Frightening . . . Too many stars. Too much sky. Too many . . . possibilities. I wanted to be somewhere . . . safe.

Last Where would you be safe?

Long pause.

Louise I don't know.

He begins to write. **Louise** *watches.*

Long pause.

What are you writing?

Silence.

I said, what are you writing?

He looks up, now a stranger, speaks in perfect German.

Last Entschuldigen Sie . . . ich spreche kein Englisch. (Excuse me, I don't speak English.)

He turns off the reading lamp. A few bars of the Fugue in the bass.

Louise Too many possibilities. How can anyone ever know what *really* happened? (*Very quietly.*) Let me in, Clara. Please. Why won't you let me in? (*She reaches for the book she was reading previously, but doesn't open it.*) When Schumann was dying, you hadn't seen him for two years. But you didn't rush to his bedside. No . . . you went to Ostend with Brahms instead. Why did you destroy all those letters? What was in them that you didn't want anyone else to see? They were love letters, weren't they? Must have been . . . passionate . . . shocking even. Love letters . . . it's obvious.

She reaches for a notepad, begins to write, speaking the words aloud:

'My love . . . my dearest darling . . . my own love. Sitting here alone . . . lonely . . . thinking of you, wanting to hold you. (*Pause, thinks.*) Your long, pale back, your

mouth hot and open against mine, your tongue . . .'

She becomes aware of **Rhea** *standing next to her. She slams the pad shut.*

Are you following me?

Rhea Perhaps. Fancy a cup of tea? I owe you one.

Louise You got some money then?

Rhea I've been busking.

She pulls out a wooden pipe, plays a few notes. Lights come up on various other seats. We see **Laura** *and* **Marilyn**, *reading, writing, absorbed. They whisper.*

Laura Shh . . . people are working.

Marilyn It's only music.

Laura You mentioned tea.

Louise I really don't have the time. We can't all be gypsies . . .

The women laugh.

Rhea That's OK.

She takes **Louise***'s notepad, reads aloud.*

Thinking of you . . .

Laura *looks at the book.*

Laura Wanting to hold you . . .

Rhea Your long, pale back . . .

Marilyn *looks.*

Marilyn Your mouth hot and open against mine . . .

The women laugh. **Louise** *snatches the notebook, stuffs it away into her briefcase. She is extremely embarrassed.*

Rhea I'm sorry.

Louise That's quite all right.

Louise *rubs her neck and shoulder.*

Rhea Here . . . let me.

She crosses to **Louise**, *stands behind her, gently massages her shoulder. For a brief moment* **Louise** *indulges herself, then stiffens.*

Louise I really must . . .

Rhea Of course.

She very lightly touches **Louise***'s face. Exits.* **Louise** *touches her own face, then her shoulder. A long pause. She looks around, sees only people reading, writing. She reaches for a manuscript, reads from it. Her voice is strained, formal.*

Louise 'Sir . . . in reply to your communication, I request to say that it is quite impossible for me at so long a distance of time to bind myself by a promise which my engagements might render it impossible to keep . . .'

Marilyn/Laura (*murmuring*) Impossible.

Louise 'In this consideration, you must excuse my giving you a positive answer at present, though I am fully sensible . . .

Marilyn/Laura (*murmuring*) Sensible. Fully sensible.

Louise *rests her head on the desk, exhausted, depleted. The other women do likewise. A few notes of the Fugue played on* **Rhea***'s pipe. Enter* **Anna**, *carrying a pile of books. She sits down. Enter the* **Polythene Woman**. *She sweeps soundlessly with a large soft broom. The women watch her, heads on the desk, and all softly, sadly sing the words of the letter in harmony, a capella, to the tune of the Fugue.*

In reply to your communication
I request to say
It is quite impossible for me
To bind myself by a promise
Which my engagements
Might render it impossible to keep.

In this consideration
You must excuse my giving
A positive answer

Though I am fully sensible
Though I am fully sensible

Though I am fully sensible, etc., etc.

As they sing, **Polythene Woman** *sweeps and the lights fade to blackout.*

In the darkness, the voice of **Johannes Brahms**. *He is a young man in his twenties, blonde, beautiful. He is obviously played by the same actor who played the* **Porter** *and the* **Young Guard**.

Brahms Clara . . . Clara . . . I *must* talk with you.

Lights come up slowly on **Clara**, *sitting on the end of her bed. She is in her thirties, dressed in a long nightgown in the style of the 1850s. She has a tense, tight quality, an air of suppressed emotion.*

Clara I have told you a million times. You may not come to my room.

Light **Brahms** *standing outside the door. He speaks with considerable passion. There is a hint of exaggeration, of stylised romanticism about the scene.*

Brahms Tonight, at dinner, I saw you look at me. I saw what was in your eyes. Clara . . .

Clara I am a married woman, and besides, there are the children to consider. What kind of example would it be for them to see their mother fly in the face of all that is decent and proper?

Brahms So you turn your back on love?

Clara This is not love. Love is more sober. Love lasts for a lifetime, not just for a night.

Brahms Let me in and I will prove you a liar.

Clara I have a concert to give tomorrow. Nothing can come of this except grief, regret and madness.

Brahms Is madness the worst that can happen? Perhaps great art can only be born out of chaos. Let me in. You *must* let me in.

Clara (*to herself*) At dinner I looked into his eyes and felt I would drown in their blueness. I pray to God to give me strength. (*Pause. Aloud.*) Music is not chaos. Music is order, a mathematical equation. When I was a child, I practised every day, four hours, sometimes five. There was not time for dolls or games. I am still practising. Every day without exception. Practising to be perfect. Genius is a romantic myth. There is no substitute for hard work and devotion to duty. That is the price. (*Shouts.*) Go away. I cannot afford you. Go away.

Pause.

Brahms If I go now I'll only come back . . . tomorrow, or the next day . . . or next month . . . or next year. Don't ever ask me to forget you. Don't ever ask me to pretend that none of this has happened. I love you, Clara, and I want you. And there can be no end to it . . . no end . . .

A door opens revealing **Louise**, *her hair wet, dressed in a robe. The light goes out on* **Clara** *and* **Brahms**. **Louise** *stands very still for a moment, as if listening, then, rubbing her hair vigorously with a towel, walks into the room. She turns on the bedside lamp, then the overhead light. She stands, very still. She rubs her hair, then, fetching a comb, begins to comb it through. Going to her bag, she takes out a small cassette player and some tapes. She looks for a particular tape, puts it on. It is Brahms Piano Concerto No. 4. She stands listening for a moment, rubbing her hair, then turns it off abruptly. Going to her briefcase, she takes out some photographs of Clara Schumann, lays them side by side on the bed. She looks at them very hard.*

Louise So bloody unhappy. (*She picks up the rag doll. Holds it against her. She crosses to the desk, turns up some notes, reads from them, rather fast.*) 'Work and duty always took precedence over personal happiness or self-expression. Even her much vaunted defiance of her father to marry Robert was,

in fact, simply the transference of allegiance from one patriarchal figure to another. All too soon the excitement of courtship gave way to the drudgery of child-bearing and the trauma of a husband whose early depression soon turned to suicide attempts and chronic schizophrenia. Remarkably enough she bore him eight children in thirteen years while undertaking a punishing schedule of concert tours both in Germany and abroad. And always she was the devoted and faithful wife, the dutiful provider to her children, the gifted and selfless interpreter of her husband's work . . .'

Light **Vera Frampton**, **Louise**'s *mother. She is arranging tulips in a tall vase. She is very tight. Quietly well-spoken, discreetly dressed. She bears an obvious resemblance to* **Laura**, *seen in the train.*

Vera I wouldn't describe him as a cruel man. Simply rather detached. And *very* methodical. (*Pause.*) You were such a good baby . . . no trouble at all. (*Pause.*) Not that *he* had all that much to do with you. But he always wanted you to do well. Bought you the Encyclopaedia Britannica on your sixth birthday, that sort of thing.

Louise I didn't *want* the Encyclopaedia bloody Britannica.

Vera Language, language.

Louise I wanted a doll that said 'Mama'. (*Laughs. To the rag-doll.*) You don't say 'Mama', do you? You don't say anything bloody much. (*She looks at the doll.*) Sorry . . . sorry . . . it's not your fault.

She goes to the bed, lies down, curls up clutching the doll, pulls the cover over her. After a while, puts her thumb in her mouth, holding the doll close to her face.

Cold . . . so cold.

She lies there very still. **Vera** *watches. Long pause.* **Louise**'s *voice becomes childish.*

I used to like playing with mud. By the river. The bank was all muddy. I went there after school once. I wasn't supposed to, but I did. I think I was eight. Something like that. Eight or nine.

Vera You were nine. I remember.

Louise Do you? That's funny.

Vera *smiles faintly.*

It had been raining all week. So the mud was all thick and squelchy. First of all I just squatted down and picked up great big lumps of it and squeezed it through my fingers. Then I started smearing it on my face and some of it got in my mouth and it tasted all funny – a bit like chocolate, only different. The next thing I was plastering it all over myself . . . imagine, in my school uniform! Covered in mud . . . sticky, warm, lovely dirty mud. And then . . . and then . . .

Light **Last**, *sitting at* **Louise**'s *desk.*

Last Yes.

Louise's *voice now adult.*

Louise My father came looking for me.

Last *nods.*

Last Did he find you?

Louise Of course.

She sits up.

Louise We walked home together in this terrible silence. Then he locked me in my room.

Last Still covered in mud?

Louise *nods.*

Louise He locked me in my room and the mud dried and I smelled like a pigsty and my skin cracked and then . . . and then . . .

Last Yes?

Long pause. **Louise** *looks at* **Vera**.

Vera I'm sorry, I'm afraid I don't quite . . .

Louise Nothing. And then nothing.

Pause. **Louise** *looks at* **Vera**.

I don't want you to blame him.

Last It's not my job to blame anybody.

Louise Not even me?

The Fugue played as if by a child, picking out the notes on a piano, very faltering. Light fades on **Last** *and* **Vera**. **Louise** *sits on the edge of the bed.*

There was another time. But I'm not going to tell you. Why the hell should I? There was another time . . . nearly. I knew I couldn't afford it. A child can be forgiven for wallowing in mud. Forgiven or punished. Being an adult means to be in control. Well, doesn't it? (*She rubs her neck.*) Rhea . . . what an odd name. Such dirty feet. (*Pause.*) I wonder why she stayed with him? My mother. She couldn't have been happy. (*She picks up a picture of* **Clara**, *studies it.*) But perhaps happiness isn't everything. Perhaps it's more important . . .

A knock at the door.

Perhaps it's more important to do the right thing.

Another knock.

Yes?

The door opens a little. The **Porter** *stands there with a silver tray.*

Porter Schokolade?

Louise I told you . . . I didn't order anything.

Porter (*coming in*) It is a present. Everybody like presents. It is like . . . what you say . . . Geburtstag . . . birthday. (*He puts the chocolate down on the bedside table.*) You are busy?

Louise Yes.

Porter You don't look so busy.

Long pause. **Louise** *gets up.*

Louise It was very kind of you to bring me the chocolate, but I'm afraid I really must ask you to . . .

Porter You are looking always tired.

He touches her face, near her eye. She jumps.

Louise I'm quite all right.

Porter Then why you are crying?

Louise I am *not* crying. I never cry. (*She rubs fiercely at her eyes.*)

He picks up the Clara Schumann book, studies the cover.

Porter She also is looking not so happy.

Louise *sighs deeply, starts to rub her neck. The* **Porter** *sees this.*

You have pain?

Louise Sometimes. A little.

Porter My mother also. I make it better. So . . .

He stands behind **Louise**, *gently massaging her neck. She allows this.*

Always she say: 'Please to rub my throat. You do it so nice.'

Louise Neck. This is throat. (*Indicates.*)

Porter This I can rub also. (*He touches her throat very gently.*) If you like it.

Long pause.

Louise The chocolate will be cold.

He smiles, goes to the chocolate, pours it out, hands it to her. She warms her hands around the cup, then sips it. He watches.

It's . . . it's very nice. Thank you.

Porter Then please to sit down. Relax. Enjoy.

Louise I really should . . . (*Pulls at robe.*)

Porter Please . . .

She sits down. He watches. She drinks.

Your hair is wet.

Louise Yes . . . (*She touches hair.*)

Porter You are looking like . . . how you say . . . woman she has tail like fish.

Louise A mermaid. Oh . . . (*Laughs.*)

Porter In my school we always sing song. She is sitting on a stone and singing. (*Sings Lorelei.*) 'Ich weiss nicht was soll es bedeuten . . .' (I don't know what it means . . .')

Louise *joins in.*

Louise/Porter . . . Dass ich so traurig bin.' (. . . that I am so sad.)

Porter You know.

Louise *She* wrote the music.

Indicates the Clara Schumann book.

Porter She is friend of yours?

Louise Oh no. (*Laughs.*)

Porter When you are laughing, you are looking like a small girl.

Louise And when I'm not?

Porter Then like old lady.

Pause.

You finish?

Louise Finish?

Porter With the Schokolade?

Louise Oh . . . oh yes. Thank you.

He takes the cup. Their hands touch. He puts the cup down.

Porter You are frighten?

Louise I don't think so.

Porter Then why you are shake?

He takes both her hands very gently in his. They look at each other.

Louise You must go now.

Porter You want?

Louise I have a great deal of work to do.

Porter At night you are working?

Louise I've been in the library all day and now I must collate my notes. Tomorrow I must go to the museum. I have a very tight schedule.

Pause.

Porter You have husband, children?

Louise I don't see that's any of your . . .

Porter You don't have.

Louise No.

Porter You like to have children?

Louise I haven't given it that much thought.

Porter Who you are trying to phone always? Always trying. Never succeed. Even at night you are trying and he is not there. Is someone you love?

Louise I . . . no . . . no . . . it's nobody.

Porter *smiles.*

Porter If you are phoning nobody, this is why nobody is not there. (*He holds out his hand.*) My name is Johannes.

Pause. She is startled.

Louise Don't be ridiculous.

Porter Perhaps in England you don't have this name. How you say it? John? So . . . you can call me John . . . John is OK. What is your name?

Louise Louise. My name is Louise.

A few notes of the Fugue. Suddenly she stands watching him. A long pause.

You have the most amazing eyes. Blue like the sea. I was looking at you during dinner. I was looking at your eyes and I thought, 'If I don't turn away I shall drown in their blueness.'

Porter Dinner?

Louise Music is order. A mathematical equation. All my life I have been taught to do as I am told. There is no room for chaos. My father was an excellent teacher. John . . . my father's name was John.

Porter Johannes is John. The same. Come. It will be easy. Once you begin it will be very easy.

Louise Perhaps that's what I'm afraid of.

He kisses her. She experiments with how it feels.

Porter You see?

Louise Yes.

Porter You want? If you don't want, I go now.

Pause.

Louise Perhaps just once more.

He kisses her. She responds with passion, then breaks away.

This isn't me . . . not me . . .

Porter Yes . . . you . . . Louise . . . Louise. With the wet hair . . . Louise . . . Lorelei . . . Lorelei.

Louise Not Louise.

Porter What it matter who? Maybe I am not Johannes. Still I am here. You are here. Lorelei. Louise. Somebody.

Pause. She looks at him, then reaches across, dips her fingers into the empty cup.

Louise When I was little I always wanted

to do this, but my father said it was bad manners.

She sucks at her fingers, dips them in again, a pause, then she offers them to him. He hesitates. She pokes them into his mouth. Then she pulls him to her, smears chocolate from the cup onto his lips. A pause. Then she kisses it off. She laughs, a joyful laugh of pure pleasure. Then she dips her finger in the chocolate again and watching his face, smears some onto her breast. He laughs, she laughs. Then pulling him to her, she kisses him very passionately, deliberately. The lights fade.

After a while, the lights come up slowly. It is still night. The bed is utterly dishevelled. **Louise** *lies across it alone, naked, grubby, covered only with a sheet. She comes round slowly, sits up. She seems disorientated. She finds her robe on the floor, pulls it on. She goes to the bedside table. It is bare. She goes to the door, opens it, looks out, closes it. She goes to the mirror, looks at herself.*

Extraordinary dream! (*Laughs.*) Chocolate. The flavour was definitely chocolate.

She turns, her foot knocks against something. She bends to pick up an empty cup. She dips her finger into it, licks it. Puts the cup down. Then she pulls aside the robe to look at her body. She goes to the mirror, examines herself.

I didn't order chocolate. I didn't order anything.

Pause.

I must get to the museum. Before it closes. (*Picks up watch, shakes it.*) My watch has stopped. 3 o'clock. It's dark outside. It could be today or tomorrow. No idea what time it is. Richard . . . where are you? I need to talk to you. There was a man. He played me with his fingers. Someone was singing. The song about the mermaids. Clara's song. Was it me? Who was it? He put his tongue into my mouth. And between my legs. Sticky. Sweet. Chocolate. Like the night of the thunderstorm. Whatever he did, it wasn't enough. Whatever he did, I asked for more. Cried

out like a child who is always hungry. Child at my breast, child in my belly. Now my belly is full of him. He is inside me now, growing. Like a flower . . . like a tree. Soon he'll be born. I shall have him soon. My child. My lover. Johannes. John. It was a dream, wasn't it. Only a dream. (*She pulls on her raincoat over her robe.*) Must go to the museum before it closes . . . Lorelei . . . he called me Lorelei . . . drowned in his eyes . . . Lorelei . . .

She runs out.

Lights change. In the street. Night. A flash of neon, a blare of the juke box, sudden, too loud.

Enter **Louise**, *running, wild-eyed, barefoot. In the shadows,* **'Marilyn'** *standing at the street corner.* **Anna** *passes, pushing an empty push chair.*

Anna Clara . . . Clara . . . Clara . . .

Louise *runs up to her.*

Louise Excuse me . . . can you direct me to . . .

Anna *looks at her fiercely, weeping.*

Anna Dead. Starved to death. Do not ask me anything.

She exits, pushing the chair.

Light **'Marilyn'**. **Louise** *runs up to her.*

Louise Excuse me, do you know the way to the museum?

'Marilyn' *turns. It is a man in drag, grotesque but alluring.*

'Marilyn' Fünf und zwanzig. (Twenty-five.) Halbe Stunde. (Half an hour.) Twenty five. You like it standing up?

Louise *turns away. Light* **Laura** *standing at a bus stop reading her letter.* **Louise** *runs up to her.*

Louise Excuse me . . .

Laura (*turning to her*) Unimaginable bliss
. . . unimaginable despair. (*Turns away.*)

Louise *stands, isolated, lost. Light the*
Polythene Woman. *She is surrounded by*
various bundles, sits on the ground.

Polythene Woman I was beautiful once.
More beautiful than you. You don't believe
me? Look at this photo. (*She points to a photo*
in the newspaper.) The more you get, the
more you want. Opens you up like a tin-
opener, like a hole in your tooth that won't
stop aching till you plug it up. But it soon
runs out. That's the trouble. To begin with
it's in good supply. When you've got your
looks, your pretty eyes, then you can get all
you want. Hook them in, use them up,
chuck them out. You're in charge.
Afterwards, you start to dry up. Skin goes
papery; in here too. (*Indicates genitals.*) Then
they don't want to know. Throw you out
like yesterday's papers. (*She grabs hold of*
Louise.) I can smell him, you know. Dead
fish. Did you pay him or did he pay you?
Not that it makes no difference. Dead fish.

She laughs raucously. **Louise** *pulls away.*

Louise I've got to get to the museum. It's
very important. No one seems to
understand.

Polythene Woman Eating is important.
Dying. A bed for the night . . . A fire is
nice, or at least a dry place out of the cold.
Music. I used to like music.

She starts to hum a few bars of the Fugue. Enter
Richard Last *in a peaked cap and*
indeterminate uniform. **Louise** *runs up to him,*
speaks very rapidly.

Louise I am engaged in a research project.
The life and work of Clara Schumann
1819–1896. She was the daughter of
Friedrich Wieck 1785–1873.

Puts her hands together.

Our Father, which art in Heaven,
Hallowed be thy name,

Thy Kingdom come
Thy will be done . . .

On September 12th 1840, she married
Robert Schumann against her father's
wishes. A composer of some note and a
virtuoso performer . . .

Sings suddenly, childishly.

All things bright and beautiful
All creatures great and small
All things wise and wonderful . . .

Last The museum is closed. Geschlossen.

Louise Richard? Richard . . . Listen . . . I
had this terrible dream . . . How can it be
closed? Daddy promised. He promised. It
can't be closed.

Last Das Museum ist geschlossen. (The
museum is closed.) Verstehen Sie nicht?
Sprechen Sie kein Deutsch? (Don't you
understand? Don't you speak German?)

Louise (*softly*) The Lord God made them
all. So that's all right. Daddy said it was all
right. Everything will be all right.

Last Geschlossen. Alles geschlossen.
(Closed. Everything closed.)

Louise Daddy promised. He *promised*. I
always say my prayers. *Always*. Drowning.
Eyes blue as the sea. My mother didn't
remember. She *said* she didn't. (*Pause.*) I
have been commissioned. My deadline is
imminent. Not my fault. Say it's not my
fault. I never ordered chocolate. Nor tea.
Nor coffee. There wasn't a thunderstorm.
On earth as it is in heaven. For ever and
ever and ever and ever and ever. Amen. It
was only a dream. Knickerbocker glory.
(*Laughs.*) Only a dream. (*She batters against*
the wall with her fists.) Clara . . . Clara . . .
tell them Clara. Tell them to open the
museum. Tell them it's not my fault. Tell
them I always say my prayers. Tell them,
Clara. Tell them.

She continues to bang violently and to shout as the
lights fade to blackout.

Act Two

In the darkness, the Fugue played as by a child on a glockenspiel. Light the hotel room. It is in total chaos. The bed is a tangled heap of sheets. The floor littered with papers, many of them crumpled, various trays with cups of chocolate half drunk, sweet wrappers. **Louise** *sits on the floor in the midst of all this, picking out the notes. She looks totally dishevelled, vulnerable, childlike. Her hair hangs in scruffy little bunches; she wears a short nightgown. Her feet and legs are filthy. She plays a wrong note. When she first speaks, it is in a parody of Friedrich Wieck.*

Louise The note is G. How many times must I tell you the same thing.

(*Own voice, rather childish.*) Sorry. Shall I do it again.

(*Wieck's voice.*) Indeed you shall. And again. And again. Till you can get it right.

She plays it again, very carefully. She makes a mistake.

(*Wieck's voice.*) You are a wilful child. Wilful and disobedient. If you had attended to your practice as I requested, you would, in due course, achieve results. Perfection is not a mystery; it is a simple equation. If we do as we are instructed we eventually achieve all our goals . . .

She begins to giggle, tries to control herself.

(*As Wieck.*) But . . . if we succumb to idleness, temptation and disorder, then we can expect nothing but disappointment . . .

She breaks into uncontrolled laughter, then jumps up, holds out her nightie, curtsies, smiles sweetly.

(*Reciting.*) I am a good girl, a nice girl. I always do as I am told. I've got very good manners and I always look . . . nice. (*Pause.*) I have a degree in English Literature . . . (*Carefully.*) a 2.2 . . . and soon I shall be awarded my PhD. I am an acknowledged expert in my field. There are few who can touch me. Very few. (*Pause.*)

No one can touch me . . . that is the truth. I can hardly touch myself. I am untouched. Perhaps untouchable. Except in dreams. (*Pause.*) Only in dreams. (*Brighter.*) But I can do a dance for Daddy, dance for Daddy – (*She takes a few steps.*) Pretty as a picture in my pretty little frock . . .

The sound of the mazurka from the opening sequence of Anna Karenina. **Louise** *stops, startled. Light* **Anna.** *She is dancing like a gypsy, slowly turning on one heel, very sensuous, knowing, dramatic. She speaks with passion.*

Anna 'I Love you, Alexei', I said, 'I love you.' I knew at the railroad station. Nothing else has mattered since.

She whirls around.

Anna/Louise (*in unison*) I feel pain. I feel tears. Because I am so happy.

Louise *speaks now in her normal voice.*

Louise But you lost everything . . . your home, your child, even your life . . .

Anna Of course. How could I steal such passion and be allowed to survive? I was marked out from the start to be totally extraordinary.

Anna/Louise (*in unison*) To feel more than most, to suffer more than most, to weep more than most, to die in a most spectacular fashion.

Louise *sighs deeply.*

Louise I like trains.

Anna I also . . . Who knows where they come from or where they go. (*Pause.*) I was lost from the very first moment I saw him, striding towards me out of the mist. I contained in me such fire, I thought I must burn at his touch. And later, as I walked out amongst the ordinary people, people who led normal, uneventful lives, I pitied them – every one of them, because they had not felt this extraordinary passion, had not caught this glimpse of paradise, experienced this moment of ecstasy. And yes, in exchange, I was prepared to lose everything, even my life.

A few bars of the Rachmaninov piano concerto, as used as the theme for the film Brief Encounter. *Light* **Laura**, *dressed as before. She stands twisting her wedding ring, she speaks softly, sadly.*

Laura (*to* **Anna**) I'm an ordinary woman. I didn't know such things could happen to ordinary people.

Louise (*softly*) 'I love you,' I said, 'I love your nice eyes, the way you smile, the way you laugh at my jokes. It's no use pretending it hasn't happened, because it has.'

Anna But you let him go. How could you do such a thing?

Laura Guilt. Decency. Self-respect. All those plain, tight self-righteous little words.

Anna 'Forgive me.' That's what he said.

Louise 'Forgive you for what?' I asked.

Laura 'For everything. For meeting you in the first place . . . for loving you . . . for taking a bit of grit out of your eye.'

Anna Grit?

Laura That was how we met. A piece of grit flew into my eye on the railway station, and I couldn't get it out. He said he was a doctor and offered to help. It all seems so trite, so utterly improbable. That was only the beginning.

Anna And the end?

Laura The end was like everything else in my life . . . At first I couldn't believe it. I said to myself: 'He didn't go. Any minute now he'll come walking back, saying he's forgotten something.'

Louise But he didn't. He'd gone . . . gone for ever. Done the decent thing. Resolved all those moral dilemmas with one supremely grown-up decision.

Laura I felt numb, cold as ice, as if my life was over.

Anna But you did not kill yourself?

Laura *shakes her head.*

Laura I *meant* to do it. I *intended* to do it. I rushed to the platform as the express thundered in. I had no thoughts. Only an overwhelming desire not to feel anything ever again. But the train rushed past and I was still standing there. So I went to the Ladies Room and I looked in the mirror and I saw the face of a madwoman and I thought: 'Now you must put this face away. You have no further use for this face. I opened my bag and took out the lace handkerchief . . . the lace handkerchief he'd used to take the grit from my eye. I held it under the cold tap and I scrubbed my face till it hurt. Then I threw the hanky into the waste bin and went home to my husband.

Louise You see, I didn't want to be naughty. Do a dance for Daddy . . . do a little dance for Daddy. Round and round the garden like a teddy bear. One step, two steps and a tickly . . . and a tickly . . . a tickly under . . .

She picks up the rag doll, slaps it viciously, then throws it against the wall with force.

Speaks deliberately, quietly.

I wanna be loved by you, by you and nobody else but you, I wanna be loved by you alone. (*Pause.*) I like that song.

Light **Marilyn**, *lying on the bed. She holds a whiskey bottle, from which she takes swigs. She is dressed in the pleated white dress of the classic photograph of Monroe. She speaks with an American accent.*

Marilyn Remind me to sing it to you sometime. By the way, I *did* kill myself. I mean it was *me* that did it. Oh they tried to pin it on the Mafia, Kennedy's men. They wouldn't even allow me *that*.

Louise Crushed underfoot by so many men.

Anna Like a mirror broken into a million fragments.

Louise Each one reflecting a different face.

Marilyn They loved me all right, if entering my body was love . . . breaking and entering. They loved me like they love a railroad. Where the trains always run on time.

Louise Like a star always shining in the same part of the sky.

Anna Burning bright, burning bright.

Louise I dreamt of you once. Or perhaps it was me. My dress rode up my thighs and I was special, very special.

Anna How could such beauty be allowed to live?

Louise Golden body, dressed in white.

Anna Adored.

Louise Worshipped.

Anna Ruined.

Marilyn Sacrificed.

A few notes of the Fugue played on the piano. Light Louise's Mother, **Vera**, *in the doorway. She is dressed in deep mourning. She carries a bunch of wilting tulips. She walks towards* **Louise**.

Louise The flowers are dying, mother. You always liked the flowers to be fresh.

Vera Everything's dying . . . (*Pause.*) I hated him. Did you know that? Your beloved father. Hated him with a passion you would never believe me capable of. Colourless Vera, drained of colour. Blotted out by years of his total indifference. Parched as an orange he had sucked dry.

But I was bright once. Red as these tulips. Even my hair was red and gold where the sun caught it. Tongues of flame. Until he bled me . . . until he chewed me and spat out the bones. Years of listening to his platitudes, his sermons in and out of church, his careless cruelty. Large, cold hands when he wanted, long cold back when he didn't. If there was something I needed to say, something I wanted to say it was this.

The women speak in unison.

Marilyn/Anna (*in unison*) Tear life open, Louise. Tear it apart. Pull out its wings. Never be afraid of cruelty, fury, fire or anguish. Run only from calmness, compassionate endurance, silence. Scream, Louise, scream. Scream with pain or passion. Only scream for God's sake, scream!

Blackout. Light on **Louise**.

Louise Mother . . . Mother . . . there was something I wanted to . . . there was something . . . please . . . I need to . . . I *must* . . . Mother . . . Mother . . .

The Fugue played very musically on the piano. **Louise** *looks around.*

Clara?

Light **Marilyn**. *She sits at the piano, playing.*

Marilyn There you go again. Categorising. This in one box, that in another. Maybe I taught myself to play. Who knows? Jazz and that classical stuff too.

She improvises gently on the Fugue, talking as she plays.

She sure must have hated you. Your Ma. If it weren't for you, she could have left your Dad . . . Kids . . . they tear your heart out. I seen it a million times . . .

Louise How would you know . . . you never had any.

Marilyn You think I didn't try? I wanted a baby more than anything in the whole world . . . a little girl . . . Jeannie . . . I'd have dressed her in blue denim dungarees. She'd have been a garage mechanic, proper little tough guy . . . stronger than me . . . fit to take care of herself. If she'd have been born, I'd never had to kill myself. My Jeannie . . .

She stops playing abruptly.

If you don't have no dreams, you might as well be dead. And if you're going to have them, you might as well go the whole hog.

Louise You should know.

Marilyn Don't you fucking despise me, little Miss tight ass! What did you ever have to fight for in your whole goddam life? Everything handed to you on a fucking plate, by a woman who cut off her right arm to do it. And you so full of loathing and spite and pride you can't even find it in you to love the poor bitch.

Louise That's not true.

Marilyn Ain't it?

Light **Vera**. *She sits sewing. Mending a sock.*

Vera It was raining the day you were born. Not a heavy downpour, just a fine persistent drizzle out of a heavy grey sky. It was a cottage hospital. December. I lay there in a little room, high window like a cell, feet freezing. Terrified. Once through the open door I saw an orderly. I heaved myself to my feet and stumbled after her. 'Help me, please,' I said. 'I think I may be dying.' Because that's how much pain there is. (*Pause.*) They say afterwards you forget. But I never did. It came back to haunt me often. Especially when you seemed such a cold little creature. But then you always *were* your father's child. Never any doubt of that. (*Pause.*) There was a young curate once. Peter. He used to hang around the church when I was arranging the flowers.

My hair was still red in those days. He liked to touch my hair. Your father had him transferred to Wokingham. Not that anything was ever said. I taught myself to love you, as one might teach oneself a foreign language. And later, on those drizzly days, I'd wait by the window for the school bus to arrive and I'd think: 'I suppose this is something. Nothing much, but something.' And that perhaps, was all I could expect, given the circumstances.

Long pause.

Louise Why didn't you say?

Marilyn Maybe you never asked.

Louise You always seemed so . . .

Vera Self-contained?

Louise Yes. And all the time you were . . .

Vera Dying.

Pause.

Louise I wanted to touch you.

Vera Did you?

Louise But I didn't know how.

Long pause.

Louise I never cry.

Vera Me neither.

Anna I always. Once I am starting, I can never stop.

Marilyn Me too. Like the Niagara Falls. (*She looks at* **Louise**.) What the hell you waiting for?

Louise *looks at* **Vera**. *Makes a tentative move towards her.*

Louise I'm sorry.

Vera *nods.*

So many questions.

Vera I know.

Long pause.

Louise Perhaps . . .

She stretches out her hand very tentatively. **Vera** *does likewise. Their fingers don't quite meet. The others watch intently. The lights fade to blackout. In the blackout,* **Marilyn** *continues to improvise on the Fugue. Lights come up slowly on* **Louise**. *She stands alone, bereft, isolated.* **Marilyn** *plays, watches her.*

Marilyn You could do it.

Louise What?

Marilyn Same as I did. I got the pills. Look in the handbag.

Louise *looks around, sees a black leather bag, picks it up.*

Louise That's . . . that's my mother's bag. (*Turns it over, examining it.*) My mother had a bag like this. Good black leather. 'You should always have one good black leather bag,' she says, 'to go with everything.'

Marilyn Open it.

Louise *opens it, takes out a bottle of pills, looks at them.*

Louise Everything's going really well for me. Absolutely according to plan . . .

Marilyn If you're so fucking happy, why the devil don't you ever crack your face?

She plays on. Light **Anna**, **Laura**.

Anna (*to* **Louise**) So you have never thought of this suicide?

Louise Of course not.

Laura Never?

Pause.

Louise Perhaps once.

Marilyn After he ditched you.

Louise Who?

Marilyn There's gotta be somebody. You got the look of someone who's been ditched once or twice too often.

Long pause. **Louise** *clutches the handbag.*

Louise I meant to do it, but I didn't have the courage. I had no thoughts at all . . . only an overwhelming desire not to feel anything ever again. Not to be unhappy any more. (*Pause.*) What was that? What did I just say?

Marilyn Something about a girl who nearly threw herself onto the railroad.

Louise *looks at* **Marilyn** *as if for the first time.*

Louise Your skin . . . it's so white. It's as if the light shines right through it. And your hair . . . it's like spun sugar . . . candy-floss. We went to the seaside once on my tenth birthday. I asked for candy-floss. My father said it was a wicked waste of money.

Marilyn Just like the knickerbocker glory.

Louise The first time he saw me wearing lipstick, he wiped my face clean with the corner of a wet towel.

Laura That must have been extremely painful.

Louise Yes. (*Pause.*) I couldn't make love. I wanted to in my head but my body had other ideas. I was . . . I was too tight inside. I couldn't let him in.

Marilyn So he left you?

Louise Yes.

Anna He was undoubtedly married.

Louise That's right. The head of my department. And old enough to be my father. (*Pause.*)

Marilyn Yeh, I tried that too.

Louise I read your biography. *Goddess*, it was called.

Marilyn *laughs with huge enjoyment, turns.*

Marilyn Come over here.

Louise Why?

Marilyn Does there have to be a reason for everything?

Louise hesitates, but then goes to stand next to **Marilyn**. **Marilyn** *looks up at her.*

Marilyn You got eyes like a cat. Cat's eyes. (*Pause.*) You can kiss me if you want.

Louise I . . . I . . . all right.

She pulls **Marilyn** *to her feet, then kisses her, very passionately.*

Louise I love you. I think I've always loved you.

The others gather round.

Laura The first time I saw you I wanted to look at you forever.

Anna You were like an angel, a child, like a mermaid, more beautiful than anything in the whole world.

Laura Flesh, yet not flesh.

Louise Pure light, light as air, invisible as breath.

Anna Yet warm and damp and rich as earth.

Louise I wanted to eat you, to give birth to you, to swallow you alive . . .

Marilyn Feel me in your flesh, taste me in your mouth, let your womb open wide and let me in or out. You can have me, or be me. You can take me or leave me. I am all that you have ever been or will ever be.

They kiss again. Then **Marilyn** *begins to dance, provocative, girlish, laughing. She hums the Fugue as accompaniment. The others join in, laughing.* **Louise** *watches, bemused, enchanted. They whirl out of sight. The sound of the humming continues till the music is taken up on the piano. Light fades on* **Louise**, *till she is in semi-darkness.*

Light **Clara Schumann**. *She sits at the piano playing. She looks tired, old, grey.* **Louise** *goes*

to her. **Clara** *now speaks with a heavy German accent.*

Louise I'm sorry.

Clara Again you are sorry. Why you are always apologising?

Louise It was probably none of my business.

Clara My life is public property. And was from the very start. 'Performing monkeys' . . . that is what he called us, my father. Performing monkeys.

Louise I read your letters. The ones you wrote to Brahms, *and* all the others.

Clara They were written in German.

Louise I bought a dictionary.

Clara You feel free to plunder my diaries, my correspondence, and you do not even speak my language. Even if you read every word written about me, still you will know nothing.

Louise I've heard almost all of your music.

Clara Childish exercises intended to impress. Displays of technical skill, virtuoso performances. The music is not great. It is polite, well-behaved, well-ordered. Greatness was not a possibility open to me. I was the mother of eight children. My husband died in an asylum. I had to earn a living, to put bread in their gaping mouths. If you want greatness, look to Beethoven, Mozart, Tchaikowsky.

Louise Brahms?

Clara Him also.

Louise *Did* you love him?

Clara What is love? Can you tell me what this word means? A mother loves her child so much she is ready to die for it. Is *that* love? (*Pause.*) I cried on the grave of my poor mad Robert. Is *that* love? But Johannes . . . love? I don't know. I wanted him once or twice quite badly, but he was more involved with dreams than flesh and blood. Now . . . if you will excuse me . . . I cannot waste any more time with this conversation.

She starts to play scales, fiercely, angrily. **Louise** *stops her.*

Louise You've been lying to me. And I believed you. You made love to him the first night he came to your room. You opened the door and let him in. Didn't you? You let him in. It was worth the risk . . . the possibility of pain. And afterwards you snatched every opportunity to be together. That's the truth, isn't it. Why else would you have gone with him to Ostend when you knew Robert was dying. You thought you had me fooled, didn't you . . . along with all the others. But I *know* you . . . I *know* who you are.

Long pause.

Clara What do you know and what concern is it of yours, anyway? You create nothing. You understand nothing about the pain of creating. You have made no music, neither have you given birth to a single child. You plunder the lives of others only to try to make sense of your own. You twist every fact to make it mean what you want it to mean. You look for me everywhere and yet you cannot find me. Why? Because your eyes are closed, your heart is closed, just as the museum is closed. Sieh dich selber, nicht mich an. Stelle dir selber die Fragen, die beantwortet werden sollen. (Look at yourself, instead of me. Ask yourself the questions you want to be answered.)

Louise What was that? What did you say?

Clara *laughs.*

Clara You see . . . we don't even speak the same language.

Long pause.

You are good girl, Louise. Just as I was a good girl. But virtue is not genius. Duty is not creativity. (*Pause.*) There *was* one piece I loved. One piece I believed in more than all the other compositions.

Louise The Fugue . . .

Clara So you understand *something* at least. (*Pause.*) Tell me . . . how did I compose it? What was the process?

Louise You . . . you sat at your desk . . . You had an idea . . .

Clara Wrong. I sat at the piano. Why would I sit at the desk when the notes are at the piano? It was not a question of ideas. There was a structure laid down, very precise, mathematical almost. Subject, counter subject. It begins with the entry of the theme in the bass. (*She plays a few notes.*) This is followed by the entry of the theme in the alto. (*She plays a few notes.*) Then the soprano enters to play the theme exactly one octave higher in the same key. (*She plays a few notes.*) This is the *tonal* answer, not, you understand, the *real* answer. Tension is built up in the piece because, when we expect resolution, I develop new harmonies . . . (*She plays a little.*) This is a piece which never rests, but embarks on a path of mounting tension. (*Pause.*) Some might even call it autobiographical.

Louise He came to my room. It was *my* room he came to. It was *not* a dream. Forget her . . . *him* . . . them. Me . . . I . . . Louise. I let him in. His tongue was in my mouth. He came right inside me. (*Touches self.*) My body burned. I burned alive. Such joy in it. Impossible bliss. I don't know anything about him . . . He had no biography. No past, no present, no future. We didn't even use the same language, no language . . . we tore through words. And all the places I'd been hiding, wasting, holding, suddenly burst open like an old scar yielding and blood streamed out and I was wet and flowing, round and hot, silenced for once or screaming. And I did it. Louise did it. It happened.

Clara Who is coming to your room? Why do you tell me such terrible things. I thought we were talking of music.

Louise (*sobbing, laughing, shouting*) Fuck you, Clara Schumann, fuck you. Never said that before. Never ever. Because I hate you. Love and hate you. Look at me, mother. Scream, you said. Scream . . . can I . . . can I? Can I? (*Touches neck.*) I was my painful neck. Pain in the neck. (*Touches back.*) Knotted back. Not back. Never going back. Clara . . . Clara . . . I wanted to eat you up, chew you up, spew you out. I thought you could make me big . . . my child . . . first born . . . only born. Stillborn. Look at me, Richard Last. My last dance, here at last. Never dance for Daddy again. Never ever ever ever. But whoever came through that door played me like a piano . . . and I was black and white and red all over . . . (*Laughs.*) 'Why don't you ever crack your face?' . . . I cracked it, see. Joke . . . I laughed. Louise laughing. And it was me lying across my bed with a bottle in my hand. And me with the red hair like tongues of flame. Dead tulips . . . throw them away. Bless them, thank them . . . then throw them away. And me standing on the platform as the train comes in, and the clink, clink, clink of steel on steel, and the swirl of smoke and the sound of the whistle blowing. Me with my white dress and my little black bag, and my fur-edged cloak. All that travelling . . . never getting anywhere. You were right, Clara, it wasn't the *real* answer . . . (*She crouches on all fours.*) Because here is the answer . . . all of the answers . . . and here is I . . . Louise . . . all of me . . . all of these . . . yes, even you. Louise is I . . . I . . . I . . .

She screams, an immense, liberating wonderful scream.

Blackout.

Coda

Lights come up slowly on the railway platform. Early morning. **Rhea** *sits on the luggage wagon, leaning against her back-pack. She is eating an apple. The sound of a train in the distance. Enter the* **Older Guard.** *He checks his timetable. Enter* **Louise.** *She wears her raincoat over crumpled clothes, no shoes, carries her briefcase. She looks dishevelled, dirty, a little wild.* **Rhea** *sees her. A pause.*

Rhea Hi.

Pause.

Louise Hi.

Rhea *notes* **Louise**'s *bare feet.*

Louise I lost a shoe. When I left the hotel. Couldn't find it anywhere.

Pause. **Rhea** *bites into the apple.*

Rhea How's Clara Schumann?

Louise She's . . . she's dead.

They look at each other. Then both laugh.

Louise I'm starving. I forgot to eat.

Rhea *hands over the apple.*

Rhea Here.

Louise *looks at it, makes a decision, takes a huge bite. She speaks with her mouth full.*

Louise That's the first time I've ever done that.

Rhea What?

Louise Bitten someone else's apple.

Both laugh.

Rhea Where's your luggage?

Louise At the hotel. I couldn't be bothered.

Rhea But you brought your work.

Louise Yes.

She opens the briefcase, draws out all the papers, files, etc. Looks at them.

Rhea It's a lot to carry.

Louise Yes.

They look at each other. Then **Louise** *goes to the waste paper basket and slowly, systematically, puts the papers in. She then returns to pick up her briefcase. She turns it over, examining it.*

Louise My father gave me this case for my twenty-first birthday.

Rhea It's a very *serious* kind of case.

Louise Yes.

They look at each other. **Louise** *takes her wallet and passport out of the case, then reaches inside and pulls out the rag doll. She then crosses to the bin, stuffs the case into it, under the papers.* **Rhea** *watches. The* **Guard** *watches.* **Louise** *stands looking at the doll. Enter the* **Polythene Woman***. She comes up to the bin, rummages in it. She tears off a piece of newspaper. Shows it to* **Louise***.*

Polythene Woman That's me with the pretty little ringlets. Clara, they called me. Little Clara. Men ate me like chocolate. They could have whatever they wanted. I called it love in those days. In, out. In, out. All wet and sticky. Feels lovely for a minute, then all you can think about is a hot bath and a nice long sleep.

Louise *looks at her. Realising.*

Louise My father used to touch me. The first time was after I played in the mud. He sat me in the bath and scrubbed me clean with a rough flannel. Then he pushed his thumb inside me as far as it would go. It hurt like hell. I thought it was a punishment because I'd been such a naughty girl.

Polythene Woman All the kids I ever had took off as soon as they could walk, fell under buses, got killed in some war or other, or learnt to swear they'd never seen

me before in their lives, and men I'd fucked to death one day, turned their back on me the next till my body closed up shop for good and I wrapped it up in polythene and let it rest. And these lines on my hands are railway lines. All the journeys I almost made I'll never make now. Because I'm not going nowhere. Nowhere. Not any more. (*Pause.*) I was beautiful once . . . more beautiful than you. You don't believe me . . . look at this photo . . .

She tears off a bit of newspaper, shows it to **Louise***.* **Louise** *studies it, hands it back.* **Laura** *approaches out of the smoke, comes towards* **Louise***.*

Louise I wanted to ask her if she knew. My mother. But I suppose I was afraid of the answer.

Laura *hesitates, then passes by, showing no sign of recognition.*

Rhea Perhaps it doesn't matter anymore.

Louise I didn't cry. I never cry.

A pause.

Rhea Come here.

Louise *hesitates.*

Rhea Come here, I said.

Louise *approaches.* **Rhea** *puts her arms around her. Holds her very tight.*

A long pause. The **Older Guard** *approaches, coughs discreetly.* **Rhea** *gently pulls a little apart from* **Louise***.*

Guard If you are wanting the train to Ostend, it is already gone. It is leaving from Platform 5 on Sundays.

Rhea Were you going to Ostend?

Louise I don't know.

Rhea What do you *want* to do?

Louise Want? What do I want? (*Considers.*) I . . . I want . . . I want to walk beside a lake . . . I want to swim in a river . . . I want to look at mountains . . .

Marilyn *hurries by on high heels, passes out of sight.*

Louise I *don't* want to find my shoes.

They laugh.

Rhea (*to* **Guard**) When's the next train to Lucerne?

Guard Lucerne? Lucerne is the opposite direction. Ostend. (*Points right.*) Lucerne. (*Points left.*)

Louise Good.

Rhea, **Louise** *smile. The* **Guard** *consults a big timetable.* **Rhea** *and* **Louise** *sit on the luggage trolley.* **Rhea** *takes out the wooden pipe and begins to play the Coda from the Fugue.* **Anna**, *shrouded in her cloak, comes into view, approaches the* **Guard**.

Anna Is there a train to Vienna please?

He looks it up in the timetable.

Guard At 11.53 you can go, yes.

She thanks him, moves on, stands waiting. The **Polythene Woman** *returns to the bin, sees the briefcase, considers it, throws it onto the ground. She eagerly pulls out some of the papers and stuffs them into her shoes, then pushes the remains back into the bin. Taking some matches from her belongings, she sets fire to the papers in the bin, warming herself at the blaze.* **Rhea** *plays on, watching.* **Louise** *goes to the bonfire, warms her hands. The* **Guard** *joins her. He too warms his hands.*

Guard Journeys. Everybody is making journeys. First, oh yes, they are asking me the way please . . . what time the train is? I tell them. Where is coffee, tea, sandwiches? All this I am telling them. Soon . . . you will be surprised. Soon they are learning to read timetables. Soon they are finding out where is coffee, tea. So they don't ask me no more. Toilet, they can find. Newspapers they can find. Where to catch train to Düsseldorf they can find. Everything they can to do alone. (*Pause. He warms hands.*) Bonfires not allowed. This is the rule. This is the law. Item 51. No fires. Verboten. Forbidden. And still they are lighting fires. (*He warms hands, turns to* **Louise**.) So . . . you can to go your own way, Fräulein. If you know where you are going, you can go your own way. Maybe you are getting lost sometime . . . but . . . never mind. (*Pause.*) There is something still you like to say?

Long pause.

Louise I let him do it because I was afraid he wouldn't love me. But he didn't love me anyway. So I was broken inside and out. (*Pause.*) That's why I had to find a place to hide. A safe place.

Pause.

Guard Was a long journey. And not so easy.

Louise *nods.*

Guard And still you are travelling.

Louise Yes . . .

Long pause.

Louise Goodbye Richard . . .

She holds out her hand. He takes it.

Guard I am not Richard. My name is . . .

Louise Johannes . . . I know.

He holds her hand for a moment. Then lets it go. He exits. **Louise** *watches him go.* **Rhea** *begins to play again.* **Louise** *looks at the rag doll, kisses it tenderly, then, throwing it into the fire, watches it burn. A whirl of smoke.* **Anna**, **Laura** *and the* **Polythene Woman** *disappear into the shadows.* **Louise** *takes off her raincoat, begins to dance in time to* **Rhea**'s *music. She dances for herself, slowly, with intense pleasure. A private ritual, as the lights gradually fade to blackout.*

Variations

During rehearsals of the first production of my play *Self Portrait*, Anthea Gomez, who composed and played the original music, handed me a copy of the biography of Clara Schumann saying 'This would make a good play.' It took me a while to get round to reading the book and, when I did, I felt that the subject was both too obvious and too impenetrable for me to consider.

Clara Schumann, born Clara Wieck, was a child prodigy. By the age of 8, under her father's tuition, she was composing competent pieces for the piano and giving public recitals. Later she married Robert Schumann, whose psychological illness and early death left her with six children to support. The composer Brahms, several years her junior, was a lifelong friend and, possibly, lover.

I had no musical knowledge: I couldn't even read music, let alone play an instrument. How could I hope to find an empathy with this woman whose life was dominated by music and by the men who composed it? Nevertheless, something in the subject matter began to obsess me. Was it the picture of the child Clara, too clever for her own good, trying desperately to please her father? Or was it the adult woman, her face a mask of pain and tension who spoke to me? Or was it both?

I had recently become interested in Jung's writings on the process of individuation and the search for wholeness. These describe how within each of one of us there are many different women, and that the dialogue between these 'sub-personalities' is potent and real and must be heard. We all unconsciously internalise female archetypes while, in the adult woman, the child and the girl are still present and alive.

Not knowing what any of this might have to do with a play about Clara Schumann, I began to take piano lessons. I watched old films: *Anna Karenina, Brief Encounter, Some Like It Hot*. I listened to concertos and fugues, feeling that Clara would speak to me through music rather than words. I went by train to Berlin. I thought that I was looking for Clara Schumann, but my search was leading me into dangerous and uncharted territory.

When, eventually, I'd finished a legible draft, I knew that something in the subject was still eluding me. A rehearsed reading was arranged. I also took the unusual step (for me) of seeking the opinion of a few friends whose judgment I value. Among them was Annie Castledine, who had directed *Self Portrait* and who had been instrumental in bringing the text of that play to fruition. I remember her saying something about a journey in therapy. I went back to the text, took a deep breath, and plunged in . . .

Sheila Yeger has written for stage, television and radio. Her stage plays include *Self Portrait* (Theatre Clwyd 1987, Derby Playhouse 1990, Orange Tree, London 1991. Pub. Amber Lane Press); *Watching Foxes* (Bristol Old Vic 1982); *Alice and Other Reflections* (Soho Poly 1982) and two community plays: *The Ballad of Tilly Hake* and *A Day by the Sea*. Plays for radio include *These Animals are Dangerous, Heart of England* and *Yellow Ochre*. She is the author of *The Sound of One Hand Clapping*, a guide to writing for the theatre (pub. Amber Lane Press).